McGILL-QUEEN'S STUDIES IN THE HISTORY OF RELIGION
G.A. Rawlyk, editor

Volumes in this series have been supported by the Jackman Foundation of Toronto.

The Dévotes

Women and Church in Seventeenth-Century France

ELIZABETH RAPLEY

McGill-Queen's University Press
Montreal & Kingston • London • Buffalo

© McGill-Queen's University Press 1990
ISBN 0-7735-0727-2 (cloth)
ISBN 0-7735-1101-6 (paper)

Legal deposit first quarter 1990
Bibliothèque nationale du Québec

First paperback edition 1993

∞

Printed in Canada on acid-free paper

Originally published with the help of a grant from the Canadian Federation for the Humanities, using funds provided by the Social Sciences and Humanities Research Council of Canada.

Canadian Cataloguing in Publication Data

Rapley, Elizabeth
The Dévotes: women and Church in seventeenth-century France

(McGill-Queen's studies in the history of religion; 4)
Includes bibliographical references.
ISBN 0-7735-0727-2 (bound)
ISBN 0-7735-1101-6 (pbk.)

1. France – Church history – 17th century. 2. Women in the Catholic Church – France – History – 17th century. 3. Monasticism and religious orders for women – France – History – 17th century. I. Title. II. Series.
BV639.W7R36 1990   261.8'344'0944   C90-090335-2

To my husband

Contents

Maps and Graphs

Acknowledgments

The author wishes to thank Jean-Claude Dubé for his advice and guidance; also (in Canada) Jacques Barbier, Didier Cencig, Mark Olsen, and Victor Wallwork for their technical assistance, and Harriet Doherty for reading and advising on the manuscript; and (in France) the archivists of the Soeurs de l'Enfant-Jésus, in Paris, Rouen, and Reims, Marie-Thérèse Notter of Cloyes, and Sister Lucienne Plante CND, now of Troyes.

The education of the Virgin. This statue comes from the monastery of the Visitation, Nancy. Courtesy Musée Historique Lorrain, Nancy

The child Jesus. Seventeenth-century holy picture. Courtesy Archives Soeurs de l'Enfant-Jésus, Reims

Mary, Queen of the Apostles. This painting by LeBrun, which was commissioned by M. Olier, hung behind the high altar of Saint-Sulpice in Paris. It was probably seen by Marguerite Bourgeoys and Jeanne Mance when they visited the seminary in 1659; certainly its composition harmonizes perfectly with Marguerite's writings on the subject of the Blessed Virgin. The painting shows the scene of Pentecost with Mary at the centre and above all the apostles, a clear depiction of the position of importance which she was assigned by Catholic tradition. M. Faillon, *Vie de M. Olier*, vol. 3 (Paris 1841)

T.IV. p. 172.

Ursuline de la Congrégation de Toulouse en habit ordinaire les jours ouvriers.

40.

Ursuline of Toulouse. Even working-day dress bore the characteristics of the full religious habit. Bibliothèque Nationale, Paris

Madame de Miramion

Decedée à Paris le 24.ᵉ Mars 1696. Âgée de 66. ans.

Madame de Miramion, dressed (despite her rank) in the distinctively bourgeois dress
of a *maîtresse charitable*. Bonneau-Avenant, *Madame de Miramion* (Paris 1875)

Authentic portrait of Margúerite Bourgeoys painted by Pierre LeBer, Montreal, 1700. Her dress closely resembles that of the various *maîtresses charitables* in France. Courtesy Congrégation de Notre-Dame, Centre d'archives, Montreal

Madame du Buc, one of the first superiors of the Soeurs de la Providence of Rouen. Note that her dress resembles that of other *maîtresses charitables* and, indeed, of other respectable women of the bourgeoisie. Courtesy Archives Soeurs de l'Enfant Jésus, Paris

Portrait of a *maîtresse charitable*, presumed to be Marie Hayer, dressed for her formal reception into the community. Courtesy Archives Soeurs de l'Enfant-Jésus, Paris

Dame Religieuse de S.ᵗ Cyr.
*Ces Dames Religieuses sont au nombre de trente six engagées par vœu de s'employer
tout le temps de leur vie a instruire et former a la pieté et autres vertus les 250. Demoi:
selles nommée par le Roy, et entretenuë a tître de fondation dans la maison Royale de S.ᵗ
Cyr proche versailles.*

A schoolmistress of Saint-Cyr. The aristocratic dress, designed by Madame de Maintenon, reflects the character of the Academy. While the Dames de Saint-Maur taught
at Saint-Cyr they dressed the part. When they withdrew, they resumed their bourgeois dress. Bibliothèque Nationale, Paris

Madame de Maintenon, second wife of Louis XIV, a dedicated patron of feminine education. Bibliothèque Nationale, Paris

Louis XIV's formal visit to Saint-Cyr in 1690, several years after the departure of the Dames de Saint-Maur. The mistresses in the foreground are now full religious, as can be seen by their dress. Courtesy Archives Soeurs de l'Enfant-Jésus, Paris

A sister dressed as a working woman. This portrait of a Soeur de la Providence, Rouen, dates from the eighteenth century, but probably reflects a long-standing tradition of dress. Courtesy Archives Soeurs de la Providence de Rouen

Soeur de la Charité

Aimer Dieu jusqu'au point de lui être fidèle,
Et soulager sa faim dans le necessiteux,
C'est former l'inébranlable échelle
Qui seule peut escalader les Cieux.

Sans Charité Chrétien point de vie Eternelle,
Soulage sans cesse le pauvre malheureux,
Et partage avec lui tes biens avec zèle,
Je le veux, que tu sois à nombres bienheureux

A fille de la Charité. The *marmite* in her hand is the symbol of her calling. Her headdress is not the original *toquois*, on which Vincent de Paul insisted so firmly, but the variation which came into use in 1685. Bibliothèque Nationale, Paris

The varied activities of the Filles de La Charité. Bibliothèque Nationale, Paris

Beggars on the road to "the great Hospital" (1660). After an engraving by Lagner.
Bibliothèque Nationale, Paris

The Dévotes

Introduction

Nowhere has the metaphor of war between the sexes been more liberally employed than in describing French society in the seventeenth century. Almost every indicator of social relationships which historians have examined – religion, politics, the law, medical practice, literature, business, and marital and family relationships – has supported their thesis of a growing male-female dichotomy, an aggressive antifeminism, an irresistible trend towards patriarchy. The picture emerges of a society like an armed camp, with men in control of all strategic points. Yet it also appears that the men lived in a constant state of anxious vigilance, always alert to the other sex's efforts at usurpation. The image that haunted their thoughts was that of the "world turned upside-down": the mule riding the muleteer, the woman commanding the man, a thing against all nature and reason.[1]

Many explanations have been given for this situation. Perhaps the most persuasive explanation is fear: the profound psychic aftershocks of the Black Death, which continued to rumble in "great mortalities," in schisms, wars, and social disruptions – and finally, in the devastating experience of the Reformation. To allay this mood of fear, scapegoats were sought and found, and among them were women.[2]

Though misogyny predated the Christian era, it was easily transplanted into Christian thought. "In Paradise, between Adam and God there was only one woman; but she did not rest until she had succeeded in chasing her husband from the garden of delights, and condemning Christ to the agony of the cross."[3] And the daughters of Eve had inherited all her weaknesses: her credulity, frivolity, inconstancy – and carnality. In medieval thought woman was fundamentally sensual and lascivious, and in constant need of firm control. "Your yearning will be for your husband," said Genesis, "yet he will lord it over you."[4]

If the strong points were all in the hands of men, then the citadel at the centre of their commanding position was the Church. Catholicism's marginalization of women, it is argued, was a practice made venerable through the centuries. The Church of feudal Europe had grown up in distinctly male form. The secular clergy was, of course, reserved for men. Women were excluded from the service of the altar, from handling the sacred vessels;[5] from teaching or preaching the Word, even from understanding the liturgy.[6] As for the monastic life, it had never been made available to any but a few women, almost all of high birth. They remained a small minority,[7] observing customs which were, in fact, hand-me-downs from their male mentors. The very clothes that they wore were adopted from the male monastic habit – an inconvenience to which Heloise, abbess of the Paraclete, objected vigorously.[8] "In the great majority of cases," writes an historian of medieval nuns, "they were subjected to rules elaborated by men for men."[9]

The male monastic orders accepted their female subsidiaries with mixed emotions. While the women's appeal for a share in the religious life was hard to resist, the work of guiding and advising them was seen as a serious distraction to the brothers. After an initial period of support, they tended to draw back from the responsibility.[10] The official Church maintained a certain reserve towards its religious women – or so a recent study of canonizations seems to suggest. Of the seventy-one saints canonized between 1198 and 1431, only thirteen were women, and of these, only four were nuns.[11]

The same exclusion of women is detected in the ordinary religious life of the laity. Women seldom took part in the organized activities of the religious confraternities.[12] They received communion less frequently than men. Girls were less likely than boys to receive religious instruction. "The Lord," said a bishop of Troyes, "when speaking to Saint Peter, asked him twice to 'Feed my lambs' but only once to 'Feed my sheep.'" Lambs being in the masculine and sheep in the feminine, the bishop concluded that "it was more necessary to attend to the education of boys."[13]

Reform in the Catholic church tended to be accompanied by a hardening of its attitude towards sexuality. In the years after Trent, in the heat of the drive for clerical celibacy, a war of words was declared against the female sex. With increasing frequency, preachers and confessors treated women as agents of the Devil, and warned male audiences against their wiles. To be sure, there were preachers who issued the same warnings in reverse to female audiences – but somehow, the message does not seem to have been as powerful. The discrediting of sexuality meant, in general, the discrediting of women.[14] True virtue, in the vocabulary of early seventeenth-century preachers, was always male.[15]

These are the unfavourable terms in which historians have described the status of women in the Counter-Reformation years. However, in the very area of male-female relationships that seemed the most unpromising, a radical change was already in the making. In the early years of the seventeenth century the Gallican church was prized open, to admit women into its inner life. How serious a breach this was, and how unexpected, the following pages will show.

It began, as so many things do, with the printing press. The last quarter of the sixteenth century had seen the translation and publication in France of most of the great works of religion. Among these works were the writings of the Carmelite mystic, Teresa of Avila. Their appearance in the vernacular put them, for the first time, within the reach of ordinary upper-class women.[16] The effect was electric. When in 1601 a small group of Spanish Carmelite nuns appeared in Paris, the ground was already prepared for a revolution in female contemplative life. The Carmelites exercised a remarkable influence upon the life of contemporary high society. The community which they established, and the fifty-five other Carmelite convents which appeared in the next forty years, became the focal points of a profound religious revival. The "mystical conquest," as it has been named, owed much of its inspiration to women – the *saintes âmes* who acted as the confidantes, and often the spiritual guides, of the great religious leaders of the times.[17] From this time on, the Catholic Reformation in France, for all its clericalism and its insistence on masculine authority, bore the distinct imprint of feminine spirituality. A process was begun which very swiftly gathered momentum. By mid-century there were more nuns than monks and friars in France. The Church, in the words of one historian, had been "feminized."[18]

Religious women, then, registered an advance during a period that for most other women was characterized by retreat. Against a general background of feminine weakness, the feminine religious life became a nucleus of real, though always discreet, strength. The "great Catholic females of the Counter-Reformation" enjoyed opportunities for organizational activity far beyond anything that Protestant women were allowed.[19] Their power and influence were transferred to the collectives which formed around them: their religious communities.

Women were intent on invading not only the Church's prayer life but also its active life. In the early seventeenth century they made a determined move into the field of activity which is known as the Church's apostolate. France was still in crisis, still suffering from the effects of the religious wars. In the battle to restore Catholicism there was a very real need for female catechists, to stem the stream of women into the reformed religion. The women who offered themselves for this work came from the ranks of women known in their time as *dévotes* – deeply religious women, very often unmarried, and with time and leisure to devote themselves to the exercise of piety. Their "rush"[20] into religious life during these first critical years was a phenomenon in itself, which preceded the existence of convents in which to live, or even suitable jobs to perform. Even before they were settled, they began to participate in the work of catechizing the faithful.

They believed that the value of their work was self-evident, but here they were wrong: they met with serious resistance, on the grounds that they were exceeding the limits which had always been assigned to women. They redeemed themselves by retiring into the cloister and accepting the more unassuming work of schoolteaching. And here they proved so successful that society swiftly accepted them and supported their effort.

The appropriation by religious women of this new and expanded teaching function was itself a tremendous novelty. According to custom, the profession of teaching was left almost entirely to men. It was certainly considered inappropriate for nuns. Contact with young people of the world was seen as a threat to their chastity. Girls could be instructed in monasteries only if they remained within the cloister, quarantined from all outside influence. The teaching of day pupils, permitted by the Holy See for the first time in 1607, on conditions that preserved clausura as much as possible, was a significant advance. But the Church of the Counter-Reformation closed the door on a feminine teaching apostolate.

At mid-century, the resistance of the traditionalists began to fall apart. A second "rush" of women into religiously inspired activities took place, surprising and sometimes alarming the authorities. Again, however, the women's fervour carried the day and broke down opposition; a massive complex of charitable institutions began to rise, built upon their support and service. As the work expanded, some women emerged from the crowd and began to take on the character of professionals. This raised the question of their support, protection, and training. Communities and seminaries began to appear. What was clear from the start, however, was that as long as these women wished to work in public places, and to move about freely, they could not be considered nuns. Caught between its appreciation of their work and its old prejudices against uncloistered women, Catholic society still held firm. The women compromised, by renouncing the title and appearances of religious life but following many of its practices all the same.

With this, the female religious life entered a new phase. The first active *uncloistered* congregations were born. Their members – "filles séculières," as they were called – knew full well that they were nuns in all but name. However, they accepted secular status, so as to remain free to pursue their active vocation. They adopted the "intermediate state," part religious, part secular, which was already being practised in some masculine congregations, but which had previously been forbidden to women.[21] Their freedom to work outside the cloister represented a serious challenge to traditional thinking, but the services which they offered to society went far towards allaying old prejudices. And among these services – legitimated now by a deep change in social needs and attitudes – was the service of public religious instruction. By the end of the century, women had become not only nurses and teachers, but also catechists.

What did all this signify? Not much, according to some historians. The work was too humble, too servile. "Religion peopled the convents with poor servants of God, proletarians of the faith whose only value, from the point of view of feminine action, was that they were free to choose their charitable vocation."[22] But this viewpoint does not do justice to the value, and power, of dedicated work. Other historians are closer to the truth when they argue that, by gaining the power to participate in the Church's activities, women experienced a true promotion.[23]

But who did the promoting? According to the older texts, the Church. But in that case we must define what we mean by the Church. The papacy and the hierarchy were ambivalent about these new women. While some churchmen became their most powerful protagonists, as many, or more, other churchmen were antagonists, particularly in the early years. The same can be said about society as a whole. If all our historians do not lie, the majority of institutions in seventeenth-century Catholic France were unfavourable to the promotion of women, and many of them were actually dedicated in principle to their demotion.

Until recently, there has been little interest in explaining how the promotion took place. The older literature, which consists largely of the work of the historians of religious congregations, does not concern itself with dynamics. Providence "called forth" the women, so of course they came. A founder/foundress drew up the blueprint for a new community and almost at once, miraculously, it was filled with women. Modern historians have found a new word for "providence"; they call it the *conjoncture*. Society needed nurses and teachers, so nurses and teachers appeared. These two interpretations have one thing in common: they assume that women had only a passive role in the process.

In fact, the evidence suggests otherwise. An examination of the sequence of events leads to the conclusion that the complex of social services which developed in the seventeenth century, and especially feminine education, was the creation rather than the creator of religious congregations. The religious energy of the women came first, and the need to channel that energy into meaningful action came second. Then came the need for institutions within which the women could be protected and maintained while they carried out their new activities – in other words, communities. At this stage the involvement of Catholic society, as provider and supporter, became imperative. It was usually in the course of this last stage that the secular and ecclesiastical authorities gave their approval.

What were the lasting effects of this movement upon society? The active congregations became an integral part of modern France. The vast majority of schoolgirls of the Old Regime were educated by them. The hospitals depended on them absolutely. Society grew up around them, to the degree that it developed no alternative sources for the services which they provided. When the Revolution forced the sisters out, the country's schools and hospitals broke down. Municipalities looked for *citoyennes* to replace them, but without success. Napoleon wasted no time in inviting them back in, and they continued their hegemony throughout the nineteenth century. Doctors and educationists of the Third Republic inveighed against the nuns, but could not do without them. Many famous anticlericals quietly sent their daughters to convent schools.

The contribution of active nuns to French Catholic life is incalculable. For three centuries they acted as the Church's teachers, nurses, and social workers, and the parish clergy's strong right arm. But even in the nineteenth century, when their numbers had increased tenfold,[24] their importance could not have been greater than in the seventeenth century, when they first appeared upon a scene of general religious breakdown and became the mediators between the Church and their own sex – the "devout sex" as it had once been and was soon to become again. There is historical evidence of a close correlation between areas of female schooling and areas of practising reformed Catholicism.[25] If this is correct, then the primary purpose of the *dévotes* was served.

The history of feminine education, of the girls who benefited by it and the nuns who dispensed it, intertwines with the history of the Church's changing attitudes towards the women in its service. A third strand, another history, runs alongside these two. This is the history of women. How did the changing vocation of religious women affect the lives of women in the wider world?

Historians agree that as the seventeenth century gave way to the eighteenth, there was a certain mellowing of attitudes towards women. But it is impossible to give religious women credit for this warming trend, since it was more marked in the Protestant world, where nuns, of course, did not exist. The growing army of religious women undoubtedly had their effect upon female education and upon female religious practice; but whether in the final analysis they contributed to the strength of women in general, or to their weakness, it is impossible to say. What has been posited, however, is that in the two different worlds there was a different evolution of male-female relationships: Protestant societies were "assimilationist," Catholic societies "pluralistic."[26] This pluralism must be attributed to the choice which the congregations offered Catholic women, between marriage and the religious – and single – life. And it must also not be forgotten that, in Catholic France, girls and boys were schooled from their earliest years in separate environments, a situation which the existence of the feminine congregations made possible.

But the study of seventeenth-century social behaviour is always heavily dependent on conjecture. Accurate measurement of cause and effect eludes us, and will probably continue to do so. What does seem certain is that the very size and scope of the religious women's movement in the seventeenth century – a movement in which tens of thousands of women were directly involved and hundreds of thousands of other women affected – made it an important factor in the development of French society.

An historian of the nineteenth century has remarked that "the feminine congregations have their place in the history of the Church. They belong, also, in a wider sense, to all our history."[27] In exactly the same sense, the teaching nuns of the Counter-Reformation, and the *filles séculières* who followed them, belong to a wider history.

CHAPTER ONE

Women and the Counter-Reformation in France

Historians of religious life in early seventeenth-century France have often commented upon its two contrasting faces. It was a "confusion of light and shadows": the light of this age of saints made all the more brilliant by the surrounding obscurantism and decadence.[1] It was a time of mystical greatness; yet it was also a time of trauma and menace and pervasive fear.[2] The growing sophistication of knowledge went hand in hand with an obsessive concern with the supernatural – the tens of thousands of witches burnt across Europe are evidence to this.[3] "The age of humanism was the golden age of demonography";[4] far from banning Satan, the early modern mind seemed to welcome him in. The faithful were conscious of living within a barricade, outside which the Evil One was forever on the prowl.[5]

Behind the Counter-Reformation was the Reformation. The crisis of the early seventeenth century can be understood only in the light of the events of the sixteenth century. It was this great rupture, with its accompanying upheavals, that brought the collective fear and anxiety of two centuries to an almost unbearable state of panic. Yet modern historiography, setting aside the agonies and hostilities of the past, now sees Reform and Counter-Reform as two thrusts of the same movement, in which the very violence of their confrontations was an indicator of a certain underlying unity.[6]

It follows from this interpretation that, since the two reforms had a common root, they had many characteristics in common. During the sixteenth and seventeenth centuries, it has been pointed out, both camps experienced the same spiritual movements: of humanism, of mysticism, and of the "agony of salvation" which accompanies the interiorization of religious faith.[7] Thus Catholic reform paralleled Protestant reform for many years.

However, there can be no doubt that Luther and Calvin moved ahead of their opponents in several important areas. The Counter-Reformation, properly speaking, began only with the Council of Trent (1545–63) – a generation after the appearance of the first reformers. Many of the questions which the Fathers of Trent were called upon to address were already accomplished fact in Protestant jurisdictions. They had therefore the choice either to imitate them or to anathematize them. For the most part, they chose to do the latter. The Counter-Reformation, in its conscious decisions, was highly reactive. To most Protestant challenges it responded by a hardening of its positions: a greater respect for the sacrament of the Eucharist, an enhanced devotion to the Virgin and the saints, a more hierarchical and clerical ecclesiology, and a renewed emphasis on the superiority of the clerical over the lay state.

On the other hand, wittingly or unwittingly, the Catholic church absorbed many of the attitudes of its antagonists. When François de Sales wrote that "it is not only erroneous, but a heresy, to hold that life in the army, the workshop, the court or the home is incompatible with devotion,"[8] he was drawing from his personal experience of Calvinism, and he himself was called heretical;[9] but his promotion of the laity became, in time, a Catholic orthodoxy. Similarly, Luther's principle, that all Christians, in order to be saved, must be capable of a conscious, and informed, assent to the call of faith, was adopted without reservation by the seventeenth-century Catholic church.

Underlying unity but deep antipathy, mutual rejection but selective imitation – these contradictory movements were enough in themselves to cause deep trauma in the European mind. As long as the boundaries between heresy and orthodoxy remained fluid, the tension continued unabated.[10] And to these psychological strains must be added the experience of decades of fratricidal war, and the consequent breakdown of normal life. In France, between 1562 and 1598, eight wars in succession disrupted social relationships and destabilized the population. They also raised religious partisanship to unprecedented levels. This was to have its consequences even after the wars were over. The leaguers of one decade became the *dévots* of another, and impressed a deeply fervent character on the revival of post-war France.[11]

"Anguish went along with dynamism ... Fear created its own antidotes."[12] The Counter-Reformation period was, indeed, an anxious and a dynamic period, and the supreme antidote which it offered for the collective fears of the people was absolutism, both civil and religious. The admonition made to Martin Luther at the Diet of Worms, that "the only safe course is submission to established authority," expresses to perfection the spirit of the age. The road to an ordered society was being prepared long before the advent of royal absolutism; it received much of its direction from the Counter-Reformation. Obedience to authority was the cornerstone of tridentine Catholicism, the supreme virtue, the Church's response to the disorders and deviations of the sixteenth century. Since it served the purpose of the centralizing monarchy, it became in turn the supreme civic virtue. Since it answered well to the needs of society, it was readily accepted and internalized. Absolutism was more than a system imposed from above; it was the answer to a craving by respectable people of all social ranks for the law and order that they had lacked so long.[13]

By the end of the seventeenth century French society was more orderly and law-abiding than it had been at the beginning. Much consideration has been given by historians to the process by which social control was applied to the many different social layers. Among the groups to be subordinated were women – all women. Their destiny of obedience stemmed not from rank or from economic status, but from the perceived inherent inferiority of their sex. The theological, medical, and social reasoning which supported this perception appears strange to the modern mind. But in its own time it was believed by everyone – even, apparently, by women themselves. A female, in the tradition of Aristotle and Aquinas, was nothing but "an imperfect male," and this accounted for the inconstancy of her nature. Woman, like the rib of Adam from which she was made, was essentially frail and weak – or bent – of will.[14]

It has been suggested that, from a legal point of view, the seventeenth century was part of a *longue durée* of feminine subordination, which lasted till the end of the nineteenth century.[15] Before the law, women were actually in the process of being devalued. The concessions which medieval jurisprudence had made to them were being negated; their condition, especially in marriage, was being reduced to something very close to perpetual minority. Wives were held to be *in manu mariti*: they could be corrected, even imprisoned, at their husbands' will.[16] From a political point of view, the Salic Law, which barred women from succession to the throne of France, remained firmly entrenched, despite the two feminine regencies. "The people of God," wrote Bossuet, "would never allow the succession to pass to the sex that is born to obey."[17] Power was patriarchal, and it allowed for no division.

As in the sphere of politics and the law, so in the sphere of family relationships. One of the most widely read family manuals of the seventeenth century gave this advice: "All must be subject to one head. Just as the world cannot have two suns, so the family cannot have two masters. If sovereign power were divided, the division would engender the jealousy which is the ruin of all governments."[18] Indeed, the small society of the family prefigured all other societies. According to Bossuet: "the first subordination and order in government among men, was that of husband and wife, parents and children."[19]

Throughout seventeenth-century Europe, this model of marriage prevailed. Even in England, where women were considered to be exceptionally privileged, subordination of wives to their husbands was the accepted norm. After all, had it not been ordained for Adam and Eve in their *Paradise Lost*? "Not equal, as their sex not equal seemed; / For contemplation he and valour formed, / For softness she and sweet attractive grace, / He for God only, she for God in him."[20]

Certainly in France, with its strong leaning towards authoritarianism, the principle of patriarchy went from strength to strength. "As for us," Madame de Maintenon told her young ladies in 1700, "we are here to obey, all our lives."[21]

How closely did reality conform to theory? In a country such as France, with its many different regions, there were as many variations as there were customs. Broadly speaking, women in the north enjoyed more freedom and more social participation than their sisters in the south.[22] The same diversity can be found in the various social strata. But one generalization can safely be made: the important unit was the family, and individuals fitted into its strategies according to need. Among peasants, necessity tended to make for a certain equality: men and women were partners in the business of survival.[23] Among artisans, women were associates in the family enterprises: they worked beside their men, minding the business, keeping the accounts, sometimes even earning independently.[24] The same thing applied among the bourgeoisie. Marie Guyart, the future Ursuline of Quebec, worked as an overseer in her brother-in-law's shipping business.[25] Jean Maillefer, bourgeois of Reims, recalled his mother's early career: "She was taken out of school at the age of fourteen years, to be married and to work in a shop under close supervision, and her first jobs were ... to keep the accounts and to work selling haberdashery."[26] Urban women of the lesser classes worked in a number of different employments, and though their status (and their pay) was generally lower than that of men, they nevertheless enjoyed a certain independence, at least of movement and of association.[27]

The situation was different for women of the aristocracy. They had suffered during the wars of religion. The normal restraints had been destroyed, and they had become vulnerable to rough treatment at the hands of men.[28] Well into the seventeenth century, the kidnapping of marriageable girls was a serious social problem. "In 1625, in the middle of Paris and in the middle of Lent ... persons of quality amused themselves by carrying off young girls in their carriages."[29] Seduction was as great a threat as abduction: the fortunes of upperclass families were endangered by clandestine marriages. With the restoration of law and order, the protection, and circumscription, of the young became a matter of central concern. Gradually, the authorities moved to subject all marriages to the will of the parents.

The subordination of individual to family interests was not an inspiration of the Counter-Reformation. Indeed, the Church strongly maintained the right of young people to dispose of themselves. Canon law had always held marriage to be a consensual act. In spite of the arguments of the French bishops, the Council of Trent had upheld the validity of unions concluded without parental consent. But this ran counter to the wishes of the ruling classes of France, and in the course of the sixteenth and seventeenth centuries French civil power undermined the Church's definition, to the point where the parlements were annulling such marriages.[30] Through the combined efforts of Crown and Parlement, marriage was changed from an act of mutual consent between partners into a family pact. As a prominent jurist wrote in 1643, "Marriages are made not for the pleasure of the parties involved, but for the honour and advantage of families; contracts are passed not as personal agreements, but as agreements that involve all the relatives."[31]

Both bride and groom were at their families' disposal. But whereas he had a life outside the home, she was bound entirely to the family. Barred by her rank from any exterior profession, her only function was the production and supervision of children, the upkeep of the household, and the care and support of her husband. This arrangement received full approval from the Church. François de Sales wrote: "Saint Paul assigns the care of the house to the women, which is why many people believe that their devotion is more fruitful to the family than that of their husbands who, since they spend less time among their families, are consequently unable to direct them as easily towards virtue."[32]

An aristocratic girl married much younger than her counterpart in the lower classes: sometimes at the age of twelve, more often at sixteen to eighteen, when – according to some learned opinion – she was most likely to produce strong (and male) children. By twenty-two she was considered an old maid. The daughter who did not marry remained under her father's roof, and was in time bequeathed to the heir along with the property. She could do nothing to advance her own marriage prospects, since these depended heavily on the provision of a dowry, and on the interests of the family.

Marriages contracted in this fashion might not be unhappy, but they were likely to be cold. In fact, passion was not recommended in the ideal marriage.[33] Almost universally, the literature of the day presents marriage as a sorry state. The accepted wisdom may be found in collections of proverbs, in the popular *Bibliothèque bleue*, in the books read by the upper classes, in drama, and in clerical writings and sermons. Most often, the sympathy went to the husbands, but, in fact, their position was easy compared to that of their wives. Madame de Maintenon, at the end of the century, presented the case against these gentlemen:

They come and go more than once a day, always making sure that everyone knows they are the masters; they enter with a terrible noise, often with I don't know how many other men; they bring in dogs, which ruin everything. The poor wife has to put up with it; she is not mistress enough even to have a window closed; if her husband comes late, she must wait up for him; she must dine when it pleases him; in a word, she is counted for nothing.[34]

Obviously, not all upper-class wives were prepared to renounce frivolity and live within their homes, or to be totally subject to their husbands. The very vehemence of the clerical literature against wifely independence, extravagance, waste of time, neglect of the home, gossip, and the sinful use of low-cut dresses and make-up is witness to this. The collapse of family fortunes was regularly attributed to their improvidence and mismanagement. However, all the evidence suggests that the seventeenth century saw a clear trend away from the relaxed social mores of the reign of Henri IV, and the development of a distinctly housewifely ethic.

What, then, was expected of the upper-class wife? First, that she live with her husband (a legal obligation) and that she be faithful to him (a moral duty, not necessarily reciprocated). Second, that she give him heirs and supervise their upbringing – in the case of boys, until the age of seven or eight; in the case of girls, until they left home. She was expected to help plan their future, and her consent was required for their marriage or entry into religion. Third, that she manage the domestic affairs – no small matter, whether the household numbered many servants or few. Fourth, that she assist her husband in his efforts to ascend in society. Clearly, the fulfilment of all these expectations required skill and application. Yet, in law, she remained a "demi-incapable."[35]

Did women see any anomalies in this situation? Some historians contend that they did. They base their argument on the evidence of the Reformation years, when aristocratic women joined the Protestant churches in remarkable numbers. They hypothesize that such women, already partly emancipated from old conventions, adhered to the religion of the Bible, because it represented for them an escape from a male-dominated world.[36]

If this was so, it would not have been without precedent. It has been frequently observed that throughout Christian history women have been attracted to "deviant" religious movements. "From the Montanist movement onwards," writes R.A. Knox, "the history of enthusiasm is largely a history of female emancipation."[37] Women had figured largely in the medieval heretical movements,[38] in English Lollardy,[39] and, more recently, in the Protestant Reformation. "In the diffusion of Reform," writes Febvre, "the capital role was held by women; they threw themselves body and soul into Reform, they served it with all their heart, with all their instinct."[40] Yet, where Protestantism became the established religion, as in England, and its structures became more authoritarian, many women again moved on, to become prominent in the sectarian movements.[41] The more egalitarian the sect, the higher the proportion of women.

At the same time, women also became the backbone of the Catholic recusant minority in England. It has been suggested that without their resistance the English Catholic community would not have survived.[42] Catholicism under persecution needed them, as much as did Quakerism or Anabaptism. It would seem that it was not doctrine that attracted women to minority religions but structures: structures that, being by necessity more relaxed and more inclusive, offered them a certain promotion.

Some historians have maintained that what attracted women to the reformed religion was the possibility of improvement which it offered in husband-wife relationships. Marriage, so the argument goes, was elevated as celibacy was devalued. Protestantism, at least in its early stages, seemed to offer a more equal partnership and a more genuine companionship.[43] In any case, many women, when given an opportunity, decided against their old religion and, with it, the patriarchal society.

Women of the Counter-Reformation seem to have sought in their religion not a improvement of marriage but a relief – temporary or permanent – from it. The case was put by a newly widowed lady of high rank: "Please pardon my frankness, if I tell you where marriage is concerned I obeyed once, and in obeying I bound myself to love the world more than Heaven, and vanity more than piety ... I shall stay in the freedom that my condition allows me."[44] Her opinion of marriage was not unique. Many pious women vowed their widowhood to God, even before the death of their husbands. Marriage was a "bother," a "subjection"; with François de Sales, they exclaimed: "Oh my God, how sweet it is to a widow to have only one heart to please!"[45]

The practice of their religion gave them an outlet. The early seventeenth century saw the awakening of upper-class Catholic women to the possibilities which religion offered them. The change in their attitude was so marked and so sudden that François de Sales, an infrequent visitor to Paris, commented on the progress in virtue of "these good ladies."[46] They rediscovered the practice of charity: under the influence of Madame Acarie,[47] the ancient custom of hospital visiting was again made respectable. They crowded the churches. Suddenly, "devotion" became the style. Women forsook frivolity for piety, and signalled their conversion by wearing sober clothes and, when they went outside, an enveloping black cape. "This became so common in Paris that almost all the girls and women one saw on the streets were wearing the cape," wrote one observer.[48]

However, this change in feminine behaviour created some awkwardness. Complaints were heard against "certain outlandish dévotes."[49] Their sober black dress and modest walk invited malicious imitation. Their behaviour was mocked openly. The doggerel ran: "If you are going to play the dévote, / wear the cord of Saint Francis / Communicate each month / Vespers at the Oratory / Know which are the Stations / and what is the Meditation, / Visit the Order of Saint-Ursule / Get to know the Père Bérulle / ... Have some aunts and some cousins / In the house of the Carmelines."[50]

More serious than the taunts of the impious were the scoldings of the Church. Until recently, preachers had castigated women for their failures of piety. Now they began to warn them against overzealousness. Madame Acarie herself was reproved from the pulpit for neglecting her duties as a wife and mother.[51] And yet feminine devotion continued to gather strength, and women continued to prefer it to their duties at home. Moralists were forced to give the problem further consideration, and to make some new definitions on the subject.

The Church had long been distrustful of the married state. In the early seventeenth century, in reaction to the position taken by the Protestant reformers, and consequent to its own elevation of the state of celibacy, its distrust was stronger than it had ever been. According to one of the most popular preachers of the time, "Virginity [is] the Sun, chastity the dawn, and marriage the night; marriage is the sea, chastity the port, and virginity the homeland."[52]

However, it now became necessary to formulate a moral argument to protect the married condition against the counter-attraction of the devout life. This argument was shaped out of the main thesis of François de Sales's book, *Introduction à la vie dévote*. According to this, every state possessed its own particular virtues, the practice of which could lead to holiness. It was incumbent on every Christian to accept his allotted state, and to turn it to his sanctification.

According to the moralists, the particular virtues of the married woman were "Modesty, silence, keeping to the house, and obedience." Her obedience to her husband had to be absolute in all things, even in her prayer life. "Woman must conform her wishes to those of her husband, she must support all his plans, she must unite her strength to his; and in everything which does not offend God, she must accept her husband's orders as though they were the commands of Heaven ... A communion neglected for the sake of obedience is to be preferred to one made in a spirit of wilfulness."[53] This obedience was enjoined even in cases where the husband was wrong, or where he was less intelligent than his wife: "Be subject to your husbands as to God, because for you they are the images of His power ... And even when nature has made you capable of instructing your husbands,it does not give you the liberty to usurp authority over them."[54]

This counsel, which endowed the wifely virtue of obedience with evangelical proportions, lasted throughout the century. But an endorsement of marriage which likened it unceasingly to a wearisome cross was, indeed, a case of damning with faint praise. While ostensibly upholding the married state, the clerical authorities were in fact putting a highly negative interpretation on it. "Loyalty and fidelity, indissolubility, procreative intention: this, then, is your portion, and the three things to which you will remain obliged; which are, as the Doctors say, the purposes which make Marriage legitimate and respectable."[55]

The corollary of this was that, in the case of the husband's death, the wife was advised not to marry again. According to François de Sales, "the most perfect course is to remain a widow."[56] This was a release for which, apparently, many wives prayed. Nicolas Caussin, in his *Instructions pour les veuves*, wrote: "Oh, how many times while you were tied down by marriage have you said that if God would only take away your husband, you would give yourself completely to Him; that your duty as a wife and your worldly responsibilities were your hindrance and your obstacle. Now that God has taken him away, bury your heart entirely in His."[57]

The best course – and all the preachers came back to it – was not to marry in the first place. Marriage caused nothing but pain. "Marriage is a long pilgrimage with but three wayside inns, the first being false pleasure, the second, regret, the third, calamity; and if you wish to go further, you will find only despair."[58] Virginity continued thoughout the century to be promoted as both the holiest and the happiest of all conditions. "You see," wrote Fénelon, "chastity is not a hard and heavy yoke; on the contrary, it is a liberty, a peace, a pleasant escape from the cares that afflict men in marriage."[59]

For *dévotes*, the alternative to marriage was clear. The woman who did not marry had no respectable option but to embrace the religious life. "Maritus aut murus" – a husband or a cloister – these were her only choices. By custom and by law she was considered too weak to live otherwise. "The common expression which tells parents to give their daughter 'either a husband or a cloister' seems to be based on a hidden law by which woman is born to spend her life under the control and the guidance of others."[60]

It is therefore reasonable to suppose that many of the women who became nuns in the seventeenth century did so as an alternative to marrying. This was the conjecture of at least one contemporary: "Among the virgins consecrated to God, how many decided to dedicate their lives to the state of virginity only after consideration of unhappy marriages? Thus, strangely enough, marriages in some way promote virginity, and the uglier they are, the more they serve to produce the beauty of virgins. If all marriages were happy, the millions of holy women who serve God in purity in the cloisters, would perhaps never have entered [religion]."[61]

Promotion of the religious life, devaluation of marriage: this was a message delivered in persuasive tones by the preachers of the Church. Nor did the law, literature, and social conventions of the day do anything to soften the message. For women of quality, the monastic attraction, exercised through sermons and a rapidly burgeoning literature of devotion, was a powerful force, made more powerful by the negative character given to marriage. Only by an understanding of this religious dimension, built out of social and economic conditions but not entirely commensurate with them, can the extraordinary developments of the Counter-Reformation be understood.

In the first half of the seventeenth century the cities and towns of France experienced what has been called "a fantastic conventual invasion."[62] In the space of some fifty or sixty years, the urban religious population, which had remained reasonably static for generations, soared. "For the last twenty or thirty years," complained an official of the Parlement of Rouen, "so many different religious orders have entered this city, that they outnumber all those of the previous thousand years."[63] This was an almost universal experience. By mid-century many municipalities saw the larger part of their urban space in the hands of religious orders. The drain of property became so serious that most cities looked for ways to prevent or limit the establishment of further communities.

The "conventual invasion" was occasioned partly by the revitalization of old communities, but even more by the establishment of the new congregations. The attraction of these new religious groups was seemingly irresistible. As Pierre de l'Estoile wrote in 1606: "It was not unusual, in Paris and everywhere else, for the sons and daughters of good houses – men and women of quality – to go off and enter these orders."[64]

The increase of female religious was even more striking than that of male, because traditionally there were far fewer women than men in religious life. An observer wrote in 1659: "This century is a century of new establishments of nuns. One sees their monasteries everywhere; there is no town, however small, that does not have one or two."[65] In Troyes, the one female abbey that had sufficed for centuries was joined by such a variety of convents that in 1695 there were 320 nuns in the city.[66] In Blois, where the ancient monastery of the Véroniques with its handful of nuns had accounted for the entire female religious population, three new convents raised the number to 236 by 1670.[67] In Reims, which had a total population of ten thousand, the number of cloistered nuns rose from sixty in 1619 to between three and four hundred in 1658.[68] In Saint-Denis, on the outskirts of Paris, three separate convents were built between 1625 and 1629; one of them alone, the Ursuline community, came to number seventy-four members in the 1670s. This approached the entire population of religious women in the diocese of Paris in the year 1600.[69]

In increasing numbers, from the start of the century until its middle years, women crowded into the convents. The massive influx has been explained in a number of ways: social pressures, anxiety, the desire for flight from the world. But the motive power that must not be discounted is enthusiasm and a sense of mission. The word that appeared with greater and greater frequency was "apostolate." The Counter-Reformation Church envisaged nothing less than a total rechristianization of society. The new congregations were, in the large majority, specifically designed to be instruments in this rechristianization. As so much of the religious art and literature of the age shows, they saw themselves as fighters in a spiritual war. Their members were being invited to participate in this war. The feminine congregations considered themselves included in this invitation.

For women, the experience was absolutely new. For them, the monastic ideal had traditionally been an inward-turning life, complete unto itself, its isolation from the world made concrete by the enclosing walls and grilles. Now, quite suddenly, this life began to turn outwards. Even as some women re-established monastic life in all its austerity, others began to look for a means to participate in the work of the Church. "To do all the good that is possible"[70] – this intention, as enthusiastic as it was imprecise, was typical of the spirit in which women of the early seventeenth century offered their services to the Church. As opportunities to do this good opened up, the number of women entering religion burgeoned so rapidly that within a few years it equalled, then surpassed, that of men.[71]

It would be a mistake to see this as an integral part of the tridentine reform. This burst of feminine energy was neither foreseen nor welcomed. The congregations of the seventeenth century grew out of a sort of anarchy of religious activism. To a significant degree, the act of their creation was performed by the women themselves. Groups of dévotes all over the country joined together in impromptu communities to live, work, and pray, sometimes for years, before developing a rule of their own or placing themselves in an authorized congregation. These women do not fit the stereotype of the adolescent nun, safe behind her convent walls, which was so much a feature of later seventeenth-century society.[72] In fact, the congrégées[73] of the Counter-Reformation period were more likely to enter religion in their twenties than in their teens.[74] The communities to which they bound themselves were often extremely tenuous, and in their early years were dogged by uncertainty and lack of funds. In other words, life in most of the new congregations involved several years of risk and discomfort. And yet it was often during these very years that the number of entries was highest.[75]

From all the appearances it may be argued that, however important other factors may be, the "conventual invasion" in the early years of the century must finally be related to the fervour of the entrants themselves. But the dévotes had already attracted criticism by what was seen as their excess. How did such further enthusiasm come to be tolerated by the Church?

It has to be remembered that the Counter-Reformation came late to France. Only in 1615 did the Assembly of the Clergy officially accept the discipline of the Council of Trent. The old structures of the Church had been in ruins for some years before the new structures were put into place. This meant that, in the religious life of

the country, the early years of the century were years of interreg-
num, and, therefore, conducive to individual initiative. It was during
this period, and especially after the publication of the *Introduction à
la vie dévote* in 1608,[76] that lay action "took off." "Catholic reform,"
remarks one Church historian, "was the work of the saints, not the
politicians."[77] Before the French church even found its feet, a strong
apostolic current was sweeping through France.

In this current many women found, or thought they found, their
calling. By 1615, new feminine communities were appearing all over
the country. As the French church began to prepare for reform, and
for the rechristianization of the people, the women were already
there, seeing themselves, in some way not yet fully articulated, as
participants in the apostolate.[78]

This sudden invasion by female volunteers of an area that women
had not trodden before forced Catholic reformers to define and clar-
ify the place of women in the Church. The clarification was mostly
negative. The very strength of Catholic Reform lay in its respect for
tradition. Tradition had always allowed for feminine religious life,
and indeed piety had encouraged it. But before the sheer weight of
numbers of women who were now seeking admission, some people
in the Church took fright. Furthermore, certain groups of these
women had ideas of exceeding the boundaries of religious life and
taking up an active life; and the same people found this unacceptable. According to tradition, the female sex was weak and flawed,
and unfit to enter religion's inner courts. A powerful antifeminism,
raised through time almost to the level of Christian doctrine, awaited
women at the church door.

CHAPTER TWO

The Defence of the Status Quo (1563–1631)

Catholic reform was, by its very nature, an effort to return to a more perfect past, to correct the faults which had caused its deformities and incurred the divine wrath. "We frankly confess that God permits this persecution to afflict His Church because of the sins of men, and especially of the priests and prelates," wrote Pope Adrian VI in 1522. "All of us (that is, prelates and clergy), each one of us, have strayed from our paths, nor for a long time has anyone done good; no, not even one."[1] The punishment for this scandalous infidelity was the spread of heresy; and the only cure for heresy was a return to virtue.

Virtue could be found in the *status quo* – the way Christendom used to be before sin and division came to it. Catholic reformers looked back to a golden age, an age of faith, and hoped to recreate it by returning the Church to its pristine state, and by rooting out the novelties which they considered akin to heresy. In this spirit they prepared themselves to admit guilt but, at the same time, to resist change. For the first implied fault in themselves, which they could accept; and the second implied fault in the Institution, which they could not accept.

This concept of reform as a return to the past found strength in the natural bias of Catholic society in favour of tradition, and the deep outrage which it felt at the innovations and iconoclasms of the Protestants. In the century of the Reformation, ordinary Catholics did not take kindly to any tinkering with ancient customs, no matter how outdated. A deep-rooted conservatism lay in wait for every innovation, every new experiment in religious practice. Yet at the same time, and in response to the same experience of Reformation, new energies were being released in the Church and a new militancy was making itself felt. In many different ways, Catholics looked at the reformed churches, envied their dynamism, and absorbed their values. The current of apostolic movement thus created met and mingled with the current of reform, creating a turbulence which would eventually transform the Church.

It is the purpose of this chapter first to examine the context of monastic reform, and then to study the cases of two feminine religious congregations of the early seventeenth century which were caught in this clash between reformism and apostolic fervour. The characters of these two congregations were altogether dissimilar. The English Ladies of the Institute of Mary were extremely ambitious. They hoped to create a female order in imitation of the Society of Jesus, with powers to teach and to evangelize. To achieve this, they rejected clausura outright, as unapostolic. "All of ours should know," their memorial ran, "on entering this life, that they are not called to a life in which they can devote themselves only to themselves."[2] The Filles de Sainte-Marie, or sisters of the Visitation, had far more modest aspirations; they simply wished to combine the monastic life with care of the poor and sick of their neighbourhood. Yet even in this humble measure of service to the world they invoked the example of the apostolic women of the early Church: "the illustrious ladies of antiquity, the Paulas, the Marcellas, the Eustochions, the Mellanias."[3]

Their proposals created a storm of opposition. Both congregations were dealt with: the Institute of Mary was condemned and suppressed,[4] the Visitation was put firmly into enclosure and deprived of its opening to the world. What happened to them subsequently is not our principal concern. What is important here is the nature of their opposition, for from it we can gauge the strength of the *status quo* in the first decades of the century, and also identify who was most concerned with defending it, and why. Only if the *status quo* is fully appreciated can the change that later did take place be given its real weight.

European monasticism was already ten centuries old when the Council of Trent undertook to reform it. For many of those centuries it had been the heart, and indeed the muscle, of western Christianity. But in recent years the heart had faltered and the muscle grown slack. Along the paths by which the Reformation had moved, monasteries – if they had survived at all – had been left in shambles, their finances disrupted, their populations dispersed. Elsewhere, where the old religion still prevailed, the distress was of a different order: monasteries were held *in commendam* by absentees, or granted as benefices to the friends of princes, and buildings that had once been full were now half-empty, occupied by men and women who no longer had the will to live up to their original purpose.

While the council was prepared to address the problems of the monasteries, these were not its priority. It was through reform of the bishops and the secular clergy that it intended to save the Church. Only in 1563, during its last session, did the Fathers turn to the question of monastic discipline; and then their purpose was restorative, rather than innovative. The monasticism which Trent hoped to re-establish was essentially still the life that Benedict had instituted, the life of retreat, in which the unchanging round of prayer and labour, lived out within a community of brothers or sisters, was its own end. To this purpose the great religious rules of the Middle Ages were reinstated without alteration. The council insisted that there could be no modification of established monastic practice. "For if those things that constitute the basis and foundation of all regular discipline are not strictly observed, the whole edifice must necessarily fall down."[5]

Medieval monasticism was built around the ideal of "flight from the world." Strictly speaking, there was no other true religious life.[6] Only by renouncing the world altogether could the soul aspire to perfection. Therefore a monk left all temporal affairs behind him, to belong to his monastery, and to devote himself to the daily round of prayer and praise which is known as Divine Office. His life was self-contained, and separate from the world.

The only entry into the state of religion was by the profession of solemn vows. In a public ceremony before the Church and the world, the aspirant solemnly vowed himself to the perpetual observance of the three evangelical virtues of poverty, chastity, and obedience. This public profession, made in front of witnesses, signalled his death to the world, and the beginning of another life that would end only in eternity. Solemn vows had a binding, quasi-sacramental quality; only the Holy See could grant dispensation from them.[7] Between the religious and the secular states, canon law and theology had posed a sharp and clear demarcation.

With the passage of time the demarcation had been blurred. This was the consequence of relaxation, of a centuries-long process of self-compromise by the religious orders. Even where they remained free of outright scandal, they had accepted involvement in secular affairs, and a private, often propertied, lifestyle which conflicted with their vows. But another development had had equal and possibly greater effect on the old monastic ideal. This was the appearance through the later Middle Ages of semi-religious communities which continued to act "in the world." Throughout Europe, brothers and sisters – many of them tertiaries under the aegis of the mendicant orders – worked in charitable institutions, while living in community and taking only simple vows.

The Council of Trent rejected both the relaxation and the adaptation, and bound itself firmly to the traditional, and extremely radical, interpretation of the "perfect" life. The religious orders were directed to return to their primitive observance. In two constitutions issued immediately after the council, *Circa pastoralis* (1566) and *Lubricum vitae genus* (1568), Pope Pius v ordered that all tertiaries must accept solemn vows and full monastic discipline, or be dispersed.[8] Thus at its very outset, the Counter-Reformation formally rejected the possibility of an intermediate state between the wholly secular and the wholly religious.[9]

In practice, however, the same impulse for reform that inspired the council also gave rise to new associations, which eluded the medieval monastic definition but responded perfectly to the needs of the Counter-Reformation church. Foremost among them was the Society of Jesus. Ignatius Loyola and his followers offered the papacy a force with which to re-establish its spiritual authority – but at a price. In the new Society the religious and secular states so recently declared separate were merged again, in a "mixed" life of contemplation and action. Opponents of the Jesuits saw this as a dilution of the ideal of monastic perfection, while supporters argued that the new mixed life was more perfect, because it was modelled on the life of Christ himself. There was a long-running battle in Rome over the question of the Society's legitimacy. But the papacy sided with the Jesuits: in the bull *Ascendente domino* (1584), it specifically exempted them from the obligations of solemn vows and monastic stability. Although this was intended at first as a privilege for the Jesuits alone, other masculine congregations later sought and attained similar exemptions. By 1630 the existence of men's communities living under a rule, bound by simple vows only, or by no vows at all, and pursuing an active vocation in the world, was generally accepted.

For women, however, reform continued to mean only return to the rules.[10] And these rules were extremely rigid and limiting. Feminine monasticism, though modelled on its masculine counterpart, had developed its own particular ethos. Medieval nuns were seen as the "brides of Christ," and their virginity as the jewels in his crown. Their principal duty, therefore, lay in the preservation of chaste bodies and minds.[11] But innocence was constantly endangered by natural weakness, and therefore in the course of the centuries the stricter communities of nuns had adopted clausura. In 1298, Pope Boniface VIII raised their practice, which had previously been only local custom, to universal law, and ordained that all religious women, once they had taken their solemn vows, must live within an enclosure, closed off from all contact with the world.

The Council of Trent reaffirmed Boniface's legislation, and commanded all bishops "under threat of eternal malediction" to ensure the enclosure of the nuns under their jurisdiction. No nun, once professed, was to be permitted to go out of the monastery, "even for a brief period, under any pretext whatsoever," except with the permission of the bishop.[12] The only legitimate excuses for leaving the cloister were fire, leprosy, and contagious disease.[13] The monastery walls were to be high enough to exclude all view, either from without or from within. Men were forbidden to enter, except in certain specified cases of necessity; and such contact as was allowed between nuns and outsiders, through the narrow mesh of the parlour grille, was to be strictly limited, under pain of excommunication.[14] Furthermore, laywomen – with only a few exceptions – were excluded from the enclosure. To block out the influence of the world, even the young girls who were pupils in the monasteries were ordered to be kept permanently enclosed until such time as they were finally ready to leave, or to enter the noviciate. There was to be no coming and going to disturb the inner stillness of the cloister.

This was strong medicine indeed, as the long and bitter struggle to restore the women's monasteries to clausura was to prove. To enforce compliance, the council placed all communities of women, except those already subject to male religious orders, under the immediate control of the ordinaries. It is not difficult to sense the Fathers' preoccupation with the "relaxed" monasteries: nuns in their silks and furs, with their retinues of servants and their gallants in attendance; abbesses powerful enough to defy their bishops, and beyond them, the whole order of authority.

Clausura was much appreciated by Catholic reformers. It restored and protected the honour of religious women; it saved them from exposure to the influence of the world. Also – an important consideration in the sixteenth century – it gave them all possible protection from the violence of the age.[15] But it also rendered them ineffective for all practical purposes. The council in its prescriptions for female religious looked backward to the Middle Ages, rather than forward to the much more activist world that was in the making. While it opened the door to reform of contemplative communities, it closed it to the more apostolic religious lifestyles that were already taking shape. There would be no special considerations for women's congregations to match those made for the Jesuits.

Religious women were also treated differently from men in the matter of their organization. As has been seen, Trent ordered that all women's monasteries – unless they already depended on male religious orders – were to be subject to the ordinaries. This meant that they could not join with other communities in congregations. There was to be no question of self-government, of movement or co-operation between houses. Yet at the same time the Church was advancing the principle of congregation and union of houses as the means of ensuring male monastic reform. Nothing illustrates more vividly how differently the Church perceived its male and its female religious.[16] In the tradition of the Counter-Reformation, nuns were the "daughters of the bishop," much cherished, but minors nonetheless.

The half-century after Trent was a period of hesitation. It was not immediately certain that the Church would enforce in practice what it had laid down in law. Rome, after all, was not strong enough to ignore regional customs and conditions, and the personalities of local bishops and princes. In various parts of Europe, women followed the example of the new masculine congregations, and established communities which, in modern terminology, devoted themselves to social work. The initial reaction of Church authorities was not unfavourable. Beneath the surface, however, ran a deep strain of resistance. As the women grew stronger and more numerous, and their work more ambitious, anger grew against what was seen as presumption on their part. In the early years of the seventeenth century it erupted, in a case which set an enduring precedent for women's active congregations.

THE ENGLISH LADIES, 1609–31

Since the days of Queen Elizabeth, the Spanish Netherlands had been a haven for English Catholics who were dissatisfied with, or in danger from, their own country's Protestant government. Therefore it was in no way unusual when, in 1609, a young Catholic Yorkshirewoman named Mary Ward, with the help of six companions from her own country, opened a school in Saint-Omer, to teach young girls "to read, write and sew for the honour of God."[17] Their community was an instant success, and by 1612 it numbered some forty members.

They were more than simple schoolmistresses, however. Their ultimate hope was to return as missionaries to their own country, as their memorial, drawn up and submitted to the Holy See, indicated. "As the sadly afflicted state of England, our native country, stands greatly in need of spiritual labourers, and as priests, both religious and secular respectively, work assiduously in this harvest, it seems that the female sex also in its own measure, should and can in like manner undertake something more than ordinary in this great common spiritual necessity."[18]

In 1614 they put their plan into action: they opened a house in London, a base from which they went out to teach in private homes, and to care for the sick and the poor. This was dangerous work, beyond the reach of any normal Catholic conventions of the time. The England of James I, still tense in the aftermath of the Gunpowder Plot, allowed no clausura or solemn vows, and certainly no catechizing in the popish faith. To conceal their purpose the women put aside their sober clothes and conventual lifestyle, and dressed and lived as became their rank in society. In all this they took their cue from the masters of underground evangelization, the Jesuits.

The identification of the English Ladies with the Jesuits went far beyond missionary tactics. From the beginning, the women saw themselves as counterparts, for their own sex, of the Society of Jesus. They openly used it as their model. Mary Ward herself, when pondering the form that the institute should take, received an inspiration to "take the same of the Society."[19] Her plan, submitted to the pope in 1615, provided for a Jesuit-style structure, complete with a superior-general who would be responsible to the pontiff alone, "and that no religious Order whatsoever, or any person whatsoever ... should ... exercise over us authority, power, or jurisdiction."[20] To the minutest details, the practice and spirit of the new institute were to be modelled upon the Jesuits.[21] Like the Jesuits, the English Ladies would allow degrees of membership, so that many of them would live under simple vows rather than solemn vows. They would be dispensed from the obligations of Divine Office and religious habit. More audacious yet, they would be mobile as the Jesuits were mobile. Since they were women, this meant that clausura, the great protection of virginal purity, would have to be waived.

The institute received support in high places. The archdukes of the Spanish Netherlands, Albert and Isabella, gave it their encouragement. So did Bishop Blaise of Saint-Omer. One prominent theologian, Lessius, pronounced the proposed rule to be "holy, lawful and good," while another, Suarez, approved it on condition that it received the confirmation of the Holy See.[22] In 1616, this confirmation seemed forthcoming, when Pope Paul v gave the institute his provisional approval. Within a short time new communities, including a college and a noviciate, were established in Liège, Trèves, and Cologne.

But Mary Ward was too much in advance of her times, and her project aroused violent reaction. "Various persons set themselves from the first against her plans," wrote a seventeenth-century biographer.[23] As the institute grew, so did the opposition. In 1616 Bishop Blaise was forced to issue a pastoral letter, defending the Ladies; and in his defence, for the first time, the charges against them can be divined. These were, first, that they diverted other women from entering established monasteries; second, that they pretended to be true nuns; and third, that they undertook apostolic missions in England. The last charge, with its antifeminine edge, was by far the most serious. In claiming to act as apostles, the women were invading a masculine preserve. The importance of this accusation can be seen in the fact that it stayed with them until the end, fifteen years later.

The chief reason for this hostility continued to lie just beneath the surface. The rivalries within the exiled Catholic community were deep and vicious. The English secular clergy were engaged in an ongoing quarrel with the Jesuits, who, with their aggressive missionary tactics, were cutting into what the seculars considered their own territory. The unswerving loyalty of the English Ladies to Jesuit principles seemed to the seculars to be further evidence of the Jesuits' determination that "both sexes shall have a general dependence of them."[24]

For its part, the Society of Jesus was ambivalent about the English Ladies. Many of the English Jesuits supported these women "who do not content themselves to live in monasteries for themselves alone, ... but according to their measure of grace ... leave their rest and retreat as our Blessed Saviour did his Father's bosom to quench the fire of sin and heresy."[25] Their superiors, however, handled their new devotees much as they would have handled a bunch of stinging nettles. Since the days of Ignatius, the Society had attempted with more or less success to avoid the responsibility of directing women's communities. Now, in the early 1620s, the Jesuit General Vitelleschi expressly ordered his English troops to stay as clear as possible of the Ladies. "Let all endeavour not to meddle in their businesses and make the world know that the Society hath no more to do with them than with all other penitents who resort to them; whereby I hope, in a short time, the manifold caluminations which for their cause and proceedings are laid upon us will have an end."[26]

However, Vitelleschi's orders only split the English Jesuits, while it failed to allay the growing opposition. An impressive body of slander was already being concocted. The English Ladies were nick-named "Jesuitesses" and "galloping girls"; they were accused of vainglory and high living. Mary herself was rumoured to be closer than was proper to her Jesuit confessor; it was even suggested that she had lived in a Jesuit house, in male attire. The information was sent to Rome, where it was put to good use by the representative of the English clergy.

But amidst all the falsehoods, the true allegation remained the most damning: the institute aspired to do the work of men: "[it] professes to be devoted to the conversion of England, no otherwise than   as priests themselves who are destined to this end by apostolic authority."[27] The English clergy considered this intolerable, and they used it to play upon the sensibilities of Rome. The Ladies' firm rejection of clausura only strengthened the case against them. "Of clausure they will not hear," wrote the English clergy's agent in Rome, "And in other Orders there is not the perfection they aim at; and this they have not been ashamed to answer to these great prel-ates, who think of them accordingly."[28]

Mary Ward did not retreat before her critics. She was a courageous woman, who had not been afraid, while she was in England, to carry a rosary in public, and to visit the Jesuits who were in prison. She was used to carrying all before her, with her mixture of charm and natural authority. She was also completely frank – too frank, in the opinion of her biographer. In her own words, "I so greatly … loved integrity … that unless I had gone against my nature, it would have been impossible for me to act by halves in things of the soul."[29] Since she refused to compromise, and opposition continued to grow, there seemed no recourse but to take her own case to Rome. In 1621, with her protector, Paul v, dead, and still no definitive papal confirmation of her institute, she went to plead with the new pope, Gregory xv. By now the feelings against her were running high and for all her natural ability she was unable to defend herself against the bill of accusations which the English clergy drew up against her.

The document's main points were as follows: 1) "It was never heard in the Church that women should discharge the Apostolic Office"; 2) the institute contravened the decrees of the Council of Trent; 3) "The members arrogate to themselves the power to speak of spiritual things before grave men and priests, and to hold ex-hortations in assemblies of Catholics and usurp ecclesiastical offices"; 4) it was feared that they would run into errors of various kinds.[30] On the basis of these charges, a council of cardinals ruled against the institute.

Mary had not yet lost her case. The pope allowed her and her companions to open a charity school in Rome, to demonstrate the value of their work. In the following years schools were founded in other Italian cities. But in 1625 her enemies prevailed, and the schools were ordered closed, in spite of local protests. The representative of the English clergy was overjoyed. "Their schooles is tooke away, they shall stay in Rome if they will, but their habbit shall be tooke away. Their houses at Perugia and Naples shall be undone," he wrote.[31] But Mary had not yet been ordered to desist. She returned across the Alps to Bavaria, where she enjoyed the support of the Elector Maximilian, and began again to establish communities. In 1628, the institute numbered ten houses, and between two and three hundred members.[32] It was at this stage that the Congregation of Propaganda secretly ordered it suppressed.

By now there had been another change of popes, and Mary, unaware of the order against her, was already on her way to Rome to petition the new pope, Urban VIII, for authorization. She was as effective a pleader with Urban as she had been with Gregory, and she had influence in high places. But she also had enemies, and these, it seemed, carried more weight. Of the committee of four cardinals appointed to hear her case, one, Cardinal Borgia, pleaded to be released from the duty, out of his feeling for the institute: "that he held it to be of God, and that he neither could nor durst be against it; nor was his power enough to assist it, so powerful were her enemies."[33] Having presented her case, Mary left Rome and returned to Munich in 1630, only to be arrested there as a heretic and a schismatic. When she was released from prison a year later, her institute had been formally condemned, its members expelled from their houses – often without a penny to their names.[34]

The Bull of Suppression, dated 13 January 1631, declared that the English Ladies were "noxious weeds," "to be rooted out and extirpated." "We suppress and abolish them absolutely and altogether … we submit them to perpetual abolition, we remove them, cut them off, and banish them entirely from the Holy Church of Christ."[35] The bull gave two reasons for the condemnation. First, the institute had been established, and had continued to function, without papal approval.[36] Second, the women had arrogated to themselves functions reserved to men:

They went freely everywhere, without submitting to the laws of clausura, under the pretext of working for the salvation of souls; they undertook and exercised many other works unsuitable to their sex and their capacity, their feminine modesty, and, above all, their virginal shame; works which men distinguished by their knowledge of the scriptures, their experience and the innocence of their lives, undertake only with reluctance and extreme circumspection.[37]

This was the true charge against the English Ladies: they had threatened the order of things, in an age when such a threat smacked of heresy. For this, as one of their sympathizers had warned them, they were rejected, "like as the little crows left by the old ones, because not feathered like themselves."[38]

Mary, it is argued, might have saved her institute, if she had been willing to compromise her ambitions. She was advised, over and over again, to accept clausura, "on which condition," wrote her companion, Winifrid Wigmore, "she should have freedom to set up as many houses all over the world as she would. But to this fair offer our dearest Mother gave for answer that 'to obtain the foresaid grace of propagating [the faith], she would not admit of two stakes put in cross in form of enclosure.'"[39]

Although she consistently denied that she wished to usurp the functions of the priesthood, she did not hesitate to confess her high ambitions, both for her own sisters and for other women:

There is no such difference between men and women that women may not do great things ... And I hope to God that it will be seen that women in time to come will do much ... I confess wives are to be subject to their husbands, men are head of the Church, women are not to administer Sacraments, nor preach in public places; but in all other things, wherein are we so inferior to other creatures that they should term us 'but women'? I would to God that all men understood this truth, that women, if they will be perfect, and if they would not make us believe that we can do nothing and that we are but women, might do great matters ... I must and will ever stand for this truth, that women may be perfect, and that fervour must not necessarily decay because we are women.[40]

The suppression of the institute had far-reaching consequences. It has been seen as the end of post-Reformation Catholic expansion in England – and the victory of the *status quo* preferred by the secular clergy over the more dynamic missionary program espoused by the Jesuits.[41] In the Catholic world, it served as a caution to women who wished to take up an active apostolate. In the immediate aftermath of the affair, numerous active uncloistered communities of women were ordered closed across Europe, on the vague grounds that they, too, were "Jesuitesses." The teaching communities of Flanders were among those affected and only a long and stubborn defence by their bishops saved them.[42] Another group of teaching communities in Lorraine and eastern France, the Congrégation de Notre-Dame, was less successful; it was forced to accept strict clausura.[43]

The long-term consequences were equally discouraging. The papacy froze into a stance of total negativity on the question of women in the apostolate. Urban VIII later recognized that his hand had been forced, and that the information given to him about Mary and her institute had been false.[44] He redressed Mary's greatest grief, by requesting the Holy Office of the Inquisition to state that she had never been a heretic. But he could not undo what had been officially done to her institute. The Holy See had served notice that it was committed to upholding the most conservative position regarding female religious – a position which envisaged nothing but a return to the strict monasticism of the high Middle Ages. Henceforth throughout the century, no initiatives for a feminine apostolate would come out of Rome, and the advances that were made in fact received no sanction in canon law.[45] There would not be another Mary Ward, outlining her brave hopes before the pope with candour and confidence. The founders of women's active communities learned that henceforth, if they wished to approach the apostolate, they would have to use more circuitous routes.

THE VISITATION: EARLY YEARS, 1610–16

The case of the Visitation was not taken to Rome. Its fate was decided by a debate between two bishops, one of whom had the advantage of sanctity while the other had the advantage of political power. But the content of the debate has a familiar ring. Was there any justification, in the circumstances of the seventeenth century, for moderating the existing tradition of clausura for religious women? The final conclusion was a victory for what one historian of canon law has called "the narrowness of some Frenchmen in questions of canon law."[46] The new congregation was forced to adopt solemn vows, strict clausura, and the rule of Saint Augustine.

In this case it was not the Universal Church that passed judgment; it was the Gallican church, and the elites who were the backbone of its support. The reasons for French rigidity are not hard to find. Where the old religion was most embattled, innovation was most strongly resisted. The France of the early 1600s, still deeply shaken by the religious wars, was in no mood for experiments. Therefore

French canonists put the narrowest interpretation upon the legislation of Trent. The Visitation was only the first of several female communities which found that they could not enter the kingdom of France without submitting to full monastic discipline.

The Visitation of Annecy, in Savoy, was an experiment in an updated feminine religious life, attuned to the new spirituality for which its founder, more than any other single person, was responsible. François de Sales, bishop of Geneva,[47] envisaged a community of prayer without solemn vows and clausura, and without the extreme rigours of reformed monasticism. His creation, which saw the light of day in 1610, aroused a clamour of criticism.

The Visitation made its appearance just as the abbeys and priories of France began to wrestle with the problem of a return to discipline, and an end to relaxed behaviour and luxurious lifestyle. The arrival in 1601 of the first Carmelites from Spain had given a powerful impulse to the reform movement. In all these cases, reform was characterized by strict austerity and personal mortification – and, of course, full clausura. It required high motivation, but it also required great strength and stamina.

François de Sales saw the need for a community for women who were unfit for so strenuous a life, and yet had spiritual potential. He developed the idea after meeting the baronne de Chantal.[48] Widowed and the mother of four young children, she had already taken a vow of chastity when the bishop of Geneva met her in 1604, and was occupied in searching for a life of "perfection." However, her obligations to her family and the state of her health made entry into a monastery impossible. The community of the Visitation, established in Annecy in 1610, was inspired by her and designed for her.[49]

According to François de Sales, the principal virtue to be cultivated in the new community was "littleness": "Leaving the great Orders already established in the Church to honour Our Lord by their excellent religious observances and brilliant virtues, I desire that my daughters glorify Him only through their lowliness."[50] The four women who made up the community at its outset were not meant to be religious, but simply *dévotes* in the fullest sense of the word. They took only simple vows. Physical mortification, as practised in the monasteries, was reduced to a minimum. They observed no fasting beyond that enjoined on all Catholics; they slept through the night and rose at 5:30; their food was sufficient and their clothing comfortable. Their mortification was to be interior. As their founder told them, their feet were to be well shod, but their hearts were to be bare and naked of earthly affections.[51]

The life of prayer and contemplation and work within the house was to be enriched by visits to the sick and poor. However, the ultimate purpose of this charitable work was not the service itself, but the value that it brought to the prayer life of the community. The founders of the Visitation believed that the most perfect life was one in which prayer was combined with good works. This dimension of charitable action was fundamental to the primitive concept of the Visitation. De Sales proposed for their model the strong woman of the Bible: "'She sets her hand to important matters, her fingers grasp the spindle.' Meditate, lift up your soul to God ... these are the important matters. But for all that, do not forget your spindle and your distaff: spin the thread of small virtues, humble yourself to do the works of charity."[52]

The mixed life of the primitive Visitation entailed a "mitigated clausura." In other words, men might not enter the house except under the conditions prevailing in all reformed women's monasteries. Women might enter with authorization. Indeed, one of the good works of the house would be the short "retreats" which it would offer to laywomen. The sisters, when they went out to work with the sick, were to receive permission from their superiors, and only those who were sufficiently mature were allowed to leave the house.[53] More novel was the freedom, granted under special circumstances, for the sisters to leave the house temporarily, to see to their family affairs.

In allowing this breadth of action to a religious community the bishop of Geneva was drawing upon Italian experience. In particular he used, and frequently cited, the example of the community of the Torre di Specchi in Rome, which combined simple vows and community life with service to the poor.[54] Since the foundress of this congregation, Frances of Rome, had recently been canonized, he might well feel that any community following the same pattern would be in an unimpeachable position. Here, however, he was mistaken.

In 1615, a second community of the Visitation was founded, at the request of the archbishop of Lyon, Denis-Simon de Marquemont. However, less than a year later, the archbishop had had a change of mind; he had become convinced in conscience that, much as he admired the Visitation and respected its founder, he could not accept it in its present form. He wrote a memoir to the bishop of Geneva, demanding that it be transformed into a recognized religious order, pontifically approved, with solemn vows and strict clausura. And just as François de Sales had chosen the title of "Visitation" in recognition of the sisters' "mixed" vocation of prayer and action, Marquemont proposed that the name of the institute be changed to "Présentation de Notre-Dame," as a clear recognition that their life was henceforth to be confined to the holy place that was their monastery.[55]

The response came back almost immediately, written in François de Sales's own hand: a statement "for the instruction of the devout, on the dignity, antiquity, usefulness and variety of congregations or colleges of women dedicated to God."[56] The work contained three main themes. The first was an argument, based on examples drawn from the Bible and from the Fathers, for the dignity and value of women before God.

Woman ... no less than man, enjoys the favour of having been made in the image of God; the honour is done equally to both the sexes; their virtues are equal; to each of them is offered an equal reward, and if they sin, a similar damnation. I would not want woman to say: I am frail, my condition is weak. This weakness is of the flesh, but virtue which is strong and powerful is seated in the soul.[57]

Then, beginning with Christ himself and continuing through the Apostles to the early Christian centuries, François de Sales showed how the Church had always encouraged women: "The holy pastors of the early Church had a very special care for the advancement of this sex in the practice and perfection of Christian life." In the early Church, many assemblies of widows and virgins dedicated themselves to prayer and the service of their neighbour.

The third argument was based on the structure of the contemporary Church. Within the life of perfection there were various degrees, beginning with the bishops and running through a whole range of different "states" down to the simple *dévot* lifestyle practised by individuals under some form of private vow. Among these degrees there was, of course, the monastic life for women, but this might have more or less clausura according to custom. Strict clausura, in fact, was a relatively new state in the Church. "Indeed, the absolute, perpetual, strict, narrow clausura, which many people consider the only true clausura, was hardly practised among early Christians, whose saintly simplicity did not require such severity; they were content with a moderate clausura, in which the joy of the religious vocation was itself ample enclosure."[58]

Moderate clausura was appropriate to simple congregations, which had purposes other than pure contemplation. To insist that only the strictest monastic observance was permissible was to deny many people the possibility of a religious vocation.

François de Sales concluded with the argument so central to his spirituality: that the life of perfection was an interior, not an exterior, state. "If the spirit of true devotion reigns in a congregation, a moderate enclosure will suffice to make good servants of God; if it does not reign there, the strictest enclosure will not be sufficient."[59]

Marquemont gave his response early in 1616. Where the bishop of Geneva had dealt in ideas, he was severely practical: "The young women and widows who enter the Congregation will never be proper, true religious."[60] They could not enjoy the name, the merit, the perfection or the indulgences that would be their right as true nuns. This could be rectified only by converting the Visitation into a formal religious order under an approved rule. The rule of Saint Augustine was the obvious choice, since it was less demanding than the life that the sisters were already leading, and therefore could be adopted without disrupting their present usages.

Marquemont was prepared to tolerate the practice of accepting older women and women of delicate health into the congregation, and of allowing laywomen into the monastery for short-term retreats. But the other custom, of allowing widows within the congregation to go out occasionally to deal with their affairs, he adamantly rejected. The passage in which he explained his reasons affords an powerful insight into the tensions of Counter-Reformation society:

On one hand those who see a nun in the world, occupied with business affairs, will be scandalized; on another, the Monasteries which we are trying to enclose in obedience to the Council, will have something to say and good reason to complain; furthermore, Protestants and libertines will be able to criticize clausura in our Monasteries, since by the device of "congregations" we are simply by-passing it, and proving that there was no enclosure in the early Church.[61]

No matter how excellent the motives of the founder, no matter how laudable the actual life of the women, these exceptions to the rule of clausura would cause scandal, "which in these times, and in this country, is extremely dangerous."[62]

By the same token, the visiting of the poor and sick must stop. The women must accept the full implications of monastic life, without modification. "The purpose of the Councils has always been to prevent novelties and diversities in the Church."[63]

The archbishop of Lyon had another concern: the problem of juridical "state." Without solemn vows, these nuns might by reason of temptation or seduction come to contract marriage, which, regrettably, would be valid. "What legal wrangles and internal quarrels will be spread among families!" Furthermore, since they were not in a state of legal death, they might still claim succession rights. "And this uncertainty will last the lifetime of the woman."[64] Marquemont insisted that he was not speaking for himself alone, but for the families of Lyon: "Now, this is not just speculation among learned men, but a very common complaint which one hears every day in this city. Parents are already disinclined to let their daughters leave the world, or to consecrate them to the service of God; and when they do let them go, there often are many temporal considerations."[65]

François de Sales understood at once what was at issue. "I can see that by doing this [accepting full monastic status] we shall satisfy … the fathers and relatives who want to give these women to God only so that they can save on the portions which would be lost if they gave them to some wretched husband," he wrote.[66]

The archbishop was serving notice of a factor of great importance which any new congregation would have to take into account. Through the course of centuries, the act of profession of solemn vows had been incorporated into the legal and social system of the country. Monks and nuns, by acquiring the state of civil death, became, as it were, non-persons in secular society. This meant that they no longer had a claim to worldly rights – or to worldly goods. This was a comfortable thought for families with estates to consider. They valued the assurance that their children, once entered into the religious state, could not be resurrected to complicate the inheritance. The fact that their sons, by entering the Society of Jesus and the various other new congregations of simple vows, had managed to enter religion while keeping one foot in the world made them all the more determined that their daughters should not do the same. Since their support was essential for the reform program, the hierarchy, very obviously, had to take their views into consideration.

François de Sales responded by defending the legitimacy of the Visitation's existing practice, including the visiting of the sick. However, he now acquiesced "with all his heart, without even a grain of repugnance,"[67] in the imposition of formal monastic rule and perpetual clausura.

This was not an about-face. It was a recognition of the facts. Marquemont, as ordinary, had full control over "his" community of Lyon. He had warned: "If we cannot agree, Monseigneur the Bishop of Geneva may dispose of his nuns as he wishes, and the Archbishop of Lyon will dispose of his as he sees fit."[68] By coming to terms, the founder of the Visitation was able to keep his little congregation intact. There was another reason for the acquiescence. Several dioceses were already requesting colonies from the Visitation. Marquemont had enormous influence in France. On his opinion of the Visitation would depend its reception throughout the country. It seems, also, in the light of the experience, still ahead, of other feminine congregations in France, that it was Marquemont, not François de Sales, who understood the spirit of the times, and knew what was necessary to make the new congregation successful.

The two Visitation convents were erected into monasteries under the rule of Saint Augustine. Henceforth the Filles de Sainte-Marie took solemn vows and observed perpetual clausura. The visiting of the sick and the practice of allowing sisters to attend to their affairs were now forbidden. On the other hand, the principal purposes of the institute – the reception of widows and women of delicate health to a regimen of prayer without undue mortification, and the admission into the monasteries of laywomen for limited retreats – were secured. Furthermore, the nuns were dispensed, at least for the time being, from the onerous duty of singing Divine Office, and were allowed to sing the Little Office of Our Lady instead. The title of the Visitation, with all that it symbolized, was retained. Under these constitutions, presented jointly by the two bishops, and approved by Paul v, the institute enjoyed immediate success. By the end of the century the Filles de Sainte-Marie numbered six and a half thousand, in a hundred and forty-nine monasteries spread across the country.[69]

François de Sales accepted the outcome as a defeat. "I only planned to establish a single house at Annecy," he later told his friend Bishop Camus, "for young women and widows, without vows and without enclosure, whose practice would be to attend to the visiting and care of the sick, abandoned and helpless poor ... And now it is a formal Order, living under the rule of Saint Augustine, with vows and clausura; a situation that is incompatible with the original plan which they practised for several years ... So now I shall be their godfather rather than their founder, since my institution has been undone."[70]

The debate over the Visitation brings to light the powerful social forces that stood in the way of change, especially where women were concerned. The archbishop of Lyon was more than a spokesman for the Gallican church; he was a spokesman for the society to which he belonged, the elites who were as concerned with "state" and inheritance as they were with the purity of monastic discipline. The opposition which the new women's congregations encountered when they tried to dispense with clausura arose as much from legal as from spiritual concerns. Not only the Church, but society itself, had reasons to preserve the *status quo*.

It has been shown here that the Council of Trent took an uncompromising position with regard to religious women, a position which was then significantly hardened by Pius v's constitution *Circa pastoralis* in 1566. However, as popes succeeded each other and circumstances changed, the matter remained open to discussion. In the early years of the seventeenth century there were still theologians ready to argue for "mitigated" clausura. Pope Paul v, during a pontificate that lasted from 1605 to 1621, seemed favourable to the new ideas. But as the century progressed, resistance began to build against the uncloistered women, and with the death of Paul v the Holy See's tolerance came to an end. The court of Urban viii, confronted by a woman who made no secret of her aspirations, showed itself antagonistic to "Jesuitesses." The bull suppressing Mary Ward's institute in 1631 was to be the papacy's last word on the subject for many years.

But Rome's word did not automatically become law in the countries of Catholic Europe. Implementation depended on the local hierarchies. In Italy itself, in the Spanish Netherlands, and in various parts of the Empire, uncloistered communities survived because they had the protection of their bishops. The Gallican church, however, proved more than willing to enforce the law in all its rigour. It had behind it the full weight of public opinion, or at least of the elite public opinion that mattered.

"Aut maritus, aut murus" – a husband or a cloister. Every vested interest seemed to support this maxim. The Counter-Reformation began in France with an agenda which precluded the active service of women. Neither Church nor secular society saw, as yet, any need for them sufficiently strong to overturn the established order.

CHAPTER THREE

The Teaching Congregations of the Counter-Reformation (1598–1640)

From very early days, Protestantism had pinned its hopes for the future of religion upon the education of its children. The faith of the reformers soon bonded itself to the older humanist belief, that schooling was necessary to make good citizens. "In order to maintain its temporal estate outwardly, the world must have good and capable men and women, men to rule over land and people, women to manage the household and train children and servants aright," wrote Luther. Such men and such women could only be trained in the schools.[1]

Nowhere in France was this principle more earnestly applied than in the cities of the Midi, where Protestantism had sunk deep roots, especially among the elite. During the sixteenth century a network of highly respected educational institutions had passed into the hands of regents loyal to the new religion. The continuation of these schools was later guaranteed, in 1598, by the Edict of Nantes. This left the Huguenots with an advantage, and they did not hesitate to build upon it. In 1607 the Reformed church's Synod of La Rochelle ordered that primary schools be erected in every province.

Catholics, stunned and disturbed by the spread of heresy, very swiftly learned to blame it on the Protestant schools. They responded with a frontal counter-attack. In one city after another, they made determined efforts to set up their own colleges in direct competition. "To establish a college of Fathers … in order to prevent ignorance and error, which are the roots of every kind of evil, from invading the minds of the people for lack of instruction":[2] this was a central strategy of the Counter-Reformation, and one that was highly successful.

But among the people who had proved most receptive to the reformed religion was a group whom the colleges of Fathers could not easily reach – the women. Since women dominated the early years of their children's lives, their influence was crucial. And whereas their sons might be removed from their influence and given a Catholic education, their daughters, as long as they remained at home, were vulnerable to the mothers' heresy. They, in turn, would pass the contagion on to their own children. There seemed no recourse but to develop feminine institutions analogous to the masculine colleges.

Thus the first impulse towards feminine education came in the Midi, and its motive power was anti-Protestantism. Two of France's most successful teaching congregations were born in this divided countryside. The Ursulines came out of the papal enclave of Venaissin and spread first through Provence, then across the country; the Filles de Notre-Dame originated in Bordeaux and remained, with only a few exceptions, a southern congregation (See map 1). The region in which their houses were located was a theatre of war; and the spirit in which their institutions were conceived was the spirit of the Counter-Reformation.

THE FILLES DE NOTRE-DAME

The early development of the Company of Filles de Notre-Dame took place against a backdrop of ruined churches, of armed bands roaming the countryside, and of violent confrontation in the streets. The company was, in its own way, a protagonist in this conflict. Its very creation honoured the Blessed Virgin, the powerful patroness of militant Catholicism. Where her chapels had been desecrated, the nuns were installed by way of expiation, "in order to return this country to the Empire of the Queen of men and of Angels."[3] They erected her statues on their outside walls, challenging the passers-by to pay their respects; they staged theatrical processions in her honour, and rang the monastery bells on the occasion of her feasts, to call back the people to the worship that they had abandoned. But the main battle of the Filles de Notre-Dame was conducted in the schoolrooms and in the parlours, where girls and their mothers were educated and argued back into the true faith.

The company was born in the minds of the Jesuits. The Society of Jesus had founded the men's collège de La Madeleine in Bordeaux in 1572, as a direct challenge to the famous humanist collège de Guyenne. By 1605 it had far outstripped its distinguished rival, both in revenues and in student population. But two of its members, Bordes and Raymond, were convinced that its success was incomplete. "These two Fathers ... each on his own part reflected on the

Map 1   Foundations of the Filles de Notre Dame in France, 1607–50. Shaded areas show territories held by the Huguenots during the religious wars.

dissolute behaviour of the young. They remarked that it was caused by the heretic schools, and that while the evil could be remedied in part in their Company's colleges, the other part was left to ignorance and disorder."[4] By the "other part," the Fathers meant the female young. They decided to look for a suitable person to establish a school for girls.

The woman who accepted their proposition was Jeanne de Lestonnac, baronne de Montferrant-Landiras.[5] She herself was the daughter of a Calvinist mother, and in her childhood had suffered from her parents' tug-of-war for her soul. Married at seventeen and widowed at forty-one, she had entered a Feuillantine monastery, but had had to withdraw for reasons of health.[6] After two years of life as a *dévote*, she was ready to accept the difficult work of foundress. She gathered a small group of companions, who together, in the winter of 1605–6, followed Père Bordes in the Spiritual Exercises of Saint Ignatius, and a study of the Jesuit rule.

Together with Père Bordes, and after a pattern laid down by Ignatius, Jeanne drew up a "formula" of thirty articles, outlining the major features of the proposed institute. These were presented to the archbishop of Bordeaux, Cardinal de Sourdis.[7] The cardinal examined the proposals, made some changes, and in March 1606, approved the new institute. Within a year he had won pontifical recognition for his protegées. The papal bull of 7 April 1607, which confirmed the existence of the Compagnie de Notre-Dame, made it the first feminine teaching congregation to achieve official status in France.

In the provisions of the bull there was considerable novelty. First, though the community in Bordeaux was, *pro forma*, to be affiliated to the Benedictine order, its principal purpose was not that of the conventional monastery. "The aim of the religious of this Company and Order of Our Lady is not only to work, with the grace of God and in all diligence, for their own salvation and perfection, but also …, in imitation of the most holy Virgin their Mother, to procure the salvation and perfection of others of their sex, in so far as their condition allows."[8]

This was a departure from pure monastic practice. The work of education was to be the central purpose of the institute. In recognition of this, Pope Paul v himself dispensed the community from the obligation of Divine Office. However, the new creation was hedged with conditions. The monastery was to be adapted to allow for the reception of students in such a way that they would not interfere with clausura. The boarders were to have quarters set apart, though within the monastery walls. Day students were to be accepted in conditions of strict isolation. "A courtyard is to be built beside the Church and within the enclosure of this Monastery, with rooms all around; to this the mothers, sisters and mistresses will go to teach, after the last stroke of the school bell. Afterwards the two doors, which allow access to the outside and the inside, will be closed, and all the girls who are not boarders will retire to their homes."[9]

But though enclosure was preserved, the monastic spirit was changed. The constitutions elaborated further on this compromise between cloister and school: "Since the teaching function is the prime purpose of our Institute, for the greater glory of God, for the salvation of souls and for the public good, it ought to be held in highest regard by all those who are employed in it."[10] In order to release the nuns for their demanding work, most of the mortifications normally associated with monastic life were removed. They ate well,[11] performed only the penances universally exacted by the Church, and wore a habit which was designed for the classroom.[12] Their religious exercises consisted of daily mass, an hour and a half of mental prayer, the Little Office of Our Lady, and the rosary, as well as an examination of conscience after the method prescribed by Saint Ignatius – in other words, little more than any *dévot* might be expected to observe.[13]

On the other hand, the work of schoolteaching was to be taken seriously. "It must never be neglected; it must become better and better."[14] Novices were to be trained in catechetics. Classroom procedures, which were based on the Jesuit *Ratio studiorum*, were to be rigorously observed.

Even as they patterned their pedagogy on that of the Jesuits, the Filles de Notre-Dame also had another model: the Protestants. Mère de Lestonnac consciously copied the schools of the Reformed religion. The recapture of their student population was, after all, her primary purpose. "So that the girls will be attracted away from the tainted heretic schools and into this institution, we shall teach them reading, writing and various kinds of needlework – in short, all the accomplishments suitable for well-brought-up young maids."[15]

This, then, was the originality of the Compagnie des Filles de Notre-Dame. It was a Counter-Reformation congregation, in the sense that it was intended to play a part in the recapture of society for Catholicism. Consequently it owed much more to the Jesuits who presided over its creation than to the order of Saint Benedict which gave it its formal existence. Its proclaimed ideal, like that of the Jesuits, was the "mixed life," of contemplation and action. Its houses tended to locate in towns served by Jesuit colleges (see map 1). Its rule was designed to create "an Institute comparable to that of the Company of Jesus in so far as it is possible for our sex."[16] Its novices, from Mère de Lestonnac on, were trained by means of the Spiritual Exercises of Saint Ignatius.

In one respect, however, the company was not allowed to emulate its Jesuit model. This was in the matter of organization. In the original formula presented to Cardinal de Sourdis in 1606, a generalate had been called for. In other words, Père Bordes and Mère de Lestonnac envisaged an elected superior-general ruling over the order, with power to appoint the local superiors.[17] The cardinal eliminated this clause before the formula was sent to Rome. All that was officially asked for, and received, was the authority to found one monastery. Against her wishes, Jeanne de Lestonnac became the foundress of a single community – that of Bordeaux – which was subject to the ordinary. Should this house establish others, they would be unconnected with the mother house, and subject to the local bishops. For the Filles de Notre-Dame, as for other feminine congregations of their time, there was no escaping the strict interpretation of tridentine law which placed communities of women under the control of the local bishops.[18]

Nevertheless, as new communities were formed they managed to maintain at least a spiritual unity, and a recognition by all houses of the primacy of the Bordeaux monastery. Rome, perhaps unwittingly, assisted them: the papal brief of 17 October 1615, approving the new foundation of Béziers, ordered the new community to observe the rules and customs of Bordeaux.[19] Later, the company began to establish new houses without applying for new papal bulls, as though theirs was an order, and not a collection of autonomous houses. There is evidence that this action received strong support from their Jesuit advisers. "I entreat you," wrote Père de Lestonnac, Jeanne's brother, to the superior of the Filles de Notre-Dame at Le Puy, "always to remain united to the head of this body, whoever that may be. For though the person change, authority remains the same, authority so necessary for maintaining union and conformity, without which the Order would be a disorder and the body a monster."[20]

This effort to extend the authority of the Bordeaux house angered Archbishop de Sourdis, however; he suspected Jeanne of working towards an independent congregation along Jesuit lines, subject only to the pope. As a result, a subtle war of nerves continued between the two throughout his lifetime. At least twice, the archbishop openly humiliated Mère de Lestonnac in front of her community. Furthermore, he supported the second superior, Blanche Hervé, who subjected the foundress to two years of disgrace. In spite of everything, Jeanne persisted in her hopes for a generalate. Two years before her death she appealed for new constitutions, applicable to all houses. "Uniformity is the support and the base of all religious orders," she wrote, and she asked that all communities regard Bordeaux as their mother.[21] In the text of the proposed constitutions, she included a chapter entitled "Prescriptions in the case of a superior-general." The chapter was struck out.[22] The centralization of the order, which rested largely on the force of her personality, remained a matter of sentiment only. After her death in 1640 the institute lost some of its dynamism, and the pace of new foundations slowed.[23] The Filles de Notre-Dame continued without a union until modern times.

In two main areas, the creation of the Compagnie de Filles de Notre-Dame represented a continuation of past custom. The principle of clausura was never questioned, and the principle of a generalate, though suggested, was rejected. However, the founding of the Bordeaux house in 1607 did involve significant innovation. For the first time in France, the powers of Church and State officially sanctioned a monastic community of women which had as its *raison d'être* the education of girls. Convent schools, which were to be a marked feature of seventeenth-century society, were now on their way to becoming acceptable.

THE URSULINES

The Compagnie de Sainte-Ursule was to become the feminine teaching congregation *par excellence* of seventeenth-century France (see map 2). In 1700, it is estimated, there were between ten thousand and twelve thousand Ursulines in some three hundred and twenty communities across the country.[24] These communities were charged specifically with providing free instruction and education to young girls, and while in time most of them opened *pensionnats* for the daughters of better, or richer, families, there were few which did not continue to operate their free day-schools. Therefore we must reckon in the many hundreds of thousands the women who passed through their classrooms during the course of the century.

The history of the Ursulines provides a clear example of the seventeenth-century conflict between apostolic movement and monastic reform. In the course of just over a hundred years the congregation passed through a series of transformations, to meet the changing standards of time and place. By the time the evolutionary period ended, around 1640, there were new monasteries all over the country, in which the contemplative life had been altered to accommodate service to society. In the process, however, the women's early apostolic fervour was contained and reduced.

The Ursulines had first appeared in Brescia, in Italy. At the time of their foundation in 1544 they were altogether secular, living in their own homes, taking no vows other than a private vow of chastity, practising the whole range of charitable works – visiting the poor, caring for the sick, and burying the dead – as well as instructing girls and women in their faith. They were thus considerably different from the French Ursulines of a century later, who were semi-contemplatives – choir nuns – observing a monastic rule (the rule of

Map 2   Foundations of the Ursulines in the seventeenth century.

Saint Augustine, which the foundress Angela Merici had never observed), and separated from the world outside by walls and grilles.
Of the multiple works of charity that the foundress and her followers
had performed, only one remained, the instruction of girls. With
their transformation into cloistered nuns the Ursulines left their
other callings aside and became specialists in child-education.

The Ursulines of Brescia were modelled upon the tertiaries of
earlier times. Their originality lay in their dynamism – their membership grew from twenty-eight to one hundred and fifty in the first
four years – and in their innovative organization. Their constitutions,
which received papal approval in 1544, provided for a hierarchy of
officers to direct the members, all of them together ruled by a

superior-general.[25] This structure, which was modelled on that of the Jesuits, went without challenge as long as the Ursulines were confined to a single diocese. However, as the success of the company led to its expansion into other dioceses, the question of control became more prominent. In 1568, twelve Ursulines went to Milan at the invitation of the great reforming archbishop, Charles Borromeo. In so doing they found themselves absorbed into a movement which did not entirely correspond with their own. Borromeo's program for reform was centred entirely in the diocese, whereas their society crossed diocesan boundaries. He adopted the Ursulines with enthusiasm, but rejected their principle of a generalate. Appealing to the authority of the Council of Trent, he argued that female religious were the responsibility of the bishop alone; they must be subject to him and to no one else. As a result, from 1577 the concept of an internal organization was set aside, and each community of Ursulines became autonomous and subject to the immediate control of the ordinary.

Borromeo was responsible for another important innovation in Ursuline practice. He "congregated," or gathered into community, those of the sisters who so desired. This break with the primitive tradition, according to which the members lived in their own homes, was generally welcomed by the women. It was approved by Rome in 1582. By the time of the archbishop's death in 1584, five communities were at work in the diocese of Milan: six hundred Ursulines, teaching in eighteen schools.[26] These *congrégées* lived in community and considered themselves to be religious; they enjoyed some religious privileges and they were subject to some religious discipline, including the wearing of a distinctive habit. However, strictly speaking they were not religious, since they were not bound by solemn vows or the obligation of clausura, nor were they subject to any of the four great religious rules. It was this, the Milanese version of Ursulinism, that found its way into France.

The beginnings of the first French community followed a pattern which would be repeated time and time again in subsequent years. A group of young *dévotes* in Avignon gathered together to live a semi-religious life of prayer and good works. "They attracted several others, so that these young women soon numbered twenty-four, all sharing the desire to serve God and to have nothing further to do with the world ... They frequented the Sacraments and the exercises of Christian doctrine; they assisted the poor, visited the sick, and devoted themselves to all the other works of piety which their age and their sex allowed." Their ambition was to form a monastic community, and they asked the archbishop of Avignon to give them an empty monastery for their use. He answered, however, that conventional monasticism had fallen into disrepute in France; and he pointed to the superiority of the new congregation of Ursulines in Italy who, though uncloistered, were "infinitely more useful for the salvation of members of their sex."[27]

None of the women had heard of Ursulines before. They were discouraged by the bishop's response, and most of them fell away. But a few took his words to heart. They found a mentor in César du Bus, founder of the Fathers of Christian Doctrine. Under his direction, they gravitated more and more towards catechesis, and indeed for a time adopted the title of Sisters of Christian Doctrine.

Their activity aroused the kind of controversy that was to recur over and over again. While they did not lack supporters, they also did not lack critics, including on this occasion the Jesuits of the college. The leader of the group, Françoise de Bermond, received the strongest of representations from this quarter: "The Reverend Father Majorius (a Jesuit) ... always dissuaded her from this course, telling her over and over again that it was pure temptation, and that it was absolutely necessary for a young girl to have either a husband or a cloister. Therefore she did not dare to undertake this work until God gave her the model and the occasion."[28]

The opposition abated only slowly, as the group provided itself with the signs of respectability: first, a copy of the Ursuline rule, brought back from Italy by a friendly bishop, then a papal brief giving them "permission to give public instruction in Christian Doctrine to girls and even, on occasion, to women,"[29] and finally a house, rented for them by one of their wealthy members. By 1597 they were living in community, under the Borromean rule, with a superior, Françoise de Bermond, and with simple vows. The new congregation was highly successful. Between 1600 and 1610, twenty-nine houses of *congrégées* were set up across the Midi.

The early French *congrégées* were, above all, catechizers. They became full participants in the war of words that was raging against the reformed religion. Ursuline chroniclers later in the century described them as heroic figures. Thus Anne de Vesvres went like a missionary from village to village: "She would invite the priests of the villages that she visited to teach the children their catechism, and when they excused themselves, saying that they did not know how, she would readily and modestly show them the method. She even reproved the local nobility for their injustices and frankly told them that they were offending God." The crowds that gathered around her, "both men and women." were so great that she sometimes simply sat down on the ground, and taught them as the Spirit dictated.[30] Anne de Beauvais "converted a great number of sinful Huguenots and atheists."[31] Christine Peiron became the "spiritual mother" of men and women of good family.[32] Anne de Beaumont's "fervent discourses" were compared to the preaching of Saint Paul. "She communicated such a flame to her audience that women and young girls took on the appearance and behaviour of cloistered religious."[33] When Paule de Cellarier talked about God, the church of Montelimart was too small to hold all the people who flocked to hear her.[34] Such feminine activism was truly remarkable. In the front lines of the Counter-Reformation there was, for a brief moment in time, an opening for good catechists, no matter what their sex.

Their principal work, however, was the instruction of girls. It was the demand for this that drew them so quickly into the other cities of southern France. From their houses, strategically located in centres of wealth, power, and influence, they became the colonizers of their hinterlands, sending out small groups of *congrégées* to form new communities in the towns that invited them in. By 1630, some eighty houses had been opened.

This rapid expansion needs to be interpreted in terms of human and material resources. Who invited the Ursulines in? Who provided the accommodation, the funds, the very considerable effort involved in making all the necessary arrangements, and – above all – the aspirants, the young women who crowded into these communities in their early days?

First: the French hierarchy. This was a time when the princes of the Church travelled a great deal. A series of papal elections took the French cardinals into Italy, where they were able to consider, in particular, the work of the late archbishop of Milan. It has been said that it was Charles Borromeo who opened the doors of France to the Ursulines. His canonization in 1604 enhanced his reputation; he was from now on revered as the model bishop of the Counter-Reformation. A number of French bishops adopted the Ursulines as whole-heartedly as he had done. Thus Cardinal de Sourdis invited the *congrégées* into Bordeaux, and defended them fiercely against local criticism.[35] Cardinal de Joyeuse established houses in Pontoise (1611) and then in Rouen (1615), providing them with both property and money.[36] Other bishops were equally anxious to secure establishments. Mère de Pommereu tells us that an Ursuline foundress, passing through Poitiers, was detained there by the bishop until she promised that he, too, would have a house.[37]

The regulars gave the Ursulines a mixed reception. The mendicant friars were generally hostile, seeing the new nuns as a threat to the various female communities – Penitents, cloistered Dominicans,

Poor Clares – whom they directed. In Tulle, "the Devil used certain religious of the city who, quite openly, and without any reason, declared themselves enemies of the [Ursuline] monastery, and persuaded women not to enter."[38] In Langres, a friar threatened to preach against the Ursulines, and to spread the word "that it was an abuse for women to teach in public."[39] In Grenoble, "a famous preacher declaimed against them from the pulpit ... and pointing at them, and naming them openly, said many things that were highly damaging to them."[40]

The new congregations proved more favourable. The Fathers of Christian Doctrine had given them their original support. Later, the Oratorians and the Jesuits, with their considerable influence both at court and throughout the country, took up the work of advertising their existence and securing new foundations. The Jesuits very swiftly came to perceive the Ursulines as a complement to themselves in the education of children. "Our blessed Father Ignatius worked towards this end, directing our Company to the sound education of young boys. It would be a praiseworthy and useful work to establish a congregation into which one could transplant young girls, as though into a fertile soil, so that after being well instructed, they could leave to bring virtue into their families."[41] The Jesuits were prepared to act as animators wherever they saw a possiblity. New communities often appeared in the wake of their travels.

Just as a new establishment needed the consent of the bishop, it also required the sanction of king and parlement. Royal approval was not difficult to obtain. In 1611 Louis XIII, "with the advice of the Queen Regent, our most honoured Lady and Mother," authorized the foundation of the Congregation "under the name of the blessed Saint Ursula, for the purpose of instruction."[42] In the following year, letters patent were issued to the communities of Paris, Lyon, Orléans, Troyes, Pontoise, and Compiègne. It is not difficult to see the hand of the regent in the favourable treatment which the Ursulines received. Her relations with the Parisian convent were close and cordial. An Ursuline chronicler wrote that "she returned often, and frequently sent the princesses her daughters."[43] Louis himself, as dauphin, had visited the convent and attended a catechism lesson given by Françoise de Bermond. The royal favour was enormously useful in overcoming local opposition to foundations. In more than one city, recalcitrant officials had the honour of a letter from the king or the queen mother, warning them "not to make difficulties about this establishment."[44]

The parlements, though less enthusiastic, were still prepared to tolerate the Ursulines' existence. They anticipated the later, more reserved approach of Louis XIV, in valuing the institute mainly as a means of suppressing coeducation. "This religious order ... is necessary for the free instruction of children of their sex, which cannot be safely entrusted to men."[45] The reticence of the parlements is interesting, in view of the fact that it was from this milieu – the officer class and the *noblesse de la robe* – that the Ursulines would come to draw much of their support and their personnel.

To start with, however, they moved in less exalted circles. The first Ursulines were for the most part daughters of bourgeois and artisans. Though few of them were as poor as the three young girls of Clermont who, after hearing a Lenten sermon, decided to establish a community, "although they appeared to have little disposition, since they did not even know how to read or write,"[46] it is in fact estimated that almost half of the early French foundations were the work of very ordinary people.[47]

Ursuline houses were not always created from above. The process of founding an Ursuline house often began when a group of local women set up their own little community, which, months and even years later, would be absorbed into the Ursuline discipline. There are numerous examples of these spontaneous creations, and only a few can be given here. In Pontoise, in 1599, a group of *dévotes* pooled their resources and began to live together, "dressing simply, and wearing on their heads a veil of cheap stuff." In 1605 the foundation of a Carmelite house in the city caused a crisis for the community, as some of the women split off to enter this celebrated new "religion," leaving the others, who felt no vocation to the contemplative life, to an uncertain future. Several learned and pious men suggested that they disband, but their director thought otherwise: "What, gentlemen; just because the hen has laid one good clutch of eggs, do we need to strangle it?" The women were established in a new, small teaching community, which only later, in 1616, accepted the Ursuline rule and constitutions.[48] In another part of the country, five *dévotes* in Saint-Marcellin established their own community and school in 1614. Three years later, at the suggestion of the archbishop of Vienne, they went away to the noviciate at Romans, and when they returned to their home town they were Ursulines.[49] Much the same process occurred in Crépy-en-Valois, where several young women lived together in community for four years before being taken over by a colony from the *grand couvent* of Faubourg Saint-Jacques in Paris.[50] This happened over and over again, with the same ending: the women asking for, or sometimes being forced into, the established Ursuline discipline.[51]

It was imperative that these little communities should very quickly find themselves patrons, local people of substance whose donations or legacies could provide them with a house and some income. Since the Ursulines were not allowed to beg, and since the teaching of day students was supposed to be free, the support of such patrons was a *sine qua non* for a firm foundation. While some houses enjoyed generous funding from the court, the nobility, and the upper clergy, many others depended on smaller donors: prominent merchants, or curés, or wealthy ladies. These local donors did not necessarily reflect a general mood of benevolence in their towns; in fact they were sometimes in a small minority.[52] However, their support was frequently all that kept the new communities from penury.

Support grew more general as the Ursulines began to turn out their students. For a society unaccustomed to girls' schools, the Ursulines' teaching was an enormous advance; and the opinion of their patrons was that it should not be concentrated over much on the lesser people. More and more houses were persuaded to accept boarders, children of the wealthier classes, who were lodged within the convents and instructed separately from the day students. Although their numbers were always small compared to those of the day students, these boarders occupied a large part of the nuns' energy, and the expectations of their parents came to dominate the communities' policies.

This close dependence on their social environment was a source of weakness to the Ursulines, in so far as it put their original charitable and catechetical vocation at risk. And if the wealthier classes were prepared to change the character of the congregation on behalf of their schoolgirl daughters, they were prepared to interfere even more when those daughters began to seek entry into the same congregation as postulants. The question of the suitability of the *congrégées'* type of life – without solemn vows and without clausura – now became more pressing.

The absence of solemn vows left the legal state of the *congrégées* open to question. Without the guarantee secured by a solemn profession, there was no solid assurance that an individual might not return to the world at a later date, to the jeopardy of the family inheritance. Furthermore, financial arrangements were too loose and informal. The precarious condition of many of the new houses put their inmates at risk. More than once, nuns and even boarders were found to be living close to destitution.[53] The prospect of seeing their daughters thus reduced led many of the better-off families to look for a more solid establishment.

Finally, in the eyes of many families the uncloistered religious lifestyle lacked propriety and dignity. The seventeenth-century biography of the Ursuline Catherine de Veteris of Aix tells of her meeting with her father as she walked with her students to church, "her veil drawn down, her hands in her sleeves, her eyes lowered to the earth, her walk exceedingly humble." Her father, furious and embarrassed, turned away; but she was followed mockingly through the streets by the young gallants of the town. "Mademoiselle de Veteris has gone mad!"[54] Respectable society was not yet ready for these uncloistered nuns; their appearance on the streets gave rise to much scandal and derision. In Grenoble, "when they came out of their house, they were abused both by words and by actions." In Lyon, their walk to church gave rise to jeering, by passers-by who took them for women of ill repute. In Dijon, "whenever they passed on the streets, they were looked upon with scorn; the little children shouted after them and threw mud at them."[55]

Social as well as economic pressures, therefore, brought about the next phase: the transformation of the Ursulines from simple *congrégées* into cloistered nuns. The institute was embraced by upper-class society, then redesigned according to its mores. This example may have been before the eyes of Vincent de Paul when, some forty years later, he warned his Filles de la Charité: "where true poverty must be observed, people of good family are highly dangerous, because it is contrary to their breeding."[56]

This transformation owed much to the attitudes of the Church itself. Much as the hierarchy valued the Ursulines' work, the fact remained that their community life with simple vows contravened *Circa pastoralis*, the papal constitution of 1566 which ordered female religious to take solemn vows and submit to enclosure. The attitude of the bishops was beginning to harden, as French jurists finally came to grips with the legislation of Trent. Even the Jesuits were now feeling some insecurity, as their society of simple vows came under attack by the lawyers. In 1611, a tract had appeared which questioned their right to have a legal identity while not bound by solemn vows.[57] It was no time for them to risk involvement in other people's experimental communities. They took up the argument for clausura and solemn vows, asserting that it was the only way to ensure the permanence of the good work.

The direction taken by the new Ursuline house of Faubourg Saint-Jacques, the *grand couvent*, as it came to be known, was decisive. From 1607, the date of its establishment, to 1610, it had developed along the lines of a community of *congrégées*, under the guidance of Françoise de Bermond, who had been brought to Paris for the purpose. But the foundress, Madame de Sainte-Beuve, was personally convinced by her confessor, the Jesuit Père Gontery, that to be effective, the new house must become a monastery. After long debate, in which two other founding members, Michel de Marillac[58] and

Madame Acarie, took the opposite view, her will prevailed. In 1610 Mère de Bermond left with several other *congrégées*, to avoid submitting to clausura.[59] Shortly after, in a brilliant ceremony attended by princesses, duchesses, and ladies of quality, the first twelve novices received the religious habit. At the end of the celebration all visitors left, and the doors were closed with a double lock and key. Then, and only then, did Archbishop de Gondi allow the community the ultimate privilege of a religious house: the reservation of the Blessed Sacrament in its chapel.

The enormous prestige of the Paris house and its close ties to the court made it the model for the other houses of France. In 1616 the Toulouse house was erected into a monastery. In 1618 Bordeaux followed suit; and in 1619 and 1620 Dijon and Lyon took the same step. Other Ursuline communities were urged by their superiors and advisers to follow the Parisian example. This they did in increasing numbers, through the 1620s and 1630s. The decision was sometimes taken with great reluctance. The objections which many Ursulines made to monastic transformation were summarized in a petition drawn up by the community of Narbonne in about 1650. In their opinion, the particular calling of the Ursuline was to give witness to the world, to teach the children of the lower classes, and to reach out to families, as well as to train their boarders to a more profound Christian life. Their outside work would, they felt, be seriously curtailed by clausura ... Their community was transformed anyway, in 1658, and with it disappeared the last of the communities of *congrégées* in France.[60]

But it would be a mistake to imagine that the imposition of clausura was a hardship to all Ursulines. For many of them it was, rather, a progression to a more perfect form of life, one fully in tune with the spirit of the Counter-Reformation. The attraction to monasticism remained a powerful temptation for devout women, especially of the upper classes. In the spirituality of the day, the contemplative life was held to be not only the highest, but the happiest form of human existence. Contemplatives were "like the birds ... in the air of Religion, where often a thousand pleasures are to be savoured amidst a few austerities."[61] By contrast, the life of good works, even when it carried pontifical approval, did not seem to be as happy – or as worthwhile. Once committed to a life of service and bound by private vows and promises, many women felt drawn towards the holocaust of themselves that full monasticism represented. As Jeanne de Rampalle, one of the founding French Ursulines, wrote: "Vows and religious profession are among the highest and most heroic and meritorious acts that this life permits. They seem in some way to relate to immensity, encompassing as they do the height of desires, the breadth of all the spiritual riches, the length of life and of eternity, the depth of self-annihilation in the state of holy servitude."[62]

As the various communities submitted to clausura there was also a considerable interest in union, in the sense of affiliation with Paris. This would have created something resembling an order. But union was frustrated by the actual process of transformation. The congregation had no real centre. It was, in fact, a collection of congregations, each with its own customs, to which its members were fiercely attached.[63] What was more, there could be no central authority. Each group had its own papal bull, in which the houses were specifically subjected to the ordinary.[64] Each bishop had his own ideas on how "his" monastery's life should be conducted. As a result, the current of uniformity which was flowing out of Paris was counteracted by a host of particularities. "What is annoying," wrote Mère Marie de l'Incarnation from Quebec, "is that since they [the bishops] are free to impose constitutions and customs, they do it in such a way that even within the same congregation there are different ways of doing things. Add together each congregation's basic, fundamental constitutions, and all the changes made by the bishops, and everything is upset and overturned."[65] The only body which had the authority to impose union on the Ursulines was the Assembly of the Clergy, and it never got around to doing so.[66]

In the four decades since its appearance in France, the Compagnie de Sainte-Ursule had undergone profound alteration. Its members had moved away from their apostolate in the world. They had accepted a system which precluded any sort of administrative unity between houses, or interchange of members. Their collective spirituality, reinforced by their removal from the world and their intensified prayer life, drew them towards the state where they became religious first, teachers second. There remained the possibility that they might also lose that right to teach publicly which Françoise de Bermond had won in 1594. The papal bulls by which they were transformed stated that the permission to teach day students was "to last only at our pleasure and that of the Holy See."[67]

This placed them in a dilemma. The teaching of children was their *raison d'être*, the function that distinguished them from other religious orders. But they were now nuns, bound by solemn vows. "We are daughters of obedience," Marie de l'Incarnation would write, some years later, "and we must prefer that to everything else."[68] In the event that they were ordered to give up their free classrooms, the only argument they could make would be an appeal to a higher obedience. It was with this in mind that the Ursulines of Paris ob-

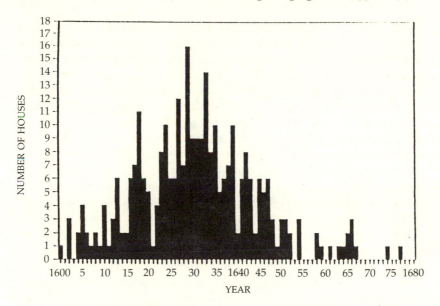

Graph 1   Ursuline foundations in the seventeenth century (houses still existing in 1699). (Four houses were founded before 1600, and one after 1680).

tained pontifical permission to take a fourth vow: that of the free instruction of girls. This vow, which many other religious congregations were to imitate, was their means of resisting interference from outside in the important matter of their teaching vocation.

By the 1630s the Ursulines of France had for the most part accepted the role which their society pressed upon them. Their reward was immediate: a rapid growth in the number of entrants, and an increase in the favours of court and nobility. The experience of the community of Dijon was typical. In 1619 the sisters were conducted with ceremony to their new monastery. They passed in procession through the streets, preceded by a hundred little girls dressed in white and an imposing array of ecclesiastics, and accompanied in this last public walk by a group of ladies of quality. There would be no more taunts and jeers, no more throwing of mud. "Once the Congregation was established in the holy religious state where there was more stability, many young women of quality presented themselves to be received into the monastery."[69] Catholic society in the aftermath of the Council of Trent had a clear idea of what religious women should be. It had guided – and where necessary had forced – the *congrégées* into this role.

A consequence of clausura was aristocratization. The evolution was natural. An enclosed monastery was expensive to build, since it had to be sufficient to all the needs of its perpetual inmates. The cost of the buildings – chapel, dormitories, infirmaries, refectories, kitchens, parlours, student quarters, and so on – as well as all the continuing living expenses of the community, had to be financed by revenue which came largely from donations and from the dowries and pensions of the nuns. The wealth of their families, therefore, became a determining factor in the admission of aspirants. The fees charged to boarders, an important source of income, also maintained the "quality" of the house. Since monasteries recruited their personnel heavily from among these same boarders, their social standing tended with the passage of time to become fixed. Overwhelmingly, and in spite of regional variations, they became identified with the local elites, and by this identification their members were protected from the hazards of poverty and of social derogation.

Once the bargain had been driven, the great period of expansion began. The majority of the approximately three hundred and twenty houses founded in France during the seventeenth century were monasteries from the start, opened in the years 1629–40.[70] The houses filled up almost as soon as they were opened. Communities of seventy or eighty nuns were not unknown; forty and fifty were commonplace. In some cities – in Montbrison, and in Rennes, for instance – second monasteries had to be established to accommodate all the aspirants.

Undoubtedly, by the sheer weight of their numbers, the Ursulines did more than anybody else to introduce seventeenth-century Frenchmen to the concept of feminine schooling. In obedience to their original purpose, they maintained their day schools, and a considerable number of girls of humble birth received their instruction. They also formed societies of laywomen, modelled on the sodalities of the Jesuits.[71] But much of their energy was now confined within their monastery walls, in the care of their boarders and in community duties.

A contemporary observer summed up the process:

The relatives, for reasons of self-interest, fearing the little problems that might occur in their families should they [the women] leave the convent and claim the part of the inheritance that might legally be theirs, decided to insist that they be enclosed. Thus were all the congregations of France heartlessly turned into houses in which, in addition to observing clausura, the women, after a year of probation, take the three solemn vows under the rule of Saint Augustine. If this is advantageous for the individuals who have daughters there, I believe that it is prejudicial to all the cities, who are thus deprived of instructions in doctrine and other works that contribute to the public good.[72]

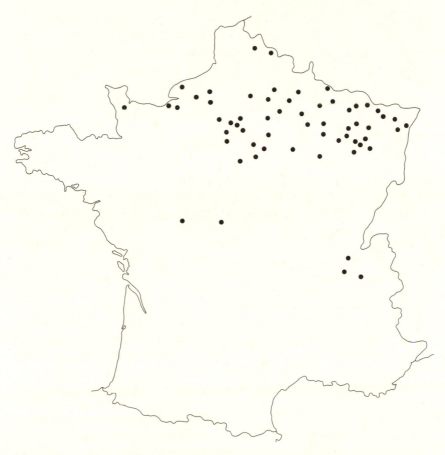

Map 3 Foundations of the Congrégation de Notre Dame in Lorraine and France, 1599–1700

THE CONGRÉGATION DE NOTRE-DAME

In 1597, virtually at the same time that the Ursuline *congrégées* of Avignon were establishing their first community in l'Isle-sur-Sorgues, another teaching congregation was being created in Lorraine. Five young women in the parish of Mattaincourt appeared publicly at the Christmas midnight mass in veils and black dresses, thus announcing to their neighbours that they intended to live as nuns, in community. This community was to develop in time into the Congrégation de Notre-Dame, a teaching institute similar in many respects to the Compagnie de Sainte-Ursule, though much smaller. Its initial field of action was Lorraine, though after 1615 it spread rapidly through the north-east of France (see map 3). Like the Ursulines, the sisters of the Congrégation started out with two simple objectives: to perform the corporal and spiritual acts of mercy, with particular attention to the instruction of girls, and to live a common religious life. Also like the Ursulines, they ended up as cloistered nuns under the rule of Saint Augustine, distinguished from conventional religious orders only by the obligations and dispensations which their fourth vow, obliging them to teach without salary, laid upon them.

Unlike the various Ursuline congregations, whose approbation by the Church came with reasonable dispatch and decorum, the Congrégation de Notre-Dame searched for legitimacy for thirty years, and was subjected to squabbling and political infighting, both in Lorraine and in Rome. Before the final bull approving the congregation was promulgated in 1628, the arguments regarding the propriety of allowing female religious to teach had all been vented in the roundest terms. The case of the Congrégation forced the opposition to go on record. This is its particular value to the historian of female religious life.

Why did the Congrégation receive such rough treatment? First, because their patrons lacked the political strength that the Ursulines' patrons enjoyed. Although the court of Lorraine favoured the new work, it and the four bishops involved – the "three bishops" of Metz, Toul, and Verdun, and the primate of Lorraine, whose seat was at Nancy – worked at cross-purposes to each other. Furthermore, in terms of influence they all paled in comparison with the court of France, which so heartily sponsored the Ursulines.

Equally important was the question of timing. The Congrégation took its case to Rome for the final time during the mid-1620s, just as the agitation over the "Jesuitesses" was reaching its climax. There can be no doubt that it was hurt by the strong wave of suspicion of all things feminine and innovative that gripped the Holy See. On the other hand the Ursulines, like the Filles de Notre-Dame of Jeanne de Lestonnac in Bordeaux, had secured their papal bulls under the more favourable pontificate of Paul v, and were no longer threatened. The political ups and downs of the papal court must never be discounted.

But perhaps the principal reason why the nuns of the Congrégation caused such offence was that they were asking for more than the other religious women. Their plan called for their houses to be joined together under a single *mère intendante*, with a general chapter and a visitor. This resembled the generalate which Mary Ward and Jeanne de Lestonnac had both requested; but the former's petition had been decisively rejected, and the latter's request had been struck out before it was forwarded to Rome. The nuns of the Congrégation asked, furthermore, that in view of the fact that their central vocation was the teaching of children, their obligation to clausura and to the other monastic observances should be moderated so as not to interfere with their work. They wished to have the maximum freedom, compatible with their state, to work with day students. This would have resembled the "mitigated clausura" which François de Sales had desired but failed to achieve.

Unlike the Compagnie de Sainte-Ursule, the Congrégation de Notre-Dame was guided by a single mind: that of Pierre Fourier, curé of Mattaincourt, a graduate of the Jesuit college of Pont-à-Mousson, a theologian and a canonist of considerable ability. He was able to give theoretical foundation to an organization of women who, though extremely able and dedicated, could never alone have understood the niceties of Church law or the nuances of Church politics, and could never have defended themselves against the censure of the experts. Fourier was dedicated to the idea that religious women could work actively in the Church without giving up their monastic standards, by observing a modified clausura which would allow them to leave their house when necessary, and to receive day students into their classrooms. "Clausura does not consist in an unchangeable, indivisible form … it is open to being more, or being less."[73] He also insisted that the congregation should remain united, with an interchange of personnel, funds, and ideas between houses. This concept was of itself bound to arouse the suspicion of the bishops, as he well knew, since the internal strength that it envisaged was designed specifically to resist outside pressures – notably theirs.

The new congregation, as Fourier proposed it, was therefore a challenge to the *status quo* in a way that the Ursulines were not, and this, as well as his adroit persistence in promoting its cause, must go far to explain the opposition that it aroused. Here were all the demands that the papacy, the episcopate, and high society as a whole found most unsettling, set out and supported by a man who commanded wide respect, both as a theologian and as a saint.[74] If in the end Fourier did not get the congregation he desired, it was because the difficulties were too many and too massive, and because his ideas outdistanced even those of the women whose work he was promoting.

The story of the congregation's beginnings is a familiar one, with youthful ideas and aspirations running against the prevailing currents of scepticism and custom. In June 1597, Fourier, a young canon regular of the abbey of Chamousey, became curé of Mattaincourt, a derelict country parish in Lorraine. He at once set about the work of rechristianizing his parish. In the best tradition of the Counter-Reformation, he soon identified the pressing need for education of the young. "He concluded that there is no better expedient than to take the children straight from the cradle ... and that there would be no work more advantageous than to establish in the Church an Order whose express duty is to break the bread of life for these little ones." Instinctively, his first thought was for boys. He collected a group of young men in his rectory, with the object of training them to be schoolmasters. "But the time had not yet come. First one broke away, then another demanded his leave; another became so fed up that in three months everything had gone up in smoke."[75] His first attempt to create a Christian school was a failure.

It was at about this time that Alix Le Clerc approached him. Later she recalled the meeting: "I was twenty years old when I received my religious vocation ... The inspiration came to me to create a new community of women to do all the good that was possible, and this idea took hold of me so powerfully that I went at once to propose it to our good Father, begging him to allow me to arrange it all; but he was unwilling, and showed me the difficulty that there would be in finding women who had what was necessary to undertake this new vocation."[76] She proved him wrong, however. Within two months she had been joined by four companions, ready to work and live together. Their undertaking was affirmed at the Christmas midnight mass.

The early days of the community were uncertain. The young women were content simply to start work. But Fourier knew that, to have legitimacy, they must receive approval from the Church. To this end he took their case to a council especially convened in Liverdun by the primate of Lorraine, Monseigneur de la Vallée.

The petition with which Fourier introduced the new community is revealing in its caution: no mention was made of the word "teaching." He simply affirmed their intention to accept a limited clausura, while working for the glory of God, their own perfection, and "the care, both corporal and spiritual, of their neighbour."[77] The council, however, was not so easily put off. It had heard of a provisional rule, which he had prepared for the women, devoted entirely to "the importance, value of and need for their schools."[78] It was over this document that the argument raged, and Fourier had for the first time to defend the feminine teaching vocation. Against the claim that the community represented an innovation in the Church, he maintained rather that they sought to restore the practices of the primitive Church. Quoting from Saint Paul and from the Fathers, especially from Saint John Chrysostom, he claimed for women the historic right to a share in the apostolic work, including the teaching of the faith "if not from the pulpit, in churches," at least "in private places."[79]

The congregation won a conditional verbal approval from the archbishop. It was enough for the present. The women taught school, first in Poussay, then back in Mattaincourt, in lodgings found for them by a wealthy patroness. They also set up an infirmary and a soup kitchen and went out, after school hours, to visit the sick. The initial reaction of the town was reserve, even derision. "Some said that they had gone mad, others that they were misled; and almost everybody agreed that their undertaking was beyond their strength, and that it would all end in confusion."[80] Even Fourier lost heart for a while, and only the women's determination to continue prevented the community from being disbanded.[81]

In time, however, scepticism gave way to acceptance. New houses were opened: in 1602 in Verdun and Saint-Mihiel, in 1603 in Nancy, in 1604 in Pont-à-Mousson, in 1605 in Saint-Nicolas du Port. Paradoxically, though the sisters themselves were at first treated with suspicion, their schools enjoyed instant success. Students appeared in such numbers "that to satisfy them, they began at six in the morning and did not come out until eleven"; they went back after lunch "and returned only in the evening."[82] Success bred further success: aspirants began requesting admittance to the institute, and among them were young women of quality. The house in Nancy, where Alix Le Clerc was superior, became the darling of the ducal court. In 1603, the cardinal of Lorraine gave the congregation, which now had houses in three dioceses, a general approval. Without questioning the ultimate authority of the bishops, he accepted the principle of union between houses. It appeared that the Congrégation de Notre-Dame might indeed become a regular congregation, after the model of the Jesuits. After that, there seemed to be nothing standing in its way. At the opening of classes in Saint-Nicolas in 1605, Fourier wrote to the sisters: "Numerous gentlemen and great ladies, people who are first and foremost in this country and in the Church of God, princes and princesses and many others, listen, ask questions, and watch to see what you are about to do in this place." But he added: "Be on your guard."[83]

Success was a two-edged sword. In the obscure parish of Mattaincourt the sisters' life could go on without much stir, but their presence in the principal cities subjected them to scrutiny and criticism. Rome had recently restated the prescriptions of Pius v enforcing the strictest interpretation of clausura.[84] What was more, Lorraine was now feeling the full force of Catholic reform. It was difficult to impose monastic discipline on the ancient monasteries when these new uncloistered nuns were seen in the principal cities, moving around in the very shadow of the hierarchy. Furthermore, the upper-class families whose daughters were now entering the congregation were beginning to ask the inevitable questions about permanence and legality. It was an appropriate time for a petition to reach the cardinal of Lorraine against these pseudo-monasteries without vows, "which they [the nuns] are free to leave whenever it suits them."[85]

The congregation required pontifical approval to establish it on a legal basis. The women needed this, to be sure that their "state" might not be suddenly stripped from them, reducing them again to lay status. But a series of deaths in 1607 – of the bishop of Toul, the cardinal, and the duke – diverted the attention of Lorrainers to more pressing affairs, and the congregation was left for several years to conduct its schools and build its community life as best it could. In 1611, however, there was an abrupt change. The new primate of Lorraine, Antoine de Lenoncourt, offered to speak for the congregation in Rome. Fourier, anxious to gain pontifical approval for the work, hastened to provide him with a plan which represented a consensus of all the superiors. Now, it seemed, the Congrégation de Notre-Dame would receive its juridical existence.

However, Lenoncourt had ideas of his own. He was building a new monastery for the sisters in Nancy, which he hoped to make the showpiece and the mother house of the congregation. The bull that he obtained from Rome in 1615 was drawn up in total disregard of the wishes of the general chapter of the congregation. It authorized the nuns to teach, but made no mention of day students.[86] Furthermore, instead of including the entire group of communities in his request, Lenoncourt sought, and received, approbation for a single monastery only, that of Nancy, with no mention of the other houses. Without any consultation with the nuns or with Fourier, he erected this monastery under the rule of Saint Augustine. At his orders Alix Le Clerc, superior of the Nancy house, was sent to the Ursuline convent of Faubourg Saint-Jacques to study their methods. Clearly the primate was considering a monastery along Ursuline lines, under obedience to the bishop, himself.

Lenoncourt had not abandoned the idea of a congregation, however; he simply planned to organize it in his own way, under his own authority. He had probably heard of the initiatives of some French bishops, to unite the female monasteries in their dioceses under their own direction. The temptation to attempt the same himself must have been very strong. If he did not do it, someone else might. The duchy of Lorraine was at this time an uneasy neighbour to France, standing in the immediate path of its political expansion. The political power struggle extended even into ecclesiastical affairs. The foundation in 1615 of a new house in Châlons-sur-Marne, in France, meant that from now on the Gallican church had its hands on a corner of the congregation. Experience already showed that where religious orders spread across boundaries, the French superiors claimed jurisdiction over the rest. Lenoncourt decided to forestall such a move. One of his advisers was set to work to draw up constitutions for the entire congregation.

However, this bid to set Nancy over its sister monasteries had disruptive effects. From now on, schismatic tendencies appeared in the congregation. Fourier had hoped, above all, for a united congregation. The "interaid" that he had recommended was undermined by the general suspicion of the nuns that a new organization and a new mother house were being foisted upon them without their consent. No longer were the ideas of a central direction appealing, if that direction came from Lenoncourt in Nancy.

The erection of the monastery of Nancy went ahead. The other houses soon followed suit in seeking the privilege of clausura from their own bishops. Very swiftly the consequences of these transformations came to be felt. Invited to Nancy to make their profession of vows together, the nuns of the French houses refused, their bishops maintaining that to do so would be contrary to clausura.[87] The natural centrifugal tendencies of the monasteries, coupled with the various bishops' jealousy of their own jurisdictions, were already destroying the prospects for a single congregation. The unity of "one heart and one soul for all" which Fourier had sought was already a thing of the past.

The congregation had survived through thirty years of change. It had functioned in favourable and unfavourable circumstances. In the aftermath of the cardinal's approbation in 1603 everything had seemed possible; after Lenoncourt's divisive move in 1615, everything was thrown into doubt. For a time, the question of "mitigated" enclosure had seemed open to discussion; gradually, this subject closed again, as religious thinkers, notably the Jesuits, came down in favour of strict clausura. As the Ursuline communities of France, one by one, submitted to monastic rule and enclosure, the hopes for a wider sphere of action dimmed also in Lorraine. As Mary Ward's cause began to fail in Rome, the tide of resistance to innovation in feminine religious life reached full flood.

The key to survival was adaptibility. And the evidence of this adaptibility exists today, in the various plans and rules which Fourier drew up for the congregation between 1598 and 1640. These represented the nuns' thinking as well as his own, since from the very beginning he was in the habit of consulting with them on all major decisions. Thus the formulae which he drew up at different times, beginning with the *règlements* for the schoolmistresses of Mattaincourt and ending with the *Vrayes Constitutions des Religieuses de Notre-Dame* – full, strict, monastic constitutions – remain for us as discrete imprints of a congregation in evolution, responding by necessity to internal and external forces of change.

Fourier was ready to accept the less perfect in order to save the essential. It is possible, therefore, to know what he still retained, and what he had already surrendered, when the congregation finally took its case to Rome in 1627. On one fundamental issue he remained adamant: "The original and principal intention was to instruct children, and then to lead as saintly a life as possible ... I have always thought it necessary to say that they were schoolmistresses first and that then, for the sake of a stricter life, they have desired and ... earnestly sought to be religious."[88] Without this central vocation he saw no reason to have a congregation. "He would rather his daughters remain in their homes without clausura, as they used to do in the past, than give up the free instruction of day students."[89] His constant preoccupation was to find strategies to make clausura and the teaching of day students compatible; but of the two, he considered teaching the more important.

The central purpose of the Mattaincourt community had been set out in all its simplicity in 1598. It was "to establish public schools in which to give free instruction to girls in reading, writing, needlework and Christian doctrine." The best, most fruitful, and most appropriate means of staffing these schools was "by *filles congrégées*, striving to live well, charging nothing, teaching piety and whatever other subjects can of themselves bring some temporal profit to those who learn them." No child should be excluded by reason of poverty. "As for us who teach, let God alone be our salary and paymaster; may He have occasion to bless and prosper our labours."[90]

There was no word here of a formal "religion." However, from the very start Fourier was committed to the principle of clausura. Not only had he promised it to Monseigneur de la Vallée at that first council in Liverdun; he had also promised it to the women themselves. Alix Le Clerc and her companions wanted enclosure. Fourier accepted this, but hoped for a "moderate enclosure," with movement outside the house for charitable purposes, and with students free to come and go. In the more favourable climate of the early 1600s it did not seem unreasonable; after all, it only meant adapting their monastic commitment to their functions as school-mistresses, just as his own vows as a canon regular were adapted to his work as a curé. Thus the congregation as he initially planned it was a compromise between their attraction to the monastic life and his own urgent desire for Christian schools.

Under this regime the new congregation prospered, and the approbation given it in 1603 by the cardinal of Lorraine seemed to sanction Fourier's ideas. As new foundations appeared, he extended his plan by instituting a general chapter which he, as director, summoned to discuss questions of general interest. He decided that aspirants should be sent away from their own home town, to undergo their period of probation in another house, preferably one that was not yet comfortably established. The nuns should be ready "like Saint Peter and Saint Matthew, to leave all else, and self, at the first word," to go wherever they were needed.[91] Clearly he had plans for a flexible organization similar to that of the Jesuits, suitable for the broad apostolate that he saw waiting for it.

By 1611 the early optimism had faded. The exigencies of monastic reform, both in Lorraine and elsewhere, were not compatible with the freedoms that the congregation had been enjoying. Increasingly concerned, as the years passed, with the problem of official recognition, Fourier and the general chapter bowed to the inevitability of full clausura. But in order to fulfil their duty of teaching the poor, and also to hold on to their young schoolmistresses, talented but poor, who would not be able to afford religious dowries, they proposed that the congregation should henceforth consist of two kinds of houses, "enclosed" and "unenclosed." The enclosed houses – the monasteries – would support and guarantee the other houses, in which secular schoolmistresses would observe the rule but not take vows.[92] This duality was the congregation's solution to the restriction of its field of action which monastic transformation would inevitably entail.

As Fourier drew and redrew his plans, the centralization of the organization, and the mobility of its members, remained a priority. The monasteries were to be joined in a federation, headed by a *mère intendante* who would be elected for a three-year term by each of the communities in turn.[93] They were to be subject to a single visitor, who, he hoped, would be taken from the congregation of canons regular of which he was a member. The aspirants were to be asked before clothing if they were ready "to live in whichever country and whichever house of the congregation was most appropriate for the service of God."[94] There was to be a seminary, supported by all the monasteries, which would train poor young women to teach in the primary schools.[95] Above all, he and Alix persevered in preparing for recognition of the congregation's unenclosed houses, which were now functioning with great success in fact, though still non-existent in law.[96]

The petition for papal approbation was finally taken to Rome in 1627, by Fourier's fellow canons regular, Guinet and Lemulier.

The introduction of the cause in the court of Urban VIII was greeted with astonishment. By what authority had the bishops of Lorraine and France erected all these monasteries? Only the house in Nancy had pontifical approval. To Guinet, who referred to the legislation of Trent which empowered bishops to erect monasteries, the response was that more recent legislation had in fact removed this power to the Holy See alone. He was advised that the best he could hope for was that the pope would confirm what was already done, and validate the religious vows which had been taken in error.[97]

Guinet's audience with the pope foundered as soon as Urban learned that the religious of the Congrégation taught day students. "Are these Jesuitesses? We don't want them in Rome!" The pope then "broke into exclamations, like a person stupefied by what he is hearing."[98]

The case was sent to the Congregation of Regulars, whose reaction was equally negative. "We are surprised that they cannot be persuaded that with schoolteaching it is still possible to maintain clausura," wrote Guinet, "but what is even more astonishing is that they believe that chastity is incompatible with this instruction, pure though it is."[99] His protests, that a suppression of the houses would lead to scandal, elicited the unsympathetic response: "Well then, let them marry. After all, it's their right, and they can use it."[100]

Under these unfavourable circumstances, mere survival of the monasteries seemed doubtful. The idea that the pope would grant a single bull to create a whole congregation together was altogether preposterous.

Fourier sent back arguments. How could the teaching of day students be unlawful for the congregation as a whole if it had already been approved for the religious of Nancy? He argued again, as he had done in 1598, for the historical authenticity of the feminine teaching apostolate, and he again used his citations from the Fathers of the Church.

The debate went on in Rome. Guinet came to the conclusion that it was the pope's personal prejudice, rather than the law, that stood in the way of approval: "He finds such difficulty in the idea of women giving instruction, and his mind is so firmly made up, that it is difficult to change it."[101]

In March 1628, Urban relented and approved the congregation, though insisting that there must be as many bulls as there were monasteries. Guinet's plea, that the houses were much too poor to pay for so many bulls, was rejected. "They can do what they want. They can take the bulls or they can leave them; let them look to their own conscience."[102] Then again, without forewarning, the pope reversed his decision, and granted the single bull to cover the entire congregation.

The implications of this favour alarmed the Roman officials. "Their reason was ... that a congregation of nuns was never to be allowed or created, because of their basic incapacity."[103] However, the pope's decision was final; the bull that was promulgated on 8 August 1628 assured the institute for all time, under the title of "Chanoinesses regulières de saint Augustin, de la Congrégation de Notre-Dame."[104]

The bull represented a compromise. The nuns had won recognition as a congregation. They had won the right to teach not only boarders, but day students. This right was secured by the fourth vow which each nun henceforth took at profession, "to devote herself to the instruction of girls ... and never to allow it to be abolished or eliminated from the monastery, or from the Congregation."[105] On the other hand, their entry into full monastic life meant a shrinking of their former apostolate. Hemmed in by severe physical and financial restrictions, they underwent a "reclassing" similar to that which the Ursulines experienced. They were forced to discriminate in favour of the wealthy, in total opposition to the founding members' wishes. The dowries of their entrants were raised, their boarding schools became more exclusive; the solidity of their status brought in more aspirants, more support from the moneyed classes. The unenclosed houses were gone. The monasteries' day schools were all that was left of their mission among the poor. The unity of the congregation, for which Fourier sought to lay the foundations by securing the single bull, was frittered away, as some monasteries accepted the visitors provided by the canons regular, and others continued in close subordination to their bishops.

Yet for all the deflection from its original purpose, the Congrégation performed a great service to its society. It established its schools widely, forming the base for a network that would keep the feminine literacy rate relatively high in Lorraine throughout the Old Regime. More to the purpose of its founders, it assisted in the christianization of a country that was to be grievously afflicted by war and social disruption in the coming years. Fourier, exiled from his homeland in the course of those bitter years, never ceased to take pride in the nuns' achievement. He wrote in their praise: "Wherever

they live, people remark with admiration on the marvellous transformation that takes place in the youth who pass through their
hands; ... on the modesty, obedience and piety of the women who
attended their schools when they were young girls." And he added,
in an aside which reveals his own educational concerns: "What is
more, people see the way that many [women] have profited in learning, in a short time and without expense, not only piety but manual
skills – especially the poor who previously did not know how to
earn their living."[106]

In 1640 he died, still in exile, still far from the women whose work
he had so faithfully advanced. In the same year Jeanne de Lestonnac
died, followed in 1641 by Jeanne Françoise de Chantal, the foundress
of the Visitation. Françoise de Bermond, the first Ursuline of France,
had been dead for well over a decade. They had all lived long enough
to see their institutes accepted, but also altered and contained.

During the first years of the century, as the Counter-Reformation
began to take hold in France, an unprecedented number of women
had flooded into "religion." Before the French church even found
its feet, they were already there, caught up in the strong reform
current that was sweeping through the country. Whereas many
women had embraced a contemplative lifestyle already well
grounded in tradition, others had found, or thought they found,
their calling in action. They had decided to participate in the apostolate, without yet knowing exactly what form that participation
could take.[107]

In the following years these *filles congrégées* experimented with all
the activities that are known as the corporal works of mercy. But
the greatest need of the times, in their eyes and in the eyes of all
dévots, was the rechristianization of the people and the elimination
of heresy. Religious instruction, in 1600, was not merely the corollary
of other good works; it was *the* good work, the basic condition for
the Church's survival. The great preaching orders, the Jesuits, the
Capuchins, and others, were covering the country with their missions. It was natural that the women should desire to participate in
these missions. For a few years they, too, moved around the countryside, teaching and indeed almost preaching the word of God.

But this turned out to be a false start. Religious women doing this
kind of work were a threat to their times. By teaching in public they
were seen to be in contempt of divine law, and dangerously similar
to some heretic women whose invasion of the preaching ministry
had shocked the Catholic world. By moving around openly in society

they were challenging the sacrosanctity of clausura, at a time when the hierarchy was working to re-establish it. "[Such behaviour] is highly dangerous in these times, and in this country," wrote the archbishop of Lyon.[108]

In one undertaking, however, the women were successful. They discovered, and then adopted, the teaching profession: not the small-scale training of boarders for the religious life which had always been a cottage industry in monasteries, but a full-time, specialized education of children for life in "the world." And in entering this profession they hit upon a service for which the time was ripe, for which society was ready. Their classrooms were filled almost as fast as they opened.

It remained for the Church to reconcile this very popular service with the demands of clausura. This was achieved, first in the bull of 1607 which gave the Filles de Notre-Dame permission to teach day students within the precincts of their monastery, then in the similar bulls which transformed the Ursulines and the sisters of the Congrégation into cloistered canonesses of Saint Augustine. By the 1630s the point had been made: religious women, whether they were contemplatives in the pattern of Saint Mary Magdalen or active in the pattern of Saint Martha, belonged in the cloister. "It matters little what the times demand, the Canon Law of the Church will not allow women to live in community unless they become religious, and as this entails enclosure, then all congregations that refuse the enclosure must be suppressed."[109]

But the problem which the congrégées had sought to address was only partially solved. Their containment within monastery walls left a broad segment of the population – women and girls who lived beyond the reach of the monasteries – without any but the barest of religious instruction.

Within a few years the problem was approached again, this time from a different angle. In 1641 and 1642, the first communities of filles séculières came into being.

CHAPTER FOUR

A New Approach: The Filles Séculières (1630–60)

Modern historians of the Counter-Reformation in France agree to divide that event into two phases: the Counter-Reformation properly speaking, strongly influenced by the Mediterranean Catholicism that triumphed at Trent,[1] characterized by a highly adversarial approach to the questions that had been thrown up by Protestantism; and what is known as the Catholic Reformation, a period of genuine religious regeneration, during which the Church recognized, and moved to redress, the immense problems within itself.[2] The turning point between these two phases is generally placed around the beginning of the seventeenth century.[3]

But this "turning point," like most others, requires qualification. The atmosphere of violence and anxiety which fostered the Counter-Reformation spirit did not die with the conversion of Henri IV and the Edict of Nantes. The Protestant presence continued to cause severe, and often brutal, reaction. Even when non-violent, the defence of the faith was conducted largely through campaigns of apologetics, mounted by the great preaching congregations.

On the other hand, the "Catholic Reformation," in the sense in which that term is usually employed, was not fully realized until later in the seventeenth century. The central drive of the Catholic Reformation was for the reform of the clergy, on which was predicated the christianization of the laity.[4] This strategy was designed by the Council of Trent, but it was not implemented in France until a full century later. The French Church's program of structural reform had to wait for its financial recovery from the losses of the Reformation years. Only in the 1670s, with the setting-up of seminaries throughout the country, did clerical reform begin in earnest. In the meantime, much of France remained poorly served by its clergy. The *grand siècle*, writes one Church historian, was not the magnificent "moment" that has sometimes been depicted, but a period of severe and continuing crisis.[5]

Thus the first decades of the seventeenth century were a period during which the country's religious reformers gathered their forces and laid their foundations. This period had its own particular characteristics. It was the time of the "mystical invasion" – a sudden flowering of religious sentiment within French Catholic society. It was also the time of an extraordinarily high level of lay participation in religious affairs. An important part of the Church's work passed into the hands of the laity, at a time when there was a shortage of qualified priests.[6] "Most priests stand aside with their arms crossed; God has had to raise up laymen – cutlers and mercers – to do the work of these idle priests."[7] So wrote a great clerical reformer, Adrien Bourdoise.[8] The laymen of whom he spoke were less likely to be cutlers and mercers than men of substance; but the point of his argument was correct. What is remarkable is that there existed a body of people capable of taking up this work. These were the *dévots*.

The *dévots* defined themselves, and were defined, in several ways. In its most general sense, the term simply described pious laymen, or, in the feminine gender, laywomen. But at the turn of the seventeenth century the *dévots* were also a religious party with a strong political purpose, under the leadership of Pierre (later Cardinal) Bérulle and Michel de Marillac, keeper of the seals to the crown. Spiritual descendants of the Holy League (indeed, many of them had been Leaguers), they represented the pure "Catholic" interest, and were therefore frequently at odds with the more pragmatic policies, first of Henri IV, then of Cardinal Richelieu. In particular they favoured alliances with Catholic powers – Spain and Austria – and were appalled at the government's *rapprochement* with Protestant princes. Their political influence came to an end with the Day of Dupes, in 1630, when Richelieu finally drove his enemies from power. Thereafter, as state policy became ever more independent of religious considerations, they separated themselves from the "world," which they now saw as intrinsically evil. *Dévots* took on the role of critics of society and guardians of its morality. Hence their battle against Protestants, libertines, atheists, actors, and every other type of deviant. Hence their conspicuously sober clothes, their theatrical services of reparation during carnival and other seasons of excess, and their unremitting battle against duelling, dancing, gaming, and the theatre. For all their status and influence, they were only a small segment of French society, and they were cordially disliked by many for what was seen as their excessive, and foreign, religiosity.

Unfortunately for the *dévots*, their memory is enshrined for us in the brilliant satire created by one of their enemies. The Compagnie du Saint-Sacrement,[9] the most powerful and political of all *dévot* organizations, pursued the playwright Molière as a threat to public morality. His reprisal was *Tartuffe*. For three centuries audiences have been regaled with Tartuffe's hypocrisy and prurience, and also with his hunger for power.[10] But there was more to the *dévots* than Tartuffe. Their influence on their times was powerful and, in many ways, beneficial.

First and foremost, *dévots* were characterized by their interior religious fervour. "No Christian epoch," writes one historian, "has been more penetrated by the supernatural than the beginning of the seventeenth century ... Never did Christian souls ponder more anxiously the ways of divine grace."[11] They practised spiritual discipline at a level hitherto unknown in laymen. They confessed frequently (a practice which had begun only with Trent), mortified their bodies, and read and meditated upon the many religious works that were now coming into print. Above all, following the advice of François de Sales given in the *Introduction à la vie dévote*, they found themselves spiritual directors, and developed the practice of methodical prayer. "This practice," writes Lucien Febvre, "which during the Middle Ages belonged to the convents ... passed into the 'world.'" He argues that to it, more than anything else, can be attributed the intense religious fervour of the time.[12] *Dévots* aspired to an other-worldly life within the world. "Those who are simply good men trudge along God's road," wrote François de Sales, "but the devout run, and when they are truly devout, they fly."[13]

Part of the activity proper to the *dévot* was good works. Indeed, it was this vocation that distinguished him from the other orders in society. In the seventeenth-century mind, charitable works were not the responsibility of the priest, still less of the religious. They fell to the layman and laywoman as their apportioned lot, the means of their salvation. "If you love the poor," wrote François de Sales to his *Philothée*, "spend time among them; take pleasure in having them at your home, and in visiting them at their home ... Make yourself their servant, go to serve them in their beds when they are sick, and do it with your own hands; be their cook at your own expense; be their sewing maid and their washerwoman."[14]

Many *dévots* undertook good works as part of their spiritual exercises.[15] For those who found personal contact with the poor distasteful, there was alternative social action: organization, animation, fund-raising. It was in these fields that the Compagnie du Saint-Sacrement and its branches in the provinces were most effective.

From the 1630s on, *dévot* spirituality was, so to speak, bonded to good works. For the next thirty or forty years, the care of the poor, in all its diverse forms, bore the stamp of a particular mind-set that was other-worldly and yet highly practical. This mind-set, which saw poverty as an evil and the poor as social problems, was a far cry from the cheerful and undiscriminating charitable outlook of the Middle Ages.[16] The social relationships of the seventeenth century were tinged with a highly pessimistic theology. "For the disciples of Bérulle," writes one historian, "nature, soiled by original sin, was fundamentally evil."[17] The poor required assistance, training, and – above all – salvation. Their future was not in this world, but the next; true charity consisted not in pampering their bodies, but in salvaging their souls.

The new attitudes towards the poor did not spring from theology alone. It has been pointed out that the same general policies were developed in Protestant societies working from a different theological base. In its war on mendicancy, France was much closer in spirit to Protestant England than to Catholic Spain, where all efforts to enclose and correct beggars were resisted, well into the eighteenth century.[18] The harsher social approach came to prevail where it had the *conjoncture* on its side. Economic and social conditions, the triumph of mercantilism and the passion for order in all things combined to change the attitude of the respectable classes towards their weaker brethren.

However, a powerful and influential section of the *dévot* movement continued to draw, at least partly, on the traditional idea of the poor as *alter Christus* – the other Christ. At the risk of over-generalizing, it may be argued that this section represented the feminine point of view, while the other represented the masculine.

In French Catholic tradition, the exercise of charity towards the poor had always been a feminine prerogative. "In these parts this ministry is usually practised by women," wrote François de Sales.[19] Wives were entitled by law and custom to give alms on behalf of their husbands. They monopolized the field; indeed, it was the only field outside the home that they were allowed to monopolize.[20] However, in the environment of the Catholic Reformation charity took on a higher profile, and pious laymen resolved to take their share. Consequently, the work was divided into two categories: the business of social control, in the sense of the supervision and training of the able-bodied poor, and charity pure and simple, such as the care of the sick and the obviously helpless. The former became the preserve of men, the latter of women. Throughout the century, each sex continued to dominate its own segment of charitable works.

It was under the auspices of the *dévotes* that the first charitable company of women – the Filles de la Charité – was born. These were, essentially, unmarried women or widows who wished to live together under one roof and dedicate themselves to good works. Their original purpose was to assist lay action, and they usually worked closely with other pious, but less committed, laywomen. The evolution and the expansion of the business of charity, however, laid a demand on them far beyond expectations. To meet this demand, they underwent organization and training, and became an officially recognized company.

Changing perceptions of poverty came, first, from changes in poverty itself. The seventeenth century was indeed a "tragic century." At the end of the religious wars there was a short breathing space; then came what has been called a "climax of misery":[21] bad harvests in 1629 and 1630, followed by bubonic plague; war in Lorraine, then in Picardie and Champagne. The years 1647–48 and 1651–52, also bad harvest years, were aggravated by the upheavals of the Fronde. These blows fell heavily upon the rural poor. Unable to survive the disorganization of their habitat, great numbers of people simply took to the road, migrating to cities that had no real means of absorbing them.

Poverty became highly visible. "One saw wandering troops of vagrants, without religion and without discipline, begging with more obstinacy than humility, often stealing what they could not otherwise get, gaining the public's attention by pretended infirmities, coming even to the foot of the altars to disturb the devotions of the faithful."[22] These vagabond poor were despised by respectable people. They were "the sweepings of cities, the plague of Republics, gallows meat, from which come thieves, murderers, and all sorts of other good-for-nothing rascals."[23] They were feared, probably with cause, as being ripe for trouble. In 1649 the bourgeois of Paris complained officially: "The poor within our city walls are constantly planning frightful sedition, and the despair which is beginning to fill their hearts convinces them that there is no other remedy for their ills."[24]

Behind these problem poor, whose wandering ways were equated in the seventeenth century with heresy, disease, and vice,[25] stood another class of poor who, though less visible, caused equal concern. These were the respectable poor. By contemporary definition, a man was respectably poor "who lives as a Christian, who cannot earn his livelihood and who blushes for shame when he is forced to beg."[26] For the majority of the poor who remained integrated into their towns and villages the danger of destitution was only too real. "Most of them have not enough to survive two days of sickness without assistance from the Hôtel-Dieu," wrote one civic official of the poor in his city.[27] The saturation of the labour market by incomers and the rising price of grain kept their numbers high. In 1651, at the peak of the troubles of the Fronde, one Parisian parish alone, Saint-Sulpice, identified 856 families, for a total of 2496 mouths, as respectable poor.[28]

A number of institutions already existed to handle the poor, but they were inadequate for present needs. The small country hospitals were mostly abandoned by the seventeenth century. The municipal *hôtels-dieu*, or hospitals, were run down and poorly maintained. *Bureaux des pauvres* had been established during the previous century in many cities, but they usually existed in name only, without funds or buildings. Operations that continued to function did so only in a desultory way. The Couche of Paris, for instance, the institution for abandoned children, was maintained by a tax on the high justices of the city under the aegis of the chapter of Notre-Dame; but the children were neglected and abused nonetheless. "They were sold at eight sols apiece to beggars, who broke their arms and legs so that people would be induced to give them alms, and then let them die of hunger."[29] Everywhere, at the end of the troubles of the sixteenth century, facilities had broken down, and the will to rebuild them was lacking.[30]

The credit for changing this situation lies largely with one man. In typical seventeenth-century fashion, his own revelation of the misery of the poor came first on the spiritual, rather than the material, level. In 1616 Vincent de Paul,[31] then almoner to the Gondi family, was travelling with Madame de Gondi on her domain when he was asked to hear the confession of a sick peasant. A few days later the peasant declared to Madame de Gondi that this confession had saved his soul, that without it he would most certainly have been damned. Madame de Gondi turned in horror to her almoner: "Ah! Monsieur, what is this? ... It is doubtless the same for most of these poor people ... Ah, Monsieur Vincent, how many souls are being lost! What remedy is there for this?"[32]

At his patron's urging, Monsieur Vincent organized a mission in the local parish of Folleville, to exhort the inhabitants to make a general confession. The response was so overwhelming that he could not handle the confessions alone, and had to call upon the

Jesuits of Amiens for assistance. This was the first of his missions. In 1625, armed with a legacy of sixteen thousand livres from Madame de Gondi, he founded a congregation of priests whose sole purpose was to convert the countryside. The method that they continued to use was the mission: an organized descent by a group of preachers upon a community, a period of intensive exhortation and instruction which ended only when everybody had received the sacrament of penance.

This method, "corresponding to the needs of the country people," as Monsieur Vincent put it, bore great fruit. But its unforeseen product was the effect it had upon the missioners themselves. "I did not learn about the state of these poor people from someone else," wrote one priest, an Oratorian who had assisted at a mission, "I discovered it for myself ... The other confessors and I found aged people, sixty years old and more, who told us freely that they had never confessed; and when we spoke to them about God, and the most holy Trinity, and the Nativity, Passion and Death of Jesus Christ, and other mysteries, it was a language which they did not understand at all."[33]

On discovering this alien world so close to its own doorstep, Catholic society experienced a profound sense of shock. Monsieur Vincent and his Mission priests consciously induced and exploited this uncomfortable awareness. Information from the countryside was relayed to the city, and disseminated by word of mouth and by pamphlet.[34] This information, acting on the tender *dévot* conscience, produced powerful results.

In the minds of seventeenth-century theologians, ignorance of the faith meant damnation. "Without a clear faith in the fundamental truths of our holy Church, it is impossible to please God and be saved, no matter what outward ceremonies one observes."[35] These neglected people, then, were in danger both of material destitution and spiritual death. And the danger extended back onto those who were guilty of the neglect. "Si non pavisti, occidisti" – if you have not fed them, you have killed them – this hard doctrine was repeated frequently by Vincent de Paul. "How shall we answer to God if through our negligence one of these poor souls comes to die and is lost? ... Ought we not to be afraid that He will call us to account for this at the hour of our death?"[36] It was a disturbing thought, but a powerful one. Beneath the good works of the seventeenth century lay, not a comfortable philanthropy, but a deep sense of anxiety and guilt.

However, this pious laity looked forward also to the temporal reordering of society, and therefore found good works attractive for highly practical reasons. Even Monsieur Vincent was ready to include the socialization of the poor among the blessings of charity: "The rich acquire a million blessings in this world and eternal life in the other ... the poor are instructed in the fear of God, taught to earn their living, and assisted in their needs, and ... finally, cities are delivered from throngs of ne'er-do-wells and troublemakers, and improved by the trade created by the industry of the poor."[37]

The two motivations – the spiritual and the practical – existed side by side, so closely entwined that nobody, then or now, could distinguish one from the other. Under their impulse a great variety of institutions and projects were launched: orphanages, hospitals, refuges, workshops, asylums, prison-visiting programs, legal aid for galley convicts, training schools for servants, seminaries for teachers, furniture depots for the destitute, seed-grain for the peasants – all maintained by voluntary effort until, with the establishment of the *hôpitaux-généraux* (workhouses) at mid-century, the direction began to pass to the government, and the spirit changed.

In short, the manpower behind the good works of the period 1620–50 was primarily secular, voluntary, deeply religious in conviction, but also dedicated to the concept of an orderly and productive society.

It had one further characteristic: it was largely feminine. Of the different organizations developed to assist the poor, the majority were female. Since the work was all voluntary, this was something over which nobody had any control. Some found the fact worrying, others found it providential.

The beginnings, and growth, of the greatest female charitable organization of the times certainly did have a fortuitous character. In 1617 Vincent de Paul, having escaped temporarily from Madame de Gondi's devoted grasp, was working as a curé in Châtillon-les-Dombes, in the archdiocese of Lyon. One Sunday, just before mass, he learned of a family that was sick, some distance from the village. He announced the news from the pulpit, then, after mass, prepared to go out to visit the family, taking with him "a worthy man, a bourgeois of the town." "On the road we found women going out ahead of us, and, a little further on, others who were coming back. And as it was summer and very hot, these good women were sitting along the side of the roads to rest and get cool. There were so many of them that you could have called them a procession."[38]

The difficulty was that they had overwhelmed the sick family with their generosity. Monsieur Vincent realized that much of the food they had brought would spoil, and then the family would be in need once more. He decided to co-ordinate the women's good will: "God gave me this thought: 'could these good women not be brought together and persuaded to offer themselves to God to serve the sick poor?' Afterwards, I showed them the way to handle these great necessities with great ease. At once they resolved to do it."[39]

This was the first parish *charité*. It was so successful that Vincent de Paul undertook to establish a similar organization wherever he preached a mission, and later instructed his Mission priests to do the same. *Charités* were legally erected as confraternities, with a superior and a treasurer elected by the members. Their funds were raised by donations, by organized begging by the members, and also from any properties that the confraternity might acquire. Many of the village *charités* owned sheep and cattle.

The most successful *charités* were those in which women of different social levels were included, because in this case the wealthier women tended to provide the money while the women of modest means did the work.[40] But the several rules which have survived show that, initially, all members were expected to take their turn preparing the food and visiting the sick. The diet was to include meat, eggs or fish twice a day, as well as wine and bread and – for the very sick – broth and more eggs. The sick poor were expected to confess and communicate, and to accept the spiritual exhortations of their benefactors. Those who died while under the care of the *charité* were to be buried, if necessary, at the *charité*'s expense, and the members were to try to attend their funeral, "thus taking the place of mothers who accompany their children to the tomb."[41]

As bigger towns became involved, the organization became more elaborate. In Mâcon in 1621, a formal meeting was held at the city hall, attended by municipal and royal officials. The confraternity, once established, was given the responsibility of enumerating the poor and of suggesting how to raise the money to assist them. The city fathers' scepticism dissolved into delight as the project began to take effect. "One no longer found oneself besieged, in church and in the streets, by these sturdy beggars who spend the whole day looking for their living, without respect for the churches, or regard for their betters, or courtesy for those who refuse to give in to their importunities."[42] The Mâcon operation achieved impressive proportions. Fourteen years later, the *charité* was still distributing twelve hundred pounds of bread and thirty to thirty-five francs per week, as well as paying for medicines, a doctor, and two nurses to watch over the sick.[43]

Vincent de Paul did not conceive of this work as exclusively feminine. As early as 1620 he set up a male *charité*; in 1621, he attempted to make men and women work together. While the women were to continue their work with the sick, the men were to oversee those who were healthy but unable to take care of themselves.[44] The women's work was more in the charitable tradition, while the men's work contained a corrective element. Monsieur Vincent warned the men to respect the women's work: "Our Lord is as much glorified in the ministry of women as in that of men."[45] However, the men's *charités* did not thrive and the mixed *charités* did not work. He later wrote: "Men and women do not get along together at all in matters of administration; the former want to take it over entirely and the latter will not allow it ... We charged the men with the care of the healthy poor and the women with the sick; but because there was a shared purse, we had to get rid of the men. And I can bear this witness in favour of the women, that there is no fault to find in their administration, so careful and accurate are they."[46]

Male membership gradually dwindled and finally collapsed, while female membership continued to grow. The enthusiasm of women for the new confraternities brought them out in numbers that were sometimes alarming. From Beauvais, the royal lieutenant wrote that "about a fortnight ago, a priest named Vincent arrived in this town, and ... called together a great crowd of women, and persuaded them to set up a branch of the confraternity which he has called a 'Charity' ... Since then it has all been arranged by the aforesaid Vincent: this confraternity has been erected and about three hundred women admitted, who meet together frequently to perform their religious exercises and other duties; which ought not to be tolerated."[47] But official sensibilities aside, the success of the *charités* was guaranteed, because the need they served was so pressing.

The first confraternity in the archdiocese of Paris was erected in 1629. Vincent de Paul was initially unenthusiastic about the city *charités*. The institution had been designed specifically for country conditions, for a certain integration of society in which members from different walks of life would still be able to work together at what were, after all, menial tasks. How could the upper-class women of Paris be expected to do the same? His fears proved justified: the high-born ladies were unable to perform the "lowly and demeaning services" that the rule required.[48] While they were ready to provide and prepare the food, they preferred to send their servants to carry it to the sick. In some cases these servants abused or neglected their charges. The sick poor were "badly served," remarked Monsieur Vincent.[49]

The solution was suggested, not by Monsieur Vincent, but by someone else. At about this time (1629), while on mission, he met a young peasant woman, Marguerite Naseau. She had heard of the *charités* in Paris, and offered herself as a servant to do the work that the ladies could not stomach. He invited her to come, which she did, to serve with great fidelity until her death of the plague in 1633. To Marguerite – the "poor uneducated cowherd" of Villepreux – Vincent would later attribute the creation of the Company of the Filles de la Charité.[50]

Marguerite brought in several other young women, who were given a two-day retreat and then placed in the parish *charités*. This caused difficulties, however: village girls, no matter how well-intentioned, were poorly prepared for city life. It was decided that they should undergo a period of training in the house of one of the *dames de la charité*, Mademoiselle Le Gras.[51] Thus the first members and the foundress appeared in reverse order, and thus began the unplanned evolution of the Company of the Filles de la Charité. Even their title was an accident. Originally christened the "servantes des pauvres malades," or servants of the sick poor, in keeping with their function, they became known to the public as the "filles de la charité" – the women who worked for the *charité*. Vincent de Paul later gave the commonplace name its transcendent meaning.

From 1633, when the first few young women entered Mademoiselle Le Gras's house, until 1658, when the company, now numbering eight hundred, received its letters of registration from parlement, the picture is the same: the founders were always led ahead by events, struggling to control and solidify their immensely successful institute. In this long-drawn-out process of foundation, it was Mademoiselle Le Gras who perceived the problems, envisaged the solutions, and begged for decisions. Monsieur Vincent, preoccupied with his other concerns, and also instinctively slow to move, preferred to wait to be sure "that the good God wishes it".[52]

Another force played a part in the creation of the company: its rich and powerful benefactors. One of Vincent de Paul's greatest successes was the establishment of the Company of Dames de la Charité in Paris in 1634. This organization very soon numbered between two and three hundred members, including some of the *grandes dames* of Parisian society.[53] As will be seen, it was always in response to the wishes of important persons such as these that Vincent sent his daughters into a new situation.[54] The *dévotes* of the upper classes, in other words, pressed the sisters into their own preferred projects, and thus deeply modified the nature of their work.

Initially the community was completely secular in character. The women wore the gray dress and white *toquois*, or turban, that was standard among peasant women of the Paris basin. They rose at a comfortable hour for working women – 5:30 – and observed no rule of silence. They were allowed to go home on family visits. They took no vows and observed no exceptional religious practices. They were, in Monsieur Vincent's words, "members of parishes, subject to the curés wherever they are established."[55]

Soon, however, the characteristics of a religious community began to appear. In 1634 the women (now twelve in number) received their first "petit règlement."[56] Their rising time was pushed forward to 4 o'clock. Their daily devotions were defined, the great silence (from evening prayers until morning prayers) was imposed. The obligation of obedience became absolute. In the mother house, Mademoiselle Le Gras was to be superior. In other communities, even those of only two sisters, a superior was to be appointed. "It is necessary," they were told, "that among you there should always be one in the position of superior." Each sister was to attend a retreat annually.[57] In time, further conventual customs were added. Weekly conferences were to be given, either by Monsieur Vincent or by one of his priests. The rule was to be learned and relearned during the period of "testing"; thereafter it was to be read aloud weekly in community, a regular practice in convents. "Let them resolve to observe with exactitude all the rules, particularly the rule of unquestioning obedience," wrote Mademoiselle Le Gras.[58] From both her writings and Vincent's, it is plain that the founders privately considered the life of the sisters to be a religious life, as perfect as any found in a monastery. "Your vocation," Monsieur Vincent told them in 1643, "is one of the greatest that I know of in the Church."[59] This conviction was repeated, with increasing emphasis, throughout the rest of his life. In 1659 he was prepared to say: "You are not religious in name, but you must be religious in fact, and you are more obliged than they to work towards your perfection."[60]

From 1640 onwards, the Filles de la Charité took vows. On the subject of these vows Vincent de Paul was highly circumspect, for fear of altering the legal status of the sisters. Living in community was one thing; living in community with vows was another: it suggested religious life, and religious life, where women were concerned, meant clausura. "To say 'religious' is to say 'cloistered,' and the Filles de la Charité must be free to go everywhere."[61] His solution was to make the vows private, without witnesses. "They are no different from the vows that devout people make in the world," wrote Mademoiselle Le Gras, "indeed they are not like these, since usually people in the world make them in the hearing of their confessor."[62] By avoiding the slightest semblance of public vows, Vincent de Paul, an expert canonist himself, turned the difficulty of canon law and put his daughters beyond the reach of the cloister-ers.[63]

The company still lacked formal status. Mademoiselle Le Gras, who was more concerned with organizational problems than was her director, kept pressing him on this issue; he kept delaying "until he could see more clearly." In 1645, he found the formula he wanted: the company could be erected as a simple confraternity, like the other *charités* which the sisters had been recruited to serve. This would put its secular character beyond question. To the sisters, who wanted a more exalted title, he later explained: "We have judged it appropriate to leave you with the name of society or confraternity … for fear that, if the title of congregation was given to you, people would some day start wanting to turn the house into a cloister and themselves into religious, as the Filles de Sainte-Marie have done."[64]

This was the heart of the problem. Vincent de Paul, who had been a friend of François de Sales and Mère de Chantal, and who had been canonical superior of the Visitation on the rue Saint-Antoine since 1622, understood well the trap in which that congregation had been caught.[65] Once his own daughters began leaving Paris for other dioceses they, too, could find themselves exchanging their life of service for confinement in a cloister.

He gave them instructions on how to speak to a strange bishop: "If he asks you who you are, and if you are religious, tell him no, by the grace of God; that it is not that you do not have high esteem for religious, but that if you were like them you would have to be enclosed, and that as a result you would have to say good-bye to the service of the poor. Tell him that you are poor Daughters of Charity, and that you are given to God for the service of the poor, and that you are free to retire or to be sent away."[66]

In this last sentence lay the bargaining strength of the company. From early days the sisters had proved their usefulness. The letters of Mademoiselle Le Gras show that the demand for their services far exceeded the supply of sisters. "You are only there on loan," she reminded them.[67] By retaining their freedom to leave a situation that had become unsuitable, they were able to avoid interference in their way of life.

The final difficulty for the company was the matter of jurisdiction. Since the time of Borromeo, all new female communities had been subject to the bishop in whose diocese they were established. As the previous chapter has shown, this rule was a deterrent to any project of a central direction, or of unity between houses. "The more houses we have," Fourier had written, "and the more dioceses they are in, the more difficulty we shall have in establishing an assured government and a perfect union of all houses."[68] His solution had been to appoint a visitor to oversee observance of the rule throughout the congregation, while still deferring to the local bishops' authority. His plan had had only small success; the majority of houses of the Congrégation de Notre-Dame had passed into the jurisdiction of the ordinaries. The other new active congregations had remained altogether under diocesan control, and the result, once the first generation of nuns disappeared, had been fragmentation.

At the time of its erection as a confraternity in 1645, the new company of *servantes des pauvres malades* had been placed by the archbishop under the customary obedience: "the confraternity is and will remain forever under the authority and dependence of Monseigneur the archbishop and of his successors."[69] It followed from this that, if the company moved into other dioceses, the communities involved would be subject to other ordinaries. Furthermore, its close ties with the Congregation of the Mission were to last only for Monsieur Vincent's lifetime. It appears that the founder himself was ready to accept this arrangement; but Mademoiselle Le Gras was made of sterner stuff. At her request the queen mother petitioned the pope, asking that the confraternity be placed under the perpetual direction of the superior-general of the Mission.[70] When Rome granted her wish in 1655, this simple confraternity obtained what no feminine religious congregation had hitherto achieved in France: unity of direction and a partial exemption from local episcopal control.[71]

The path that the Filles de la Charité took was difficult. Interiorly, their lives resembled those of religious in all but the strictly monastic aspects of clausura and Divine Office. Vincent de Paul, called upon to explain how they differed from religious, could only say that "most religious are directed only towards their own perfection, whereas these women are devoted ... to the care of their neighbour."[72] Exteriorly, however, they were simply "women who come and go like seculars." All external signs that might identify them as religious were carefully avoided. Thus they were forbidden to wear veils, or to ring bells in their houses, or erect grilles in their parlours. "It is to be feared ... especially if there is a grille, that in due course it will turn into a religious order," Monsieur Vincent explained.[73] Their language was revealing in its saintly deviousness. While privately they used the vocabulary of religious (the conferences used words like "company," "rule," and "habit"), outwardly they spoke as seculars, and the words invariably used were "confraternity," "*règlement*," and "dress." Like François de Sales before him, but for different reasons, Monsieur Vincent impressed upon his daughters the principle of interiority. "Your monastery," he told them, in what may well be called the founding charter of the *filles séculières*, "is the house of the sick ... your cell is your rented room ... For cloister, the city streets, where you must go in the service of your patients. For clausura, obedience, because obedience must be your enclosure, never exceeding what is set down for you, holding you enclosed within its bounds. For your grille, the fear of God. For your veil, holy modesty."[74]

Whereas the founder of the Visitation had desired to use the exercise of charity to perfect the inner life, Vincent de Paul gave priority to the life of service. His daughters were "to leave God for the sake of God."[75] In divesting them of all the external appearances of religious life, he was simply practising a defensive strategy. In the minds of their contemporaries, the slightest suggestion that religious women were free to roam the streets was the subject of scandal. Hence the care to maintain a secular appearance; hence the repeated admonitions to go out only when permitted, and to behave modestly while outdoors.[76] In spite of all this, scandals did occur, and the sisters were sometimes harassed in the streets; but in general, they were well received by the public.

Just as the company's community life evolved, so did its work. Originally, the women were exactly what their title suggested, "servantes des pauvres malades." They made two rounds each day with the medicines prescribed by the doctors, and a third round – at noon – with the pot of food, or *marmite*, that had been prepared by the ladies of the local *charité*. Soon their duties were extended to include bandaging, bleeding, and the making of medicines.[77] Along with this physical care, they were to give simple spiritual counselling: an exhortation to receive the sacraments and to accept the malady in a spirit of faith.[78]

Another specialization appeared: teaching. Although their principal duty was to visit the sick poor, the sisters, from earliest times, also taught catechism to little girls.[79] There were two reasons for this. The parish *charités* had always concerned themselves with catechizing,[80] and, by extension, with school classes. In the words of one historian, "they put schooling in the same category as soup for the sick, or clothes for babies, or hospital visiting."[81] The sisters inherited this work, along with the other undertakings of the *charités*. The ultimate purpose in this, as in every other good work, was salvific. "Take pleasure," Mademoiselle Le Gras wrote, "in instructing, to the best of your ability, these little creatures who have been bought with the blood of the Son of God, so that they may praise Him and glorify Him eternally."[82]

There was a second, more practical, reason for teaching school. The intended milieu for the sisters was the small town or village, where a *charité* of approximately twenty women supervised the care of the sick poor. For an operation of this size, a single servant was adequate. But the lifestyle of the sisters depended on a community of at least two. Therefore the second sister needed another occupation, and the instruction of children provided it. In her spare time, she could assist in visiting the sick,[83] or do handwork (usually spinning) to help support the house. The *fille de la Charité*, like other poor women, seldom sat without a distaff in her hand.[84]

Out of this division of labour a tendency towards further specialization developed. Those women who could read and write became schoolmistresses, while others, whose work was in nursing or visiting, remained illiterate. In time, the work of the schools absorbed more of the sisters. However, although they occasionally sought advice on teaching methods from teaching professionals such as the Ursulines or the Filles de la Croix, they did not at this time become specialists in teaching. Mademoiselle Le Gras retained her reserve in the question of the schooling of poor children. "The fear and love of God": these were the subjects to be taught, not the facility "to talk a lot about it".[85]

Another more fundamental development began, which the founders had not foreseen and did not entirely welcome. This was the diversion of the sisters into institutions. The hospital at Angers was the first: badly administered and inadequately staffed, it requested Filles de la Charité to take over the nursing. Monsieur Vincent's friend Madame Goussault pleaded with him from her deathbed to grant the request. He acquiesced reluctantly, and in 1640 nine sisters were officially installed as hospital nurses.[86] From this time on, more and more of the company's personnel were placed in the service of institutions. In Paris, by 1660, the year of both founders' deaths, the sisters were in charge of three major institutions (the Enfants Trouvés, the Nom-de-Jésus, a workhouse for the aged poor, and the Petites Maisons, an insane asylum), and heavily involved in two more, the Hôtel-Dieu and the prison for galley-convicts.[87] As well, they had been committed to more than a score of institutions in the provinces – hospitals both civil and military, orphanages, and asylums.

Their success in these institutions was an irresistible argument for continuing the work. "You would not believe how greatly God blesses these good women everywhere, and in how many places they are wanted," Monsieur Vincent told his priests. "One bishop wants for them for three hospitals, another for two; a third wants them as well; he talked to me about it only three days ago, and pressed me to send them to him."[88]

Nevertheless, the work of the hospitals was a deviation from the company's original purpose. "Well, there you are doing the work of real hospital nurses," wrote Mademoiselle Le Gras to some of the sisters, "just so long as that does not interrupt the work of the Company of Charity."[89] As she and Vincent de Paul saw it, home care had been developed expressly to save poor families from the pain and separation caused by hospitalization, "if in a poor family someone fell sick [and] it was necessary to separate husband from wife, mother from children, father from family."[90] The growing movement to build and expand hospitals contradicted the work of the parish *charités*, and in so far as it drew from the same pockets, it threatened to weaken them. "What will become of the work of the Dames de la Charité," wrote Mademoiselle Le Gras, "if their patients are forced to go to the hospital? You will see: the worthy poor will be deprived of the help that they receive from prepared food and remedies, and the little bit of money that they get now will no longer be available for their needs."[91]

However, the company could do little to resist the new trend. The *servantes des pauvres malades* were, from their inception, bound to the *dames de la charité* and to the social levels from which the ladies came. Vincent de Paul reminded them continually of their dependence on these ladies: "It is they who give you the means to serve God and the poor. What would you do without them, my daughters?"[92] This close association with the ladies, and especially with the most aristocratic confraternity of all, the Dames de la Charité of the Hôtel-Dieu of Paris, was the source of the company's strength, of its ability to expand almost without regard to expense. But it also meant that the paths along which the company was to move were largely chosen by the ladies, often with regard to their own territorial concerns. Thus the move to Angers was inspired by Madame Goussault, that to Richelieu by the duchesse d'Aiguillon, that to Vaux by Madame Fouquet, and so on.[93] The patronage of two queens, Marie-Louise Gonzague and Anne of Austria, took the sisters to Poland and to a string of military hospitals along the frontiers of France. The ladies had power to dictate not only the sisters' location, but the nature of their work. "They are like the head of a body, and you are only the feet," Monsieur Vincent told the sisters. "You must treat the ladies this way; otherwise, they will get tired of you."[94]

Thus the free-moving and flexible parish *charités* were largely overtaken by the prevailing trend towards institutionalization. In one outstanding case, however, Vincent de Paul refused to give way. This was in the matter of the Hôpital-Général of Paris, the great social experiment of the 1650s.

Renfermement, "the involuntary incarceration of groups considered marginal or potentially dangerous,"[95] had been in the public mind for some time. A move in 1611 to lock up the beggars of Paris had had the effect of clearing the streets, as those beggars mostly preferred to leave town. As the official effort flagged, however, they came flooding back in. A permanent solution would require a more co-ordinated effort, like that which established the Hôpital-Général in Lyon in 1622.

The principal promoter of the project of a Hôpital-Général for Paris was the Compagnie du Saint-Sacrement. As early as 1631 the subject was under discussion at its meetings.[96] But it was the years after the Fronde – "the high point of popular suffering" – which saw forty thousand beggars in the streets of Paris,[97] that brought the matter to a head. In 1656 mendicity was banned by royal edict. Out-of-town beggars were expelled. The beggars of Paris were ordered enclosed in one or other of a group of institutions. In 1657 the round-up began, assisted by bodies of enforcers especially enlisted for the purpose, and by a decree from the parlement forbidding the private distribution of alms. In the first year alone six thousand poor were incarcerated.[98]

Renfermement had its apologists. It saved the poor from idleness, considered in the seventeenth century to be the mother of all vices; and it taught them a trade. As the Jansenist Arnauld explained, it had a pedagogical value. "The greatest benefit of incarcerating the poor is the good education of the children. This is best achieved by watching over them ceaselessly, and, by this continual surveillance, cutting them off from evildoing."[99] Above all, it fitted in with the mercantilist spirit which now, at mid-century, was coming into its own. One of the greatest champions of the workhouses was Minister Colbert, for reasons different from those of Arnauld, as his instructions to the municipality of Auxerre show. "Inasmuch as abundance always comes from hard work, and misery from idleness, your first effort must be to find the means of enclosing the poor and of giving them an occupation to earn their living. On this matter you are to take good resolutions as soon as possible."[100]

It did not, however, impress Vincent de Paul. He was a member of the Compagnie du Saint-Sacrement. Like other men of his time, as the *règlements* of the *charités* show, he saw no harm in mixing assistance with discipline. He himself had established a workhouse – the Nom-de-Jésus – which combined a hard working day with lengthy religious devotions. However, he objected in principle to coercion. Nom-de-Jésus had only voluntary inmates, and its success was attested to by the fact that it had a waiting list.[101] Why not start the Hôpital-Général, also, on a voluntary basis? His plan was later described by his first biographer: "According to his thinking all that was needed at first was a trial: a hundred or two hundred poor should be taken in – and again, only those who would come of their free will, without any constraint. If these were well treated and happy, they would attract others, and thus the number would grow as Providence sent the funds ... and that on the contrary, the haste and fear that was being used might well be an impediment to God's design."[102]

When his point of view did not prevail, and the Hôpital-Général became an institution of confinement, he distanced himself from the project. On learning that the government had assigned the spiritual direction of the institution to his Mission priests, he declined the offer, "not being sure enough that God wills it."[103] Asked to send sisters to the women's institution at the Salpêtrière, he sent two, but only for a short time.[104]

It has been argued here that two approaches to the question of public assistance existed side by side in seventeenth-century France. The one, which found its most unequivocal implementation in the policies of the Compagnie du Saint-Sacrement and in the building of the *hôpitaux-généraux*, treated poverty as a punishment and a danger. "Social disorder was man's concupiscence writ large."[105] The other, represented by Vincent de Paul and the parish *charités*, was more compassionate. "The poor are our masters," Monsieur Vincent told his daughters. "They are our kings, and they must be obeyed. It is not an exaggeration to speak of them like this, since Our Lord is in the poor."[106]

It is not too simplistic to say that the first, and more modern, approach pertained to men, and the second, more traditionalist, approach, to women. "If the work to be done is considered political," wrote Mademoiselle Le Gras, "it seems that men must undertake it; if it is considered a work of charity, then women may undertake it."[107] The exercise of charity sprang naturally from women's position in the family and in society.[108] The nature of the work of the Dames de la Charité and, by extension, of the Filles de la Charité, was traditional. After all, it was the women of Châtillon-les-Dombes, not the men, whom Vincent de Paul had met on the road after he had made his appeal for help. This kind of action was perfectly familiar and unthreatening to the seventeenth-century world.

But the scale of the effort changed, and with it, the effect that the women had on their social environment. By 1660 charity was becoming an important part of the Church's business. In subsequent years, as Louis XIV's reign progressed and the secular powers became more concerned with the management of society, this highly practical aspect of the Church's work fell more and more under government control. In so far as women made themselves indispensable to this work, they established a new role for themselves, not only in the Church, but in lay society.[109] However, the intervention of the government in the management of the poor paralleled, if it did not actually contribute to, the exhaustion of the spiritual movement that had given birth to the *charités*.[110] At the moment that society acquired an appetite for schools, hospitals, and orphanages, the voluntary support systems established by the laity began to fall away. The *filles seculières* found themselves alone in the field, stripped of the cover that the *dévot* environment had once provided them, much closer now to a professional lifestyle than they had been at the beginning.

In 1633, a handful of village girls, armed only with their own good intentions, had worked under the direction of parish *charités* at tasks too menial for their patrons to perform. In 1660 an officially recognized company of some eight hundred women, with strong central direction and an equally strong *esprit de corps*, was spread out across the country. The women obeyed a rule, took simple vows, and wore a distinctive dress, yet remained secular. However, they were indeed religious, as their founder told them, in all but name.

This was a revolution, though a hidden one. The Council of Trent had forbidden religious women to mix with the world. The first Frenchwomen who had attempted to lead a life combining religion with service to society – the Ursulines, the Visitandines, and the Congrégation de Notre-Dame – had been firmly put back into the cloister. Yet here were other women, only a few years later, and less than a half-century after the legislation of Trent had been accepted by the French church, doing exactly what the council had forbidden.

The principal reason for their success was one of approach. The *congrégées* of the Counter-Reformation had attempted a modification of the religious life, and this was seen as threatening, both by the reforming hierarchy and by Catholic society at large. The *filles séculières* approached their goal from a different direction. They denied all connection with the religious life. They practised a modification of the secular life, adapting it to be more devout, more ordered. There was nothing unusual in this. As a respected Parisian ecclesiastic observed, "it seems that this generation wishes to live by a Rule, and that by following the example [of religious], people of the world propose to live as though they have fled the world, though this flight is only one of the spirit."[111] From the private *dévot* life to community life was a small step, and for single women an eminently sensible one. If purists stirred nervously, the rest of the world refused to be alarmed. Who could find fault, as long as they remained secular? No one was unduly concerned, any longer, with the wider canonical implications. Finally, when the new communities sent their members out to serve the poor, society remained equable. After all, the women were performing a useful service at moderate cost, and this was a conclusive argument in their favour.

Then, within a very few years more, the *filles séculières* were part of the structure of public assistance, and from that time on their position was secure.

CHAPTER FIVE

The Filles Séculières in Transition (1636–1700): The Miramionnes of Paris, The Congrégation of Montreal

Vincent de Paul described the Filles de la Charité as "women who come and go like seculars"[1] – in other words, women who, though living in community, had no pretensions to the status of religious. Although they were the largest, and among the earliest, of such groups, they were not unique. The Filles de la Croix, a group of secular schoolmistresses from Roye, began functioning as a community with simple vows a year before them, in 1641.[2] Further north, in the low countries, where the tradition of uncloistered nuns and of beguines was venerable and strong, *filles séculières* had been teaching school since the mid-sixteenth century. What seems certain, however, is that in Monsieur Vincent's circle, which was located at the centre of the Gallican church, his experiment in feminine secular community life was considered original. "You are doing something that has never been seen before," he told his *filles*.[3]

But in fact, from as early as 1630, small foundations had been springing up in towns across France: orphanages, refuges, schools, and workshops. As often as not, they were entrusted to "widows or old maids"; usually their scale was very small, the community numbering as low as two members. The women were frequently engaged by civil contract.[4] However, they often took private vows, and their founders, local persons of substance, often gave them *règlements* to ensure the discipline and religious direction of their daily lives. Thus to a greater or lesser degree, these small communities placed themselves on the verges of religious life, while retaining secular status.[5] The local authorities, opposed to the establishment of more religious houses and suspicious of these "sort of convents," kept a watchful eye on them. But because they served the public interest, they were usually tolerated.

One such group was the community of Filles de Sainte-Geneviève, of Saint-Nicolas-du-Chardonnet in Paris. It was founded in 1636 when a pious woman, Mademoiselle Blosset, was forced by ill health to abandon her vocation to the religious life in the Abbey of Montmartre, and came to settle in the parish. She took as her director the extraordinary and dynamic clerical reformer, Adrien Bourdoise. Bourdoise was, above all, dedicated to the work of reviving parish life. To this end he had set up a model seminary in the parish of Saint-Nicolas-du-Chardonnet, to train young priests in the correct conduct of the various parish services: the proper administration of the sacraments, an improved and extended liturgy, and the work of instruction, by way of catechetics both in the church and in the parish school. The parish school of Saint-Nicolas was considered a model in its time, and the book *L'Escole paroissiale*, published in 1654, which described its methods, was widely read by educators interested in the instruction of children.[6]

The reverse side of his fervour for the parish was a thorough and persistent dislike of the religious orders which, in his opinion, were drawing into their own chapels the wealthy classes whose support was essential to the material maintenance of the parish. With an outspokenness which was to earn him many enemies, he argued for a return of such people to their parish duties.[7]

It is not altogether surprising, then, that Mademoiselle Blosset was soon hearing a heavenly voice telling her "that it was not necessary to be a religious to go to heaven; that she could gain her salvation and that of many others by instructing young girls, and by taking care of the poor and the sick."[8] In 1636 she founded a community on the corner of the rue des Boulangers and Saint-Victor, not far from the parish church, and took up the work of caring for the church and teaching little girls. Within a short time there were three hundred students in the school, and a number of young schoolmistresses, learning their trade in exactly the same way that Bourdoise's seminarians learned theirs in *l'escole paroissiale*.

When Mademoiselle Blosset died in 1642, a community of only three or four women remained. They continued their work, however, and in 1650 asked Bourdoise to give them a rule.[9] Eight years later, the community was officially erected, and in 1661 it received letters patent. By this time, the community numbered about ten; but its financial condition was precarious and its future uncertain.

Since Bourdoise's death in 1655, the community had been under the direction of the parish priest, Hippolyte Feret, who was also superior of another small female community working close by at the same kind of employment. This community, known as the Sainte Famille, had an advantage that the Filles de Sainte-Geneviève lacked: a wealthy and influential foundress, Marie Bonneau, Madame de

Miramion. Madame de Miramion was a member of the prestigious company of Dames de la Charité of Paris. Like Mademoiselle Le Gras, she had led the life of a *dévote* since her husband's death in 1645. At the time of the establishment of the Sainte Famille in 1661, she had several other small foundations to her credit: an orphanage for twenty little girls, a sheltered workshop for young women, a refuge for delinquent girls, a retreat house, and a special segregated ward in the Hôtel-Dieu for sick priests.[10] Now she was preparing to take her devotion a step further, and to live in community with her five or six companions.

Feret suggested a union of the two communities, to save the one and consolidate the other. Madame de Miramion agreed, and so a new community was created, using the title and the official status of the Filles de Sainte-Geneviève, but supported by her money. In 1670 the community moved to a house on the Quai de la Tournelle, close to the parish church and large enough for the conduct of retreats, which was one of its functions. Here it continued until it was dispersed in 1792.

Because it failed to survive the Revolution, the secular community of Filles de Sainte-Geneviève has left little mark on history. There have been two biographies of Madame de Miramion, both by relatives.[11] As for the community itself, the count of Bonneau-Avenant, writing in 1867, recalled that "many of our contemporaries have heard their old grandmothers, while speaking of their youth, say with pleasure, 'That was when I was at the Miramionnes.'"[12] But little remains in the way of official record. In its time, however, the community was highly respected and widely imitated. In the later years of the century, when a number of small secular communities experienced deep demoralization and the danger of financial collapse, Madame de Miramion took up the work of reanimation. She is known to have salvaged communities in Amiens, La Ferté, and Senlis, and to have been invited to La Flèche to restore order in a religious house there. She also established at least a hundred schools. "In less than ten years," writes Bonneau-Avenant, "her community became one of the most important and respected of the religious and charitable establishments of Paris and the provinces."[13] The particular interpretation which it gave to the secular-religious life may therefore be considered as having influence far beyond the borders of the one small community.

According to Bonneau-Avenant and to Pierre Coste, the *règlements* of the new community were drawn up under the eyes of Vincent de Paul.[14] If this is true, Monsieur Vincent's contribution cannot have been much more than a general approval, since he died in

1660, shortly before the Sainte Famille started its community life. A reading of the constitutions as they stood in 1679–80 would suggest that the guiding mind was that of Adrien Bourdoise: in other words, that the rule which he had drawn up for Mademoiselle Blosset's *filles* survived the amalgamation of the two communities, and became their principal guideline.

The chief originality of this rule lies in its emphasis on the parochial orientation of the community: "The Sisters of this Community make their profession as good and faithful parishioners. In health and in sickness they receive the Sacraments in their parishes; they assist in the parishes' instructions and divine offices, and in general they render to the parish and the pastor all the duties of parishioners."[15] Although they said daily prayers in common, including the Little Office, the sisters sought no identity at all beyond that of "true parishioners": "They intend above all else to perform with fidelity … the Christian obligations that are contracted in Baptism, observing the maxims of the Gospel in conformity with their state, as well as the rules of the Church which apply to all the faithful. By the same principle they intend to assist in all the religious activities of the Parish."[16]

The parish was their priority. They had their own side chapel in the church; they performed their Easter duties there, and they were buried in the parish cemetery. One of their duties was "the decoration of the House of God … by washing the altar linens, mending the ornaments, and ensuring the cleanliness of the churches."[17] Their clinic was intended to assist the poor of the parish; the workshop which they set up was called "the parish workshop,"[18] the children in their schools were to be trained to be "good and faithful parishioners."[19] Although, like the seminary of Saint-Nicholas, the community hoped to disseminate its ideas throughout the countryside, it still did so within a parochial context. Country schoolmistresses, brought into the house for advice and training, were expected to return to their own parish schools. In this respect the Filles de Sainte-Geneviève remained close to the philosophy of Adrien Bourdoise. The "Miramionnes," as they became known, were the feminine arm of the parish of Saint-Nicolas-du-Chardonnet, the completion of that circle of spiritual and temporal services that Bourdoise had envisaged long ago. This was a much stronger identification with parish interests than Vincent de Paul had ever suggested. The Filles de la Charité were servants of the poor and assistants to the ladies of the parish *charités*, and they were expected to be subject to the parish priests; but in fact he preferred to keep their contact with the priests to a minimum.[20] In any case their first obedience was to their Company, and in cases of conflict they were obliged to obey their superiors in Paris first. "You are there on loan," Mademoiselle Le Gras told them.[21] By contrast, the Filles de Sainte-Geneviève lived for their parish, and so far as they hoped to expand, planned to set up similar parish-based communities in other towns.[22]

The other characteristic of the Miramionnes was their determination to maintain secular status, in spirit as well as in the letter of the law. The community held to the *dévot* ideal, the life of perfection lived within the world: "It wishes never to leave this state, and it is satisfied with charitable service to its neighbour."[23] There was to be no inner aspiration to the religious life: "You are different from ordinary Christians only by the exactitude with which you profess the maxims of the Gospel."[24] The sisters were not expected to renounce their property,[25] nor was their commitment to the community binding under pain of mortal sin.[26] They were not to be cloistered, and they were to wear secular dress "without ever wishing to assume any form of dress which could distinguish them from women who live in great piety in the world."[27] They were not to acquire a chapel for their own use (a privilege which implied conventual life), "but only for the sake of the sick and infirm, and the outsiders who come to make retreats."[28] Everything that might tempt them away from their parish duties was to be scrupulously avoided:

This community esteems and respects the religious profession; nevertheless, having been advised ... to consecrate itself to the secular state ... it prefers this state to all others ... And the superiors must always reject as temptations all proposals which might be made to quit or cut back these exterior functions. [They must also reject] religious enclosure, solemn vows, and everything else which could lead to the transformation of the Institute.[29]

At the time of Madame de Miramion's death in 1696 the community was functioning well according to its rules. The clinic was treating between a hundred and two hundred persons per day, the retreat house was open and active, the workshop was employing eighty girls, and a school for three hundred children was operating on the Quai de la Tournelle.[30] In her will the foundress begged the sisters to continue their life without change.[31] It appears that they succeeded in doing so, for at the time of the Revolution the community was still active, and still wholly secular.

The *fille de paroisse* was very much a creature of her time. She belonged to the *dévot* world of the mid-seventeenth century. What she practised was a modification not of the religious life (as the early *congrégées*, the Ursulines and Congrégation, had attempted), but of the secular life that was, in fact, being practised all around her by pious laymen and laywomen. By entering into community, she took the process a stage further, but still retained the protective colouring of the secular status. She avoided the apartness that religious life implied. She also avoided the apartness created by professionalization. Unlike the *hospitalière* and the teaching sister, she remained unspecialized. She practised good works in general without claiming any distinguishing expertise. Thus her service to the Church remained consistent with the old tradition of feminine charity.

When Madame de Miramion died, a contemporary, Madame de Sévigné, wrote regretting the loss to the public of "this mother of the Church."[32] The mothering function, practised to an extreme degree by the great lady herself, characterized her community and others like it; and it belonged to a special "moment"[33] in the life of the French church, a time of widespread religious sentiment and deep social concern. As the moment passed, the *filles dévotes*, or *filles de paroisse*, lost their grounding in society, and were in danger of becoming anachronistic. In the later years of the century the trend was towards professionalization in occupation, and also towards a lifestyle which was religious in all but name. "If you have the spirit of obedience, you will be more cloistered than the enclosed religious ... If you have these virtues, you are professed."[34] Of the great mass of *filles seculières* born out of the Catholic Reformation, those who, in one way or another, joined this hidden compact turned out to be the most successful.

Though unique in its circumstances, the first secular feminine institute to be established in New France nevertheless experienced, in microcosm, the evolution of ideas that was taking place among *filles séculières* in the mother country. Its foundress, Marguerite Bourgeoys, left France in 1653 with a clear idea of her vocation already formed under the influence of the great pioneers of the Catholic Reformation.[35] Alone at first, then with only four companions, she practised a type of apostolate closely resembling that of the Filles de Sainte-Geneviève and other similar groups: a generalized service, given wherever service was needed. As Madame de Miramion was "mother of the Church" – the great Church of the metropole – this simple woman "without birth and without property"[36] was the mother of her Church in the tiny colony of Montreal. But by the time the congregation really "took off," in the 1680s, new ideas and new needs were making themselves felt. Under pressure from the hierarchy and the *habitants*, and in keeping with the changing self-image of its members, the community underwent a subtle transformation. In the last years of her life, Marguerite the *fille de paroisse* became Soeur Marguerite du Saint-Sacrement, member of a congregation of simple vows, with its own uniform habit and its own chapel, and its own specialization: the education of the daughters of the colonists.

Marguerite came to Montreal through the agency of the Congrégation de Notre-Dame of Troyes. Her first biographer, Charles de Glandelet, described the connection: "In the city of Troyes there is a substantial convent of religious of the Congregation founded by the saintly priest Fourier, curé of Mattaincourt: cloistered nuns who draw to themselves a large number of secular women. These are *congréganistes externes*, who follow a life of piety, and who teach school and give religious instruction in various places, going everywhere two by two, as is the practice in missions."[37]

The monastery, like the monastery of Châlons-sur-Marne from which it had been founded in 1626, had adopted the practice so close to Fourier's heart, of maintaining an association of secular assistants to work among the poor. According to a contemporary, this association in Troyes numbered four hundred, "most of them known for the most solid virtue and the highest piety."[38] Marguerite was prefect of the group for many years, under the supervision of Mère Louise de Chomedey, sister of Paul de Chomedey, Sieur de Maisonneuve, governor of the colony of Montreal. But she longed for a more religious life. After being turned down by two contemplative orders, she placed herself under the direction of her confessor, Antoine Gendret, as one of three members of a new secular community. The community soon failed, but the guiding ideas with which Gendret inspired it remained as his legacy to the congregation later to be founded in Montreal. Years later, close to the end of her life, Soeur Bourgeoys recalled his words:

"Monsieur Gendret once said to me that Our Lord had left three states in which women could follow and serve the Church; that [the state] of Saint Mary Magdalen was observed by the Carmelites and other recluses, and that of Saint Martha by the cloistered religious who serve their neighbour; but that the outgoing life[39] of the Blessed Virgin was not honoured as it should be, and that even without veil and wimple one could be a true religious." She added: "This pleased me greatly, since I felt sorry for women who, for lack of wealth, could not establish themselves in the service of God."[40]

The two principles which Gendret laid down, sometime in the early 1640s, were as daring and as innovative as anything currently in the minds of Vincent de Paul and Adrien Bourdoise. First, that active, outgoing service to the Church was not only permitted to women but was positively enjoined, by the example of the holiest woman of all. To live uncloistered, combining prayer with service to others, was to live the holiest life possible to a woman. Second, that the trappings of religious life – the veil and wimple and the dowry that inevitably went with them – were not as important as interior disposition, and that therefore poor women were as eligible as rich to enter the service of God. Marguerite, in the words of her biographer, kept these principles faithfully in her heart.[41] For the meantime, she continued her work as a secular *congréganiste*.

The nuns of the Troyes monastery, like other *dévots* throughout the country, had been profoundly stirred by the Jesuit accounts of New France. Their contact, through Mère de Chomedy, with Montreal had given them the hope that in due course they would be able to found a house in the new colony. In 1641, when Maisonneuve first left France to found the colony, his sister had given him an image inscribed with the words "God's Holy Mother, pure Virgin royal, save us a place in your Montreal."[42] In 1652, when he returned to Troyes on a visit, she pressed him further. But Maisonneuve, in view of the precarious state of the colony, opposed the idea of a monastic foundation, and agreed to take one person only for the meantime. The person proposed was Marguerite. Thus the woman who was to found a new congregation of *filles séculières* in Montreal went in the first place as an advance guard, so to speak, for the cloistered religious who hoped to follow before long.

Marguerite arrived with the *recrue* of 1653, the hundred fighting men picked to save the faltering colony of Ville Marie. These men became the first objects of her particular mothering style. She acted as their nurse.[43] She took charge of their rations. She also gave them religious instruction. "Shortly after their arrival here, these hundred men were changed like linen that has been put to the wash," she wrote in her memoirs.[44]

Once in Montreal, she took up the role of spiritual animator, leading a work party to re-establish the cross that Maisonneuve had originally erected on the mountain. "When I arrived," she later recalled, "Monsieur de Maisonneuve detached thirty men to keep the promise that he had made to take me up the mountain; but the Indians had removed the cross. We were all moved to build another. I was assigned to that ... We were there three days in a row. The cross was set up and surrounded with stakes."[45]

Some years later she undertook to build a chapel in honour of the Virgin. "I persuaded the few people that were there to collect stones, and Monsieur de Maisonneuve had the wood cut for the frame."[46] This time she seems to have taken her talent for leadership too far. The new Sulpician superior of Montreal, Monsieur de Queylus, ordered her to stop work until further notice. The project was abandoned for years and the building materials lost.

Marguerite's job for her first five years in Montreal was the care of Maisonneuve's household. "He did not consider her as his servant," wrote her friend, the *hospitalière* Marie Morin, "but as someone whom Our Lord had given him to help him save himself, someone for whom he had a deep respect."[47] During these years, for lack of young children in the colony, she was unable to practise the work for which she had been recruited. She lived, instead, the simple life of good works. "She visited and served the sick, consoled the afflicted, instructed the ignorant, washed the poor soldiers' laundry and mended their clothes, all without recompense. She buried the dead, and deprived herself even of the essential, on behalf of the needy."[48]

In 1658, however, she was granted a stone stable on the edge of the common, for the purpose of "the instruction of the girls of Montreal."[49] This was her first school. Now, as children came of school age, she decided to go back to France to recruit more teachers. The women whom she brought back in 1659 were engaged by civil contract, though they agreed to live in obedience and chastity for the duration of their service. Marguerite was still anticipating the day when the nuns from Troyes would arrive to take over the work.[50]

However, the events of the next few years altered all expectations. In 1665 Maisonneuve was forced to return to France to defend himself against allegations of mismanagement of funds. He never returned. For his circle of associates, this meant an end to the assured protection of an influential patron. The monastery of Notre-Dame in Troyes now gave up its plans to establish in Montreal. As a result, Marguerite found herself in charge of the colony's schools for girls – and little boys. During the early years, the schoolmistresses taught both sexes, though this contravened the customary policy of the crown and the Gallican church.[51]

Fortunately for her and her sisters, Maisonneuve's patronage was replaced by another, yet more powerful: that of the royal regime. In 1667 the new intendant, Talon, visited Montreal. Within a short time, at his instigation, the colony petitioned the Crown for official approbation of its two female communities – the Hôtel-Dieu and the Congrégation.[52] By 1668 Marguerite was constructing a larger house of stone, capable of holding both a community and up to a hundred scholars.[53] In 1669 she obtained official permission from Bishop

Laval to teach school throughout the region; then, in 1670, armed with letters of recommendation from both civil and religious authorities, she left for France to find herself a group of *filles séculières* to help her with the teaching. When she returned in 1672, she brought not only six companions, but letters patent from the king, approving the establishment of the Soeurs de la Congrégation de Montréal.[54] Four years later came Bishop Laval's official authorization of the community "on condition that they do not in the future aspire to the religious life"[55] – a true community of *filles séculières*.

By the 1680s, the Congrégation, now numbering some twenty sisters, was appearing regularly in reports by church and royal officials. It was operating not only its school and *pensionnat* and a workshop for poor girls, but missions in the French colonies of Lachine, Pointe-aux-Trembles, Champlain, Sainte-Famille, and (to the delight of the court) the Indian colony of Montagne, set up by the Sulpicians. "The sisters of the Congrégation" wrote monseigneur de Saint-Vallier in 1685, "operate, in the mission of Montagne, a school of about forty Indian girls, whom they dress and raise in the French manner. At the same time they teach them the mysteries of the faith, handwork, and the prayers of the Church, not only in their own tongue, but also in ours, to accustom them little by little to our ways and our manners."[56]

The Congrégation was still, in the 1680s, very much the image of its foundress, and the beneficiary of her extraordinary reputation. "She was universally regarded in this country as a saint," wrote the governor, Perrot.[57] However, Marguerite's style was not that of all the sisters. From early days, her readiness to perform any task demanded of her had disconcerted her companions. Her chaperonage of the *filles du roi* is a case in point. Around 1663 (in her own words) "some seventeen *filles du roi* arrived. I went to fetch them at the water's edge, knowing that the door of the house of the Blessed Virgin had to be open to all women ... I stayed with them, and I had to stay there because it was for the sake of creating families. I believe that I did not please our sisters and that I failed to give them the necessary guidance."[58]

As long as she was superior of her community, her sisters continued to perform a wide variety of social services. In addition to their established missions, they operated *missions ambulantes*, preparing the outlying parishes for episcopal visits or for first communion.[59] They managed the workshop known as La Providence in Montreal, and later, at Bishop Saint-Vallier's request, opened a similar Providence in Quebec.[60] In 1689, also in obedience to Saint-Vallier, and in spite of their lack of preparation for the work, they accepted responsibility for the newly established Hôpital-Général in Quebec.[61] But after 1693, the year of Mère Bourgeoys's resignation, these peripheral activities, and the Indian mission, were closed down. The sisters' decision in 1694 to withdraw from the work of the Providence of Montreal drew an angry reaction from Saint-Vallier: he accused them of trying to "act the ladies".[62] It may be inferred that specialization led to social ascension; that in concentrating their efforts on their schools the sisters were preparing to relinquish the maids-of-all-work role implied in the title *filles de paroisse*.

Marguerite watched these changes with distress. She herself had exemplified the life which they were now giving up. Though old and infirm, she offered her services to the institutions that were being abandoned. "This was not granted to me," she wrote in 1698.[63] There were further incompatibilities. On the subject of poverty she held strong (and, to some people, exaggerated) ideas. During her 1658 journey to France she had refused the offer of a foundation, for fear it would change the character of her institute.[64] To the parent of one of her recruits, who asked how they would live, she outlined her simple plan: "I promised him that we would have bread and soup and that we would work to earn our living."[65] This, most certainly, the early sisters did. Their principal occupation, the instruction of children, was performed free, since in the view of the times any charge for such work would constitute simony. They earned money where they could, as for instance in the upkeep of the churches and the laundering of the altar linens. On occasion, also, they provided room and board in return for donations, in kind or in land.[66] But the chief source of their income was sewing. "Soeur Bourgeoys and the others also worked most of the nights, so as not to be a burden on anyone, and to earn their livelihood," wrote Marie Morin.[67] Because of the shortage of women in the colony, there was no lack of work. They sewed for the residents of the fort, the soldiers and all the other bachelors of Montreal. But their principal clients were the *messieurs* of the Seminary – the Sulpicians who were both the colony's priests and its *seigneurs*.[68]

By their own work they were able to acquire considerable property. "What I admire most," wrote Dollier de Casson, the superior of the Sulpician community, "is that these women, having no wealth, and wishing to give free instruction to the children, have nevertheless, through the blessing that God pours on the work of their hands, and without depending on anyone else, acquired several houses and properties on the Island of Montreal."[69] Once acquired, some of the sisters saw no reason why they should not take at least moderate enjoyment from their property. To Marguerite, however, this was totally incompatible with the spirit of the institute. She had always feared "relâchement" – the slackening of fervour. It had only been at the urging of her sisters, and against her better judgment, that she started the building of a larger house in 1668–69. When the house burnt down in 1683, she accepted the disaster as a punishment from heaven for her infidelity. She never changed her views. In 1697, in her old age, she rose up like a prophet to warn the community against its backsliding.

Marguerite taxed her sisters with three major failings. First, a loss of the simple community lifestyle which she characterized as "the little life." Once, all the sisters had been equal. Now, "one part of the sisters looks upon the others as servants of the house. This is altogether contrary to humility."[70] Second, a weakening in their spirit of poverty. "In the beginning," she wrote, "we sought to imitate the apostles and to work so as to be a burden to no one; and that succeeded. Now, we have to have mattresses and sheets and lots of utensils, and to live unlike the simple folk, and to have all sorts of comforts which the local people do not have."[71] Third, laxity in the observance of their rule. "The strict life, which is so necessary to the service of God, is not at all appreciated in this community."[72]

In the Montreal of the late 1690s, hers was a voice from the past. The Congrégation, like the colony itself, had survived, and now looked forward to easier times. By 1693 it owned seven hundred acres, partially cultivated, and five separate habitations.[73] The house, which had been completely destroyed in the fire of 1683, had been completely rebuilt, "large, spacious, and one of the best built in the town," according to Mère Morin.[74] The community itself numbered some fifty sisters.[75] The Congrégation de Notre-Dame had earned its position as an important institution in the colony. Nobody else accused it of backsliding. As Dom Jamet writes, "Mère Bourgeoys belonged to her times, and she felt that things were going too far, too fast."[76] And Marguerite's "times" were in France, during the great days of the Catholic Reformation, while most of the young sisters of the 1690s were born in Canada, in a much more practical age.[77] The Congrégation that entered the eighteenth century responded to the needs of its time and place.

Like other communities of *filles séculières* in the mother country, the Montreal congregation was shaped partly by forces outside itself. Marguerite Bourgeoys's institute could not have succeeded without outside assistance, in the form of political connections, or wealthy patrons, or widespread social demand. What exactly were the components of its success?

From early days, it had been welcomed by the population. The *habitants* of Montreal and of the outlying areas required, not cloistered nuns, but schoolmistresses, women who had the freedom to travel considerable distances, and live in ordinary houses, and who, like the Filles de Sainte-Genevieve of Paris, could assist in the work of the parishes.[78] The sisters filled this role to the general satisfaction. Intendant De Meulles wrote to the minister in 1683: "You would not believe how much good the sisters of the Congrégation do for Canada ... They are models of good sense and they are capable of going everywhere, and, by this means, of instructing all the girls who otherwise would have passed all their lives in great ignorance."[79] Naturally, admiration was translated into support – as far as that was possible in the colony's straitened circumstances. Donations from the colonists themselves were usually modest, and it may be argued that it was by their enthusiastic acceptance of the sisters – and especially their petition of 1667 in their favour – that they contributed most to the institute's success.

Some of the principal families of Montreal, however, became considerable patrons of the Congrégation. Their support entitled them to assist in the definition of its purpose and lifestyle. An example of this influence at work may be seen in the building of the chapel (1693–95). The sisters had always performed their religious duties in the parish church where, like the Filles de Sainte-Geneviève in Paris, they had their own side chapel. In 1692, they were offered a donation of four thousand livres by Jeanne Le Ber, the daughter of one of the leading merchants of Montreal. Like many private donations, it came with a condition. This one was that the money be used to build a community chapel, onto which was to be joined a cell, in which Mademoiselle Le Ber would spend the rest of her life as a recluse.[80] The chapel was an attribute of a more conventual lifestyle, as the Constitution of the Filles de Sainte-Geneviève, cited above,[81] makes plain. The histories all insist that the chapel fulfilled the sisters' dreams; but it is significant that the one chapel that Marguerite herself had built, years before, was a chapel for the use of the public, which she made over to the parish.[82]

In less striking ways, the principal families of Montreal were able to affect the character of the developing community. The Congrégation educated their children, as often as not in the *pensionnat* which it had set up at their request. It received their daughters into its noviciate. Like people of quality in the mother country, they felt a certain reserve towards religious women who were not bound by solemn vows. It was the character of Canada, wrote Marie Morin, to have "no esteem for vows from which one can be dispensed." The fact of being in simple vows, "and not truly religious ... prevented the daughters of distinguished parents from entering the community."[83] Although the sisters remained determined not to accept the monastic life – which was inconsistent with the purpose for which their institute had been created – they must have found it difficult to resist the social ascension which association with this class entailed.[84] The result was a compromise. The institute remained relatively democratic in its recruitment,[85] but it accepted its position of social eminence in the community. And it continued to bear, for many years, the responsibility of educating all the girls of Montreal and its environs, from the poorest to the wealthiest.

The Crown consistently favoured the Congrégation. In 1671 Colbert had written to Talon: "As for the establishment of the congregation of women and girls which is being formed at Montreal to teach persons of the same sex to read, write, and to do various handworks, the king desires that you make every effort to strengthen it, since these works of piety can do much to increase the practice of our religion."[86] There were two reasons for this approval. First, the sisters' flexible organization made them more suitable than cloistered nuns for the mission work of the *côtes* and the Indian settlements. Second, in the words of the letters patent: "the aforesaid petitioner and her associates are not a charge upon the country."[87] Montreal was a poor colony, which depended for its religious services on the private generosity of its priests, the Sulpicians.[88] Requiring neither foundation nor charity, yet teaching free of charge, the Congrégation was an irresistible bargain to the civil authorities.

As for private patrons, there were strikingly few – certainly none to correspond to Madame de Miramion, the patroness of the Filles de Sainte-Genevieve, or the phalanx of noble ladies who supported the Filles de la Charité. Maisonneuve's monetary support was limited to a testament of two thousand livres.[89] Some financial assistance was forthcoming from France, as for instance twelve hundred livres from the Princesse de Conti, donated to the Indian mission.[90] But the patrons that mattered most to Soeur Bourgeoys were the Sulpicians, in their quality of *seigneurs* of Montreal, and – more important – as a powerful influence in ecclesiastical circles in the mother country. For it was from the hierarchy of New France that the *filles séculières* faced their most serious challenge.

The sisters soon earned the Sulpicians' favour. In 1671 the Ursuline Marie de l'Incarnation, who was weighing the possibility of establishing a monastery in Montreal, wrote: "The *Messieurs* of Saint-Sulpice, who are their directors, prefer the *filles séculières*, who are free to go out and travel here and there, and to seek out and assist their neighbour."[91] The correspondence of the Montreal seminary with Paris brought the influential superior of Saint-Sulpice, Louis Tronson, onto Soeur Bourgeoys's side. "I am delighted to inform you," he wrote to her in 1682, "of the esteem which I have for your community, and how completely I support you."[92] This esteem was invaluable to the community; it is hard to see how it could have survived in its secular form without it.

The prelates of New France – Bishop Laval and his successor Saint-Vallier, and Gabriel de Queylus, *grand vicaire* from 1657 – all shared the same reserve with regard to the Soeurs de Notre-Dame. While respecting their work, they considered them temporary stand-ins, until such time as genuine cloistered nuns could be brought in. "We have sent schoolmistresses to Trois-Rivières to take care of the little girls," wrote Laval in 1661, "while waiting for a favourable time and occasion to establish the Ursulines there."[93] Though in 1669 he authorized the *filles séculières* to teach throughout Canada, it is possible that his hand was forced by the action of the intendant and the petition of the *habitants* of Montreal in 1667.[94] He obviously still continued to hope for change at a later date. In 1670 Marie de l'Incarnation wrote: "Monsieur l'abbé de Queylus, who is the spiritual and temporal superior at Montreal for the priests of Saint Sulpice, promises us his protection when the time is ripe ... Monseigneur [Laval] our prelate, who does nothing imprudent, also shares this sentiment."[95] In 1676 Laval gave Soeur Bourgeoys and her companions further hope of permanence, by canonically erecting their community as the Filles séculières de la Congrégation de Notre-Dame.[96] It seems, however, that he still entertained hopes of incorporating the sisters into the Ursulines. Soeur Bourgeoys's effort, in 1679–80, to establish her community on a more solid footing met with his firm resistance.

In 1679, she took her last journey to France. "It was more my inner distress that made me undertake this voyage, than the pretext which I used of our Rules and of [seeing] Monseigneur de Laval who was then in Paris."[97] The sisters had been without a written rule for too long, and she already felt the danger of "relâchement" in the community. In France, she resolved to seek advice from secular communities which, she knew, were operating with official sanction. "I lodged with the Filles de la Croix, on the rue Saint-Antoine ... I went to see Madame de Miramion ... She asked permission from Monsieur de Rhodes, her superior, and then from Monsieur de Laval, to cut and to add to our rules as she saw fit." But Laval had set his face against her project: "He said that I had been wrong to make the journey for our rules, and that he did not approve of my taking back more women."[98]

The situation was still unresolved in 1684–85 when Monseigneur de Laval resigned as bishop, and Jean-Baptiste de Saint-Vallier took his place. Saint-Vallier also favoured a fusion of the community with the Ursulines. On the occasion of Mère Bourgeoys's retirement and the election of a new superior, in 1693, the new bishop's attention was drawn to the question. The following spring, he presented the sisters with new rules, to which he demanded their immediate assent.[99] The sisters discovered, to their shock, that he proposed, in effect, to turn them into Ursulines.[100] They refused to agree immediately to the new rules, and asked for time to consider them. Now it was Saint-Vallier's turn to be shocked. He answered that "that they had no choice but to give their consent and acceptance, and that he wished them to observe what he prescribed for them."[101] However, he ended by softening his stance, and left the sisters time to comment on the new rules while he went to France.

The sisters, or rather their superiors at the seminary, now had the opportunity to appeal to Monsieur Tronson in Paris. He was informed of their dilemma: that in spite of their status as *filles séculières*, established by letters patent and by the previous bishop, "they were being ordered to live according to a rule which was strictly for religious."[102] He also received letters from Soeur Bourgeoys, in which she recounted again, for his benefit, the inspiration which she had received from Gendret, half a century earlier.[103] Tronson undertook to mediate with the bishop, who was an ex-seminarian of Saint-Sulpice. He later wrote to Dollier de Casson: "Monseigneur of Quebec has allowed me to see the rules of the sisters of the Congregation. I do not think that he will insist on the vows or on the other articles which Monsieur Valens [their superior] has told me distress them."[104] In 1697, finally, the modifications were achieved. "I am sending you the rules which Monseigneur of Quebec has made for the sisters of the Congrégation, which you will find much softened."[105] The bishop had renounced all ideas of turning the sisters into cloistered nuns. They were to be bound by simple vows only, and there was no further mention of a special vow of obedience to the bishop.

For their part, the sisters were asked to make concessions. Foremost among these was that henceforth they had to accept dowries: a practice which they had opposed most vigorously. Neither Saint-Vallier nor Tronson had appreciated Marguerite's earnest insistence that "the more one is anxious for goods, the poorer one will be."[106] The sisters were also required to take the three simple vows of poverty, chastity, and obedience, and a fourth vow, like that of the Ursulines, to teach young girls. After consultation, the community accepted the new rule. It was not what they had argued for, but it was better than they feared: it preserved certain parts of their traditional practice while it suppressed others. At least, as a modern member of the Congrégation puts it, "the outgoing life was not irremediably compromised."[107]

On 25 June 1698, in the presence of the bishop, the sisters of the mother house took their simple vows. Fourth in the formal procession was Soeur Marguerite du Saint-Sacrement, now seventy-eight years old.

In its first half-century, the *Congrégation de Notre-Dame* had been formed by a variety of forces. The concept which had taken shape in Troyes in the high noon of the Catholic Reformation, and had been put into practice with great success in the hardships and dangers of early Montreal, was now smoothed by success and adapted to more prosperous times. The gradual acquisition of property and the improved living quarters, the respect in which the sisters were held in the parishes, the complexities of organization in the large community with its several missions, the rising expectations of the *habitants* for their daughters, both as pupils and as nuns – all these circumstances affected the "little life" that Marguerite Bourgeoys had instituted for her community. The formality of Saint-Vallier's rule only served to complete the process. The congregation as it entered the eighteenth century, with its simple vows, uniform habit, and private chapel, was sufficiently transformed to cause surprise to the court. In 1710 the minister was to express His Majesty's disapproval of the changes that had been effected in the community.[108] However, the changes remained. Like the Ursuline *congrégées* of the early 1600s, the sisters of Montreal found that the price of acceptance by society was a certain redesigning of their early apostolate. Having made their compromise, they found a secure niche in Canadian society. The Congrégation remained for many years the only feminine teaching institute in Montreal, and its members continued to be the only country schoolmistresses in French Canada until the second half of the nineteenth century.[109]

This experience was not unique. In similar fashion across France, small clusters of *dévotes* were forming themselves – and being formed – into communities, and acquiring the characteristics of nuns. The process was more or less the same: the house was acquired and furnished, patrons were found; regulations, and sometimes further regulations, were adopted, routines were formalized, community prayers were prescribed, the evangelical virtues of poverty, chastity,

and obedience were enjoined, the taking of simple vows was institutionalized. Sometimes private chapels were built, where particular
devotions and patronal feast days were observed. Imperceptibly,
many secular communities merged into the religious life which they
so greatly admired.

In all this, the intention of the tridentine law was being subverted.
Nuns were being made where no nuns were supposed to exist. But
custom overcame canon law. Long before it recognized the new nuns
in law, the Church needed them in fact. The *filles séculières* provided
the muscle for the innumerable hospitals, orphanages, asylums, and
schools which were now an important part of its mandate. So the
compromise was made which changed the future of feminine
religious life.

Little by little these groups, born in response to pressing needs, broke the
ancient bond between clausura and the feminine religious life. These pious
women, known also as *filles dévotes* (since they were not bound by solemn
vows), did not receive the name of religious, which at that time was reserved
exclusively for cloistered nuns. But they existed, they endured, and they
made themselves known. They received their consecration through the good
that they did. [110]

CHAPTER SIX

The Maîtresses Charitables (1660–1700): Three Case Studies

The *congrégées* of the early 1600s had given offence to French Catholic society on two accounts: first, because they had hoped to escape the obligation of clausura, and second, because they had tried to teach in public. Almost as fast as society's disapproval had been expressed, and the women put behind their walls, the hard line of Trent began to erode, and change began to take place. The years of Louis XIV's personal rule (1660–1715) saw the creation at least seventeen female teaching congregations – more than half of the total number created under the Old Regime.[1] Most of these were uncloistered, secular institutes. The appearance of so many teaching sisters was the result of a radical change in social attitudes.

During the years 1600–60 there had been a considerable enlargement in the role of women in the Catholic church of France. By 1660 few, if any, of the principal towns and cities were without their monastery schools, and such schools were now generally viewed as a social necessity. Furthermore, the public's growing taste for schools, hospitals, and other institutions had overcome its previous hesitations about the "state" of the women serving in them.

The old dictum "aut maritus aut murus" was losing its vigour. A new kind of person had appeared: the *fille dévote*, the unmarried woman who practised the virtues of religion without withdrawing from the world. At the start of the century, such a lifestyle had been considered wholly unacceptable.[2] But by mid-century more and more these *filles dévotes*, or *filles séculières*, were gathering into communities, emphasizing their separation from the mass of pious women from whom they had been drawn, yet refusing the formal state of "religion." An intermediate state of religious life, which combined community life with service to the public, was developing fast.

However, the situation in 1660, though much more liberal than that of 1600, still represented a containment of the women's widest ambitions. The Filles de la Charité had achieved their first priority, the freedom to live and work outside the cloister. But they had succeeded partly because the novelty of their lifestyle was compensated for by the conservatism of their vocation. The mothering, nurturing work which they performed, in caring for the sick and small children, and in visiting the poor and the prisoners, was altogether consistent with the traditional role of women in their households and in their neighbourhoods. If the appearance of the sisters on the street caused some uneasiness, at least their occupation offended no one. Even their move into the field of teaching was unthreatening, since it was treated from the start as a function of public assistance. The pursuits of the *filles séculières*, at least prior to 1660, remained essentially conservative and suitably humble.

The *congrégées* of the early seventeenth century had been more ambitious. They, too, had moved about on the streets, in spite of the scandal that their action caused. They had visited hospitals and prisons. But even more audacious was their work as catechists. They had taught in public places, sometimes in churches, and they had instructed men as well as women.[3] These public functions had been removed from them when the papal bulls transformed their communities into monasteries, while at the same time their teaching activity had been compressed into a more traditionally feminine form.[4] Finally, the very fact of clausura had the effect of reducing their horizons. Where once they had modelled themselves on the heroic women of the scriptures and the early Church, the nuns now accepted more modest ideals: "the utmost punctuality in the observance of the rules; a docility marked by simplicity and a childlike spirit."[5] They were still called upon to practise "warrior virtues," but their field of action was the "noisy classroom,"[6] and their own engagement under a rule that became ever more detailed and pervading.

This bowing of the head, it may be suggested, was the price that, in their different ways, both cloistered nuns and *filles séculières* paid for the gains that they made. In return for a wider share in the Church's apostolate (and, in the case of the latter, a greater freedom of movement), the women accepted their limitations, acknowledged the fragility of their sex, and trod lightly – for the time being – in areas of greatest sensitivity.

What were these sensitive areas? Who felt threatened by the development of the active congregations? And for what reasons?

First, the municipalities. The multiplication of religious orders made them increasingly uneasy. What they feared was the absorption of their limited urban space. And with reason: new religious houses, once established, had a way of extending their holdings throughout whole neighbourhoods. As a contemporary observer commented, "we all know that the communities settle for an inch of land when they arrive, and then afterwards spread out by degrees."[7] City officials tended to oppose the establishment of all new congregations; and by the time the women's communities, latecomers in the "conventual invasion," arrived, their frustration was frequently boiling over. Few of them reacted as fiercely as the citizens of Troyes, who in 1631 dragged a coachload of Visitandine nuns backwards away from the city gates.[8] But in many cases they used all possible legal means to prevent communities establishing, and, failing this, constrained the religious, in advance, to limit the size of their house, and to promise never to become a charge on the city.

The second area of sensitivity was in the congregations' relations with the upper classes. Here the case against the uncloistered congregations was based on family considerations. Their daughters must not enter a religious community "which they are free to leave whenever it suits them,"[9] to become a charge on their families and a threat to inheritances. Archbishop Denis de Marquemont of Lyon was speaking for the people of quality of his city when he argued against François de Sales and for the enclosure of the Visitation. For the peace of families, he insisted, solemn vows were necessary. Women entering religion must be bound to a state from which there was no return. Otherwise there would be no end to the legal wrangling. Furthermore, he maintained, women of good family needed the cloister to preserve their reputation, and to save themselves and their relatives from "from dangers, fears, and anxieties."[10] Finally, entry into religion should not entail social derogation. The humiliation that Catherine de Veteris had caused her father by walking with her students through the streets of Aix[11] was unacceptable.

The women bowed to this all the more readily because they themselves shared this point of view. For the vast majority, religious life was coloured by the same consciousness of rank that they had known in the world. Mère de Chantal, although the soul of charity, did not wish to accept truly poor women into the Visitation, "since it is quite rare for women of this condition to have the necessary talents and dispositions to acquire the spirit of our vocation."[12] Most daughters of good family entered religious houses suitable to their rank, there to pursue, often among friends and relatives, a life nuanced to their own upbringing and social attitudes. Far from being a threat to the established social structure, the new monasteries became part of it, "quasi-necessary for the preservation of the equilibrium of families."[13] The character of each religious community was protected, not only by its grilles and double doors, but by the background of its postulants and the size of the dowries that they were required to bring in.

On the other hand, the "outdoor" work which Ursulines, Congrégation, and Visitation had all undertaken at the outset was left to the *filles séculières*, who were, for the most part, of more modest social status. For these women, working for a living was no disgrace, while walking and travelling alone was marginally, but not totally, improper. Above all, they were less likely to be involved in the problems of inheritance that so exercised the minds of the upper classes, and therefore the question of the permanence of their vocation was not so burning. The simple vows that for social reasons were denied to the earlier *congrégées* were allowed to them.

The upper classes accepted the principle of an active religious life for women, on the understanding that their own daughters would not be affected. The more aristocratic the women, the less likely they were to be employed in service to an outside group. Although there are many instances of individuals who broke ranks to join less elevated communities, it can be said that, in general, parents placed their daughters in "good" convents just as they placed their other daughters in "good" marriages. The burgeoning of the non-monastic communities was possible only because a new social level was coming into action. The majority of women of high birth remained remote from the activity of the *filles séculières*.

The third, and possibly most difficult, area of sensitivity was within the Church itself. When women left the traditional occupations of charity and entered into teaching – or, more specifically, catechizing – a new question was raised: the question of their status in the Church.

The rule according to which women might not instruct men, or teach in the Church, went back to Saint Paul:

Women are to keep quiet at meetings since they have no permission to speak; they must keep in the background as the Law itself lays down.[14]
During instruction, a woman should be quiet and respectful. I am not giving permission for a woman to teach or to tell a man what to do. A woman ought not to speak, because Adam was formed first and Eve afterward, and it was not Adam who was led astray, but the woman.[15]

The early Church, it seems, adhered to this ruling. "It is neither right nor necessary that women should be teachers, and especially concerning the name of Christ and the redemption of His passion. For you have not been appointed to this, O women, that you should teach, but that you should pray and entreat the Lord God."[16]

The Church of the Reformation years held this proscription to be all the more complete because Protestants, on the contrary, were permitting women to study scriptures, dispute, and even teach. Heretic women were dabbling in theology when they would have been better employed at their distaffs[17]: that was reason enough why Catholic women should not do the same. In any case, *all* catechizing by the laity was contrary to the spirit of Catholic pastoral reform. According to the Council of Trent and succeeding councils in France, the instruction of the people in the faith was the prerogative of the parish clergy.[18] Where priests were unavailable, clerks in minor orders could act as substitutes.[19] Laymen were admitted to catechize only where necessary, and in many places they were banned from teaching inside the church,[20] though this was where most of the formal instruction took place.

This catechizing function was most emphatically forbidden to women. Obviously, mothers were expected to instruct their children, and mistresses their domestics, in their prayers and in their duties as Christians. But women were not to teach the faith publicly and formally; above all they were not to teach the faith within the precincts of a church. Yet this was precisely where catechizing was supposed to take place. The priest stood, or sat, before the assembly – not in the pulpit, but, more informally, at the front of the church. In large parishes the duty might be delegated and the congregation broken up into small groups, which went with their catechists to the side chapels. But in every side chapel there was an altar; therefore the catechist who stood in front of the altar to teach was acting in place of a priest. For a woman to perform this physical act, with all that it symbolized, was tantamount to heresy. The condemnation of Mary Ward by Pope Urban VIII was based partly on rumours that she had preached "in pulpits and places of assembly."[21]

Though the feeling that female catechists were usurpers of the priestly function had its roots in the identification of that activity with the church's interior, it extended beyond the Sunday catechisms to the everyday teaching of the faith, even in unconsecrated surroundings. It remained an obstacle to any undue feminine apostolic ambitions. As a prominent preacher put it, "The Apostle insists that women should not have any ecclesiastical function." Their condition of subjection to men, and their natural feminine modesty, were "the reasons why, according to the holy fathers, the female sex has been excluded from the priesthood."[22] Since catechizing was a priestly function, it was sinful for women to undertake it. The teaching sisters of the 1660s, like the Ursuline *congrégées* of the 1610s, faced priests who insisted that "it was an abuse for women to teach in public."[23]

The antidote for this hostility was always the same. The women were instructed to demonstrate their humility and their deference, and to maintain their vocation within that fine boundary which divided the maternal teaching function from the teaching of the faith. Over and over again, in the school rules of the teaching congregations, we find the sisters being instructed to act towards their students "as true mothers." They were to insist that their work was only with persons of their own sex. They were to avoid every appearance of preaching. Since standing up and proclaiming the faith was suspect, they were sometimes ordered to hold an open book, or a paper, in their hands: "They were to take care to avoid all personal interpretation of the faith; when they spoke they were to hold in their hands a paper from Monseigneur, to show that they were saying nothing on their own account."[24]

But if the tact of the teaching women soothed offended feelings, their ultimate argument was the demonstration that by their work they enhanced the docility of the sex that was born to obey. It was soon realized that girls who had received formal instruction performed their religious duties better. "They have benefited greatly in their studies, but even more in their piety," wrote the cardinal of Lorraine in 1603.[25] "The confessors recognize them in the confessional, on account of their better preparation and instruction," Dom Eustache remarked in 1617.[26] The christianizing effect of the teaching sisters upon the girls of their day was the key to their own acceptance by the Church.

In the final accession of the teaching sisters to a state of full respectability we see the triumph of one set of tridentine values over another. The immediate aim of the Counter-Reformation had been a return to discipline and regularity. As Archbishop de Marquemont pointed out in 1616, "The intention of the Councils has been to prevent novelties and diversities in the Church."[27] For women, above all, this involved return to the strict observance of the rules. On the other hand, the reforming councils had also stressed the obligation of instructing the faithful. In the critical conditions of the seventeenth century, and with the Protestant example acting as a perpetual goad, it was this obligation that became the ruling passion.

"The Church is a School, of which Jesus Christ is the Master": this is the substance of what has been called "an ideology of the school,"[28] developed by the French church of the seventeenth and eighteenth centuries. Catholic reformers, following their Protestant rivals, came to believe that knowledge of the faith was necessary to salvation. No longer did blind assent to the religion of the community suffice. "The parish priests' first care will be to ensure in every possible way that all parishioners – men, women, and children above the age of reason – be properly instructed in the tenets of the faith ... They are to make their parishioners understand, through frequent repetition, that without belief in these tenets, they cannot worthily receive the sacraments or be considered true Christians."[29]

This placed a heavy obligation on the parish clergy, and one which, it soon became clear, they were unable to shoulder alone. A more systematic instruction came to be seen as desirable, especially for children. "It is by means of Christian schools that souls are prepared to receive the word of God," wrote Bourdoise.[30] Childhood instruction, he insisted, was the only way by which vice could be destroyed and virtue established.

That Catholic society agreed with him can be seen from the extraordinary outpouring of donations and legacies which took place in favour of the charity schools.[31] For the faithful of the seventeenth century, instruction and the endowment of instruction became a service to God. But whereas Bourdoise thought mainly about boys' schools, society as a whole showed at least equal concern for girls.[32] As long as the purpose of instruction was the saving of souls, then the second sex – "half of the human race which has been bought with the blood of Jesus Christ and destined to eternal life"[33] – was equally eligible. Not only did women have their own souls to save, but they were responsible for others. "The same [women], when they have grown up and become mistresses of households and mothers of families, will by their good example and wise advice instruct all their children, both boys and girls, and their servants both men and women, and bring them up in the love and fear of God."[34]

But if girls must be instructed, women must instruct. This was inevitable, since both Church and Crown forbade the reception of girls into mixed classes.[35] The widespread appearance, especially in the second half of the century, of charitably funded schools for girls involved, as a necessary corollary, the widespread employment of women as teachers. And invariably, their duties included instruction in religion. In other words, during the later seventeenth century, women became catechists, and their involvement in this sacred employment ceased to shock.

Women had shown that they could assist in the new order of things. From now on, their assistance would be actively sought where it had once been regarded with deep reserve. The majority of congregations of schoolmistresses founded after 1660 were the creations of bishops.[36] Their appearance, and their admission into one diocese after another, represents the final acceptance of women as participants in the work of catechizing the masses.

Three congregations of schoolmistresses have been chosen for closer study: the Providence of Rouen, the Dames de Saint-Maur of Paris, and the Soeurs du Saint-Enfant-Jésus of Reims. All three fit the characteristics of the post-1660 congregations: they were secular, they were apostolic, and they were primarily aimed at the children of the lower social classes. They were the beneficiaries, but also the agents, of a significant change in social attitudes towards their work, from reserve and outright disapproval to acceptance. As a result of their efforts, and that of other women like them, elementary schooling for girls became commonplace and respectable.

THE PROVIDENCE OF ROUEN

Sometime around 1652–54, during the great drive to enclose the poor, the General Assembly of Rouen ordered all young pauper children to be placed in an institution, "to be instructed in piety and the Catholic religion, to learn to read and write, while at the same time practising the works and crafts in which they are being trained."[37] This was the beginning of the reconstitution of an old and moribund charity school system in the mould of the seventeenth century, with emphasis on incarceration, war on idleness, and social control. The first schools were opened within the Hôpital-Général, with masters and mistresses fed, lodged, and paid by the hospital administration. The children, from the age of eight, were subjected to a highly structured discipline. Their day, which lasted from 5 o'clock in the morning until 8:30 p.m., included one hour of reading and writing, and approximately six of catechism and religious exercises.[38]

From there the institution's pedagogy spread out into the parishes. By 1670, boys' schools were operating in the four quarters of the city and in the *faubourg* of Darnétal.[39] Between 1670 and 1675, five "quarter" schools were established for girls. All the teachers were secular, and under the administration of seculars.

The very existence of the quarter schools represented a new phase in charity schooling, one in which incarceration and instruction were separated. Gradually, the external schools acquired more weight in the Hôpital-Général's system. By 1684–85, nine of its thirteen brothers and thirteen of its sisters were working in the quarter schools.

However, the schooling of the Hôpital-Général was intended only for the indigent. Charity scholars had been distinguished in the previous century by badges sewn onto their clothes, bearing the words "Pauvre de la Ville de Rouen."[40] While they were no longer required to be so distinctive, the principle remained. All children attending charity schools were expected to produce certificates from their curés, attesting their poverty. Any malingerers, so to speak, from more comfortable families were to be constrained to attend the private paying schools. The corporation of master-scribes maintained a vigilant watch over their monopoly, and did not hesitate to prosecute trespassers.[41] Charity schools were, by definition, for paupers, and they taught subjects suitable to paupers. The school in the parish of Saint-Maclou, for instance, which numbered approximately one hundred and twenty girls, taught religion and reading, but also stocking-knitting and lace-making; "the girls work for merchants of the city and are paid very punctually; this helps to lighten the burden of their families' poverty."[42]

The community of Soeurs du Saint-Enfant Jésus, which was christened the "Providence" by the people, took feminine education a step beyond the limitations of the quarter schools. They were unusual in two respects: they aimed to teach the children of the working poor, rather than paupers; and they saw themselves, not simply as the teachers of little girls, but as auxiliaries to the clergy in the general work of christianization.[43] In addition to their schoolteaching, they were trained to give public catechism classes, and also to work among the unconverted – "To seek out, wherever they are, older girls who are at risk, as well as those who have already been ruined, so as to prevent the former from falling, and to help the others by their zealous and charitable attentions, to forsake sin and all occasions of further fall."[44]

Their beginnings were unprepossessing and unplanned. In 1662, the Minim Nicolas Barré set off to preach a mission in the town of Sotteville, on the outskirts of Rouen. He took a small group of women with him as auxiliaries, to assist other women in preparing to receive the sacraments, and to catechize the children. These women were not nuns. They were simply "women with free time"[45]; most likely members of the comfortable classes. Their leader, Françoise Duval, was the daughter of a rich merchant of Honfleur.[46] For the rest, all that is known is that at least two of them, Marguerite and Catherine Lestocq, were members of a confraternity of prayer of Oratorian inspiration, the Famille du Saint-Enfant Jésus, whose purpose was "to belong to the Incarnate Word, to be His servants."[47] In this opportunity to assist in the mission they saw, not a permanent employment, but a good work of limited duration. They offered two sessions a day, to instruct women and children for confession and communion. Strictly speaking, their work was to be confined to their own sex, though there was an openly expressed hope that the lessons taught to the women would reach the men of their families.

As Marguerite Lestocq wrote, years later, "there were notable and admirable conversions, of both men and women, and older girls, and a number of general confessions ... I can assure you that almost all the village was converted."[48]

The classes in Sotteville were originally only a part of a mission, attached to a specific period and intended to end with that period. But Barré came away from the mission impressed both by the problems in the field and by the effectiveness of the women in dealing with them. Though as a Minim his experience had been in preaching and spiritual direction, he now showed himself to be a convinced exponent of the "ideology of the school" so characteristic of seventeenth-century thinking. The instruction of souls, in his opinion, was the supreme work of praise, "since it prepares for His Majesty spiritual dwelling places, living temples."[49] It was also the supreme work of charity. "To teach ... the poor, the sinners, and the children about salvation is assuredly more praiseworthy than to clothe or nourish their bodies."[50] Among the souls to be instructed, children had a special place, since they were particularly favoured by God:

Although God is supremely great, He nonetheless takes pleasure in bending down towards little ones. This is why, when He predestined His Son, He wished Him not only to be a man but to be a little CHILD ... When He said that whatever we do to the smallest, poorest and most contemptible of His children, we do to Him, he meant that whoever receives a poor and neglected CHILD, also receives Jesus Christ in His own person.[51]

Barré saw the schooling of children as the way to salvage the world from its present sinful condition.

But why girls' schools? "To win the parents through these little ones, to enter the hearts of the mothers through their daughters, and of mistresses through their servants, and even to convert the men through their wives."[52]   This was not an original idea. It went back to Fourier and the Ursulines, at the start of the century. Vincent de Paul had set it before his teaching sisters: "And you, my dear sisters, who work at the instruction of girls, [know that] by this means you instruct their fathers and mothers ... because the children take home what they have learned, and they teach it to those who ought to have taught it to them."[53] The rest of the Church having failed, God was going to turn to little children to serve his purpose; not only little children, but little girls, the very least of his creatures. Nicolas Roland, who patterned his own work on the Rouen experiment, was soon to express the same thought.[54]

Was it really as straightforward as this? Was there not something of *faute de mieux* in the resolution of these founders? The initial focus of most educators was on schools, not for girls, but for boys. In this spirit Fourier had first collected a group of schoolmasters, and seen them fail, before ever Alix Le Clerc came to him with her proposal. In this spirit Barré first attempted, both in Rouen and, later, in Paris, to set up boys' schools. But practical experience showed that no matter how desirable charity education for boys might be, it was limited by the shortage of men ready to do the work. On the other hand, women were available, and in abundance. The concentration on girls' schools was less a matter of choice than an acceptance of the practical possibilities.

The mission was so successful that at its end it was arranged that the women should continue their work in Rouen, in the parish of Saint-Amand. Marguerite Lestocq later recalled their early days:

We held classes for the children from 8 o'clock to 11. Then we took them to Holy Mass, to the number of 130 or more. From noon until 2 o' clock, we had the big girls … Afterwards, we went around the houses to instruct the people, teaching them the principal mysteries … We held catechism lessons on Sundays and feast days; there was such a crowd that it was necessary to open up the rooms and break down the walls to make enough space.[55]

Up to this point, there was no thought of a community life.

The young women lived at home, as the Ursulines of Brescia had done. The work was voluntary and largely experimental, under the guidance of Barré and Antoine de la Haye, curé of Saint-Amand, a reforming priest in the mould of Adrien Bourdoise:

There were four or five of us sisters, completely in the hands of Divine Providence. We did not live in community, but scattered about. Two sisters held classes close to the Carmelites, and three at Madame de Grainville's house. The reverend father Barré came from time to time to give us conferences, and he gave us a rule to live by.[56]

Only later, in 1671 at the earliest, did they resolve to live in community. It was Barré who made the suggestion:

"Do you wish to live in community, even though your living will not be assured; though you will only have the necessities, and little enough of those; and if you are sick, you will be sent to the Hôtel-Dieu? You will have to be resolved to die by the roadside, abandoned by the whole world, and to live in like manner all your lives ..."

We answered with all our hearts: "Yes, we will."[57]

The community was highly successful, and went from strength to strength. But Soeur Lestocq recalled, "After several years there were great difficulties (I find it hard to speak about them) on the part of the curés, the ecclesiastics, the religious and the laity, which caused our very reverend father much suffering."

Apart from this cryptic recollection of Soeur Lestocq, there is little information on the difficulties that Barré experienced. But it seems that, as elsewhere, the women were resented when they began to intrude into what was considered a male preserve – the catechizing of the people. "It seemed that the curés and the ecclesiastics wanted to make difficulties over our Sunday catechisms, saying that we were doing what they were supposed to do, and that this upset them greatly; but we answered them so wisely, and with so much deference, respect and submission – as was their right – that from that time on, they approved of our instruction."[58]

While some of the clergy came to accept them, it would have been most unusual if approval was general; too many priests of the day believed, with the preacher Père Anselme, that "the Apostle insists that women should not have any ecclesiastical function." Barré's identification of his schoolmistresses with the deaconesses of the early Church[59] was enough to make some of his brother Minims uneasy; it certainly was too audacious for many of the ordinary curés of Rouen.

As for the laity, it is probable that the purpose of the new community – the instruction of children of the working poor – was not to everyone's liking. The Hôpital-Général, which had been constructed to enclose and instruct the "lazy" poor, was already costing the city a great deal of money. The diversion of alms to schools for children who might otherwise be working productively was dangerous and wasteful. We shall see this idea clearly expressed later, by members of the city council of Reims.[60] Also, of course, there were persons whose interests ran counter to the charity schools: the master scribes, or private schoolmasters, whose corporation was both powerful and vocal.

Furthermore, the community does not seem to have pleased the archbishop of Rouen. Like Vincent de Paul, Barré was determined not to commit his sisters to the total control of the local clergy. He insisted that they must remain free to be dismissed, or to retire, from unsuitable situations: "The people who ask for the sisters are free to send them back whenever they wish, seeing that, since there is no foundation, the parties are left free, and without any obligation on one side or the other."[61]

This meant that although the sisters were subject to the archbishop's authority, they were not a diocesan organization. They were administered by a small group of Barré's friends – all notables in the city of Rouen[62] – through the Hôpital-Général, and their director was a Minim. Their independence had the effect of cooling the archbishop's feelings towards them. "They have always been kept in total independence of the ordinary," stated a memoir some years later. "It is this that made Monseigneur de Colbert wish to have women who would be altogether under him and for his diocese."[63] In 1699, he adopted as his own protegées a small women's community in Ernemont, which he later expanded into other parts of the diocese. Whatever success the Soeurs Barré had in Rouen was due more to the *dévot* circles from which Barré's friends were drawn than to the archbishop's palace.

The institute grew with striking speed. In 1669, three years after foundation, the six or seven women had grown to more than thirty. Ten years later, they numbered two hundred. From the seminary in Rouen they spread out through the diocese, then into neighbouring dioceses: Bayeux, Evreux, Sées, Lisieux, Coutances. Sisters from Normandy were sent to start communities of schoolmistresses in Reims, Paris, Dijon, Avignon, and Marseille.[64] They also went on mission into the rural areas, to prepare people for the sacraments. The only thing lacking to their work, wrote one appreciative curé, was time; "it would be appropriate for them to stay at least three months in each place, in order to prepare consciences entirely."[65]

Once they left the main centres, Barré's schoolmistresses lived and worked in tiny communities of two or three. The foundation in Bayeux, which survives in the local records, is typical of many others: "In the year 1676, Hélène Cauvin and Marie Forfait came to Bayeux ... There, they took up the instruction of girls, who are divided into two classes. In the first, the younger girls are taught to read; they are instructed in the faith, and they are trained in piety. The second is designed to receive older girls, who are taught to make lace, and to live in virtue."[66]

Occasionally, local volunteers were enlisted to help in the schools. The arrangement was flexible – and cheap. The Providence offered an education that poorer people, and smaller parishes, could afford. "This establishment [has] enabled artisans and the common people to have their daughters educated, and has given the opportunity to many country parishes, where the curés or the vicars teach both sexes, to request these women, so as to avoid possible problems."[67]

Unfortunately, living as they did in an extremely fluid situation, and seldom using the services of notaries, the early Soeurs Barré, like other *filles séculières*, have left little trace behind them. One piece of circumstantial evidence, however, suggests that their schools contributed significantly to the education of women. In the city of Rouen, in the period from 1670 to 1720, female literacy rose by 15 per cent, though male literacy in the same period rose only by 7 per cent.[68] These were exactly the years when the new schools began to take hold. In the late seventeenth century, girls from modest families were going to school in numbers unheard of before.

THE DAMES DE SAINT-MAUR

In 1674 Barré was sent to Paris to teach at the Minim convent in the Place Royale. He began at once to look for ways of establishing charity schools along the lines of those he had started in Rouen. He found a powerful supporter in Marie de Lorraine, Duchesse de Guise. In 1676 she financed his first school in Paris, in the parish of Saint-Jean-en-Grève.[69] In the following year she decided to establish similar schools in her domains. Barré called in a young sister from Rouen, Marie Hayer, the daughter of a doctor in Bernay. By 1678 Soeur Hayer had opened four schools in Guise.

At this time Barré recalled Soeur Hayer to Paris, and put her in charge of the house in Saint-Jean-en-Grève. There were now thirty schoolmistresses teaching in the vicinity, including twelve sisters from Rouen. In the next few years, schools were opened in five more parishes, and the community, with its noviciate, was installed in a rented house on the rue Saint-Maur, from which the sisters were henceforth to take their name. Now they proceeded to expand on the left bank, opening eight schools in the parish of Saint-Sulpice alone. By the early eighteenth century, they were operating schools in every parish in Paris.[70]

Soon the sisters were in demand in various dioceses throughout the country.[71] But the crowning success of the congregation came in 1685, when Louis xiv decided to use them in the Midi for the re-education of converted Protestants. Eight sisters were sent to Languedoc, to open schools in Montpellier and Montauban. By 1686, the king's secretary was writing to ask for more: "Monsieur de Baville, intendant of Languedoc, has reported that the eight schoolmistresses whom the King ordered to be sent to Languedoc are proving highly successful in the places where they were put; and that it would be useful to have twelve others."[72] In the general distribution that followed, sisters were placed in Bordeaux, Nîmes, Gensac, Castres, Uzès, Toulouse, and Toulon. The speed of their expansion, and the numbers recruited, were such that the mother house in Paris was soon in danger of losing control of them.

At the same time, Madame de Maintenon had other designs for the Dames de Saint-Maur. She and the king, planning the new academy of Saint-Cyr for the education of young noblewomen, and determined, at this stage, not to turn it into a monastery, invited Barré to provide "twelve of the best sisters of his Institute, to give their assistance to the Dames de Saint-Louis; to train them in their teaching method; and to instruct both them and the students of Saint-Cyr, according to the constitutions and rules of the house."[73]

The sisters stayed and worked at Saint-Cyr until 1694. However, high society began to show its bias towards the monastic life, and Madame de Maintenon was subjected to heavy pressure to change her schoolmistresses into real nuns. She wrote: "The whole company of *dévots* will revolt against me, if I do not give them an office to recite, a prayer to say, a chapter, retreats – in a word, everything that is done in religious communities."[74]

The Dames de Saint-Louis were transformed from a secular to a monastic community. Though invited to remain and take vows, the sisters now used the prerogative on which Barré had always insisted, and withdrew. They received, as reward for their work, an annual *rente* for the house in Paris of five hundred livres, and the lifelong support of Madame de Maintenon.[75]

Though the lifestyle of Barré's sisters was considered inappropriate for ladies of high family, the institute remained the object of much admiration for its work among the lesser people. A contemporary historian of religious orders called it "the final work of grace in our times."[76] The sisters were especially commended for their flexibility, their readiness to go long distances and to work wherever they were called, and their indifference to questions of financial support. They owed this to the breadth of their founder's vision. Barré, like Vincent de Paul, was determined to keep his institute free of legal and canonical entanglements.[77] His plan of organization was simple in the extreme. The schoolmistresses were maintained financially by the parish, or town, which invited them in. Their upkeep (usually between one hundred and fifty livres and one hundred and eighty livres each per year, plus house and furnishings) could be discontinued. "Those whose business it is to provide for their subsistence in all those parts of France where they are sent, are in no way obliged to continue their upkeep." But in this case, the sisters were free to leave.[78]

This freedom from permanent obligation extended to the sisters' relationship with the community. Their statutes only asked them to "live in community, without taking vows or observing enclosure, under the conduct of the superiors, whom they are obliged to obey for the sake of pure and holy love."[79] The ultimate penalty for non-observance of discipline was dismissal from the congregation. On the other hand, any sister was free to leave whenever she saw fit.

Entry into the community was equally uncomplicated. Barré relied on the institute's manifest poverty to ensure the entrants' disinterest.[80] He initially discounted the importance of a training period. "Père Barré used to say that women who are set straight to work progress much faster than if they are given lengthy instructions before being put into the classrooms and the catechisms. The need to act, he said, opens the mind, and forces the person to make beneficial efforts; and thus a schoolmistress is quickly made."[81] Many of the mistresses who joined the institute during its period of rapid expansion went straight into the schools without preliminary training, either in teaching or in community life. The results were not always satisfactory. Some years later a complaint was made, that "since they are not trained in community, they make mistakes; because of these the Bishops take over their guidance."[82] A year of noviciate was made obligatory.

Nevertheless, the appearances of "religion" were kept to a minimum. The sisters preserved their secular status and their rights of inheritance (though during their lifetime the institute received the usufruct). They wore secular dress: "black dresses, which are to be of a Christian modesty and simplicity, without any claim to gentility."[83] Yet, as in the case of the Filles de la Charité, this secular exterior covered an inner life that was essentially religious. "Although the sister schoolmistresses make no vows of obedience, poverty and chastity, and must never make them – so that what has been designed for the public good may never degenerate into a private good, closed within a cloister or a monastery, as only too often happens in the Church – nevertheless, there must be as much exactitude [in observance] as if, in fact, they had taken these three vows in all solemnity."[84] Their community life included the recitation of the Little Office, monthly retreats, regular meditation, and the frequent reading aloud of the rules and constitutions – a practice observed by most of the new religious orders.[85]

However, their principal occupation was not prayer, but teaching. Like Vincent de Paul, Nicolas Barré believed that it was possible to leave God for the sake of God. "The sisters of the Institute assure their salvation by their employment": the work that they did for others would compensate for their neglect of their own perfection.[86] Barré went further, to insist that the duty of the sisters was instruction, and instruction only. "The sisters may not ... be distracted from their schoolteaching, or from any of the aforesaid rules, on the pretext of helping their neighbour through actions of charity."[87]

Their workload was heavy. In addition to their teaching, either in elementary schools or in sheltered workshops, the sisters were obliged by their constitutions to hold Sunday catechism classes, and to instruct any women who came to them in their house.

The hierarchy of the institute, as Barré devised it, was also very simple. Temporal administrators, who were always men, together with a *dame associée*, supervised the running of the house, "so that the superior and the mistresses have no occasion to become slack in their fervour and in their duties."[88] These administrators were empowered to choose the superior, to admit and dismiss the sisters, and to send them out to their places of employment. The institute was modelled more on the communities of the *hôpitaux-généraux* than on the nationwide organization that it was fast becoming. Inevitably, the simplicity of Barré's plan was soon left behind. But its flexibility was preserved, to make it a wonder among women's congregations.

By the end of the century, not counting the establishments in Paris, the institute of Saint-Maur had opened forty houses, each of which served a considerably larger number of schools.[89] While the Rouen community's ascent was less meteoric than that of the Paris congregation, it also experienced steady growth. During Barré's lifetime the two institutes were connected, though loosely, under his direction. After his death in 1686 they were divided for administrative purposes, and an attempt in 1692 to reunite them remained a dead letter. The two separate congregations lasted through the Revolution into modern times.

Not everything that Barre turned his hand to resulted in similar success. While in Rouen, he had tried to set up a boys' school comparable to his girls' schools. This lasted only a short time. In Paris, he tried again, establishing a seminary for schoolmasters, who were known as the Frères du Saint-Enfant Jésus. The statutes which he drew up in 1685 were intended for this community as well as for the teaching sisters. However, after a promising beginning the boys' schools began to fail. Barré's successor, Servien de Montigny, gave the reason quite frankly: "a lack of candidates capable of entering into the spirit of the institute, which is total self-denial and surrender to Divine Providence. Young men usually seek to get ahead in the world."[90] After Servien's death they disappeared altogether. There was still little enthusiasm for the role of teaching brothers in France.[91]

The success of the Soeurs Barré must be attributed to the fact that in several important ways they fitted the spirit of the society of their time. They enjoyed a widely respected founder, wealthy benefactors and the favour of the Crown, as well as students in great numbers to justify their existence. But more than that, they attracted entrants. The institute's appeal to young women was the foundation of its success. Once in action, the charitable schoolmistresses were their own best advocates, as the experience of the Minim Père Giry, Barré's immediate successor as director of the community, shows:

It should be remarked that this great man did not always approve, especially at first, of Père Barré's enterprise. He could not believe that women could become capable of going out, like other apostles, to travel the provinces, and to be continually on the road and in the countryside, and to work with a zeal that did not seem consistent with their sex and their natural delicacy. But when, as a result of his duties he was obliged ... to travel frequently through diverse provinces of France, and when he realized, after painstaking investigation, that the work surpassed anything that could be humanly imagined, and that its fruits were highly admirable ... he approved the scheme, and resolved to be one of the most ardent defenders of this noble enterprise.[92]

THE SOEURS DU SAINT-ENFANT-JÉSUS OF REIMS

Reims, like other seventeenth-century cities, suffered from severe social and financial strains. Its several hospitals, and the Hôpital-Général which it had built in the wake of the fighting which had overtaken it in 1650 during the Spanish war, laid a heavy burden on the city's already strained finances. By 1660, one-half of the revenue from the city's only direct tax was being spent on its institutions.[93] Yet the problem of poverty remained unsolved. This may explain a growing exasperation felt by the citizens of good standing towards the people who were causing that problem. One such citizen, Oudart Coquault, wrote: "The rabble still complain, despite our Hôpital-Général ... After establishing five institutions (as well as the Hôtel-Dieu) we have as many of these begging rascals as we had before ... This sort grows fat and bold on alms."[94]

The overloaded municipal structures had also to cope with the Church's physical presence, always very powerful in Reims. In addition to the cathedral chapter, with its heavy endowments, there were fourteen parishes, three hospitaller communities, and two colleges. By mid-century, there were also ten masculine communities and five convents of cloistered nuns. "In the last forty or fifty years," wrote Coquault, "there have been so many new monks made ... that it is ruining the republic."[95] A great part of the city – more than half the area inside the walls – was occupied by religious houses.[96] Given the limited sources of revenue in the Old Regime, every new foundation meant that the rest of the citizens were further burdened, either by the repartition of taxes or by another demand for alms. In addition to this damage to the financial well-being of the city, the new communities tended to deplete church congregations, with adverse consequences for parish life. The desertion by the faithful, especially the affluent faithful, of parish masses for the more peaceful atmosphere of convent chapels posed a serious problem to central Catholic structures.

The serious imbalance caused in city structures by the "conventual invasion" led the municipal council of Reims to take a consistently negative attitude towards new foundations. In spite of its objections, the orders managed to move in, either by appealing to a higher authority, such as the Crown, or by agreeing to restrictive terms which, once installed, they ignored. The Cordeliers, for instance, whose contract limited their community to twelve, numbered forty by 1660.[97] The city, exasperated by a situation over which it had little control, devoted itself to doing whatever it could to keep new invaders out.

The city had one monastery of teaching nuns. In 1635, after a fierce battle with the municipal council, won only by direct intervention by Louis XIII, a house of the Congrégation de Notre-Dame had been established in the city. Once founded, it suffered no shortage of either students or entrants. When its six schoolmistresses opened the free classes in June 1638, they were met by four hundred girls.[98] As for nuns, twenty of these were professed before the end of 1640.[99] By 1650 the community was approaching the limit of fifty that the city council had set it – and the list of names was beginning to represent, ever more faithfully, the reigning merchant class of Reims. Indeed, the size of the dowry requirements – an outright gift of 2711 livres and an annual pension of 250 livres, as well as a gift of 250 livres. on the day of clothing – ensured that the convent would become an exclusive reserve for the daughters of the wealthy.[100]

Without a doubt the Congrégation, bound by its obligation of enclosure and marked with the ineradicable stamp of wealth and gentility, became more involved in its inner life, and that of the boarders, than in its day students. By 1678 the community numbered almost sixty, but the day-school had not increased. However, the idea of female education had been introduced into the thought processes of the city; and this was one of the prerequisites for the establishment of girls' free schools. The great expansion came in the 1670s, with Nicolas Roland and the Soeurs du Saint-Enfant-Jésus.

The archdiocese of Reims had come late to reform. For most of the hundred and eight years between 1532 and 1640, it had been in the hands of the Guise family, and had served as little more than a power base for their activities elsewhere. Only with the consecration of Maurice Le Tellier, brother of minister of the Crown Louvois, as coadjutor bishop in 1668, and as archbishop in 1671, did the machinery of reform begin to operate.

Therefore, for lack of a local seminary, it had been the custom for gifted young men to go to Paris for their clerical education. Nicolas Roland,[101] the son of an ennobled wool merchant of Reims, was simply following a well-beaten path when he arrived in the capital in 1660 to study philosophy. However, the contact that he made with the community of Jean Bagot – the Compagnie des Bons Amis – brought him full into the circle of the Aa, a secret society of Jesuit inspiration.[102] For several years he lived in Bagot's community. When he returned to Reims, to become, at the age of twenty-three, canon of the cathedral and theologal of the diocese, he was in every way a man of the Catholic Reformation – pious, zealous, absorbed in a life of prayer, mortification, and good works.

Within a year he left Reims again, on what might be called a Grand Tour for young *dévots*: "He made a journey to Paris, to search in the seminaries of Saint-Nicolas du Chardonnet, and Saint-Sulpice, and the community of Saint-Lazare, as well as the societies of pious persons ... for the purest maxims of the priesthood ... But his spirit was not yet satisfied, and he sought other means of self-improvement; and this impelled him to make a trip to Rouen, whither he was drawn by the odour of sanctity of a curé in this city, Monsieur of Saint-Amand, with whom he lived for six months to learn virtue."[103]

This curé was Antoine de la Haye, who was collaborating with Père Barré, Françoise Duval, Marguerite Lestocq, and other schoolmistresses and supporters, in the early operation of their charity schools. At this stage in his life Roland was more interested in the renewal of the priesthood than in schools, but the contact that he made was important later, when his mind began to move in this direction.

Sometime in the next two years he received, and read, a copy of the *Remonstrances* of Charles Démia. This work, published first in 1666 and addressed to the notables of Lyon, made an effective presentation of the case for charity education as the only means of salvaging and christianizing society. The book was promoted by the Compagnie du Saint-Sacrement, and received wide attention. A copy of it reached the theologal in Reims. "Your 'Remonstrances'" wrote Feret, the curé of Saint-Nicolas-du-Chardonnet, to Démia, "have had an effect everywhere they are read. Monsieur Roland, canon and theologal of Reims, has resolved to establish schools for the poor in that city."[104]

At the age of twenty-seven, "considering that the ordinary people and the great profit little from the best sermons, and that the lack of education and instruction of the young has always been, and still is, the source of the greatest disorders," Roland decided to work for the establishment of free schools in his city.[105] Now he turned back to Rouen for assistance.

He had received an invitation from the city council of Rouen to be the official Lenten preacher in the spring of 1670. This he accepted, though, as the "Mémoires" say, "the preaching was only a holy pretext." When he returned to Reims, he took with him an understanding that, at the appropriate time, two schoolmistresses would come from Rouen to help him set up his schools. On 27 December 1670, Françoise Duval and Anne Lecoeur arrived in Reims.

Roland knew perfectly well that his plan to establish a teaching community would not sit well with the city council. For this reason he said nothing, as yet, about his plans. Instead, he provided the sisters with a "cover," so to speak. In a nearby house on the rue de Barbâtre there was a small orphanage for thirty children, established and run by a pious widow, Madame Varlet, with the somewhat reluctant authorization of the city. This orphanage was in serious financial difficulties, "the poor children completely naked and like skeletons for lack of food."[106] On 15 October 1670, Roland approached the city council and offered to take over the care of the orphanage "if the Council saw fit."[107] The city, suspicious at first, ended by accepting his offer, and even allowing him to buy a larger house in which to install the sisters and the orphans. Madame Varlet disappeared, to set up another orphanage in another town.

A period of peace and quiet ensued. The sisters, who were soon joined by other young women, continued to take care of the orphans. However, preparations continued which indicated very strongly that a teaching community was in the making. The city, suspecting that

Roland was using the orphanage as a pretext to establish schools, decided in 1674 to test his good faith. It insisted that he accept new orphans. After an initial refusal, Roland, "fearful of disobeying the City's orders,"[108] agreed, though reluctantly. In 1675 he was ready to act on his own scheme. "Since his project did not end with the orphanage, and since that merely gave him a pretext for establishing schools," he sought ecclesiastical authorization to open classrooms in the orphanage, to teach not only the orphans but also "all girls, big and small, who came to them."[109]

The city was now fully aware of Roland's plans. In August 1674 the cornerstone had been laid for a chapel in the grounds of the property on the rue de Barbâtre. In July 1675, he invited the arch-bishop to bless the chapel, and the members of the council to attend the blessing. The building of a chapel placed the entire enterprise on a different footing; and quite clearly, the council understood the message. A new convent was being slipped in under its nose, and without its permission. It protested to the archbishop at this flouting of its authority. He agreed to look into the matter, and to consult with the council before allowing the community to proceed. How-ever, at this point the council overstepped the mark; a group of members, going to the archbishop, asked that he cancel the blessing of the chapel. René Bourgeois, who attended the audience, recorded Le Tellier's cold reply: "No sooner had M. Dallier finished his com-pliment than Monseigneur, in a proud voice and with an expression of sovereign authority, silenced him, asking if he did not have the power to perform his official functions in the city. [He said] that he had decided upon this benediction, and that it was none of our business ... and that we were not his masters to make him postpone doing what was in his full power, and lay down the law to him on the functions of his office."[110] The blessing of the chapel went ahead, despite the abstention of the city council.

It did not follow from Le Tellier's snub to the council that he was ready to support Roland. He was not yet prepared to sanction the charity schools. According to the "Mémoires," he gave Roland "many refusals on the question of this establishment."[111] The Soeurs du Saint-Enfant-Jésus still lacked official approval.

During the next three years, despite declining health, and despite the criticisms of his colleagues, Roland worked feverishly to establish and legitimate his community. "He so longed and desired that the sisters should do well in the school that he himself went into all the towns that he passed ... to learn [their methods]. He arranged for experienced schoolmistresses to come and train them in this house, all at his own expense, and on these occasions, his patience and his charity were such that, no matter how slow the women were to learn, he was never discouraged."[112]

Roland, unlike Barré, looked for financial security for his community. Perhaps because of the hostility of the council and the indifference of the archbishop, and also because of his commitment to the orphanage, he wanted letters patent, and these could only be acquired if the community was on a sound financial footing. He made his own endowment of some sixteen thousand livres, to which other benefactors added another twenty-five thousand.[113] Then, in the winter of 1677, he set off for Paris, hoping to enlist the support of the archbishop and, through him, the king. "He spent all his time pleading with more ardour than ever for the confirmation of his establishment. He spent a large part of the time in attendance in the antechamber of Monseigneur the Bishop, who frequently came and went in front of him without saying a word."[114] Finally, too sick to persist, Roland returned to Reims, where he died in April 1678.

Far from hurting the community's cause, Roland's death actually expedited it. Le Tellier, as soon as he heard the news, moved to obtain the letters patent that Roland had been seeking. "Never had Monseigneur the Archbishop of Reims used his authority in the court and his favour with the King more usefully for his diocese than on this occasion. The Letters Patent, obtained from Louis XIV as soon as they were asked for, and then registered in Parlement, all at the expense of Monseigneur Le Tellier, were put into the hands of Monsieur de La Salle, Monsieur Roland's worthy successor in the community." From now on, also, "Monseigneur the Archbishop went even further, in according his protection to a work which he considered his own after the death of Monsieur Roland."[115]

Within the bare outlines of this account there are a number of illuminating dimensions. In the first place, there is the obvious unpopularity that Roland suffered. "His life was criticized by libertines, and he was persecuted for his sermons ... He was mocked on all sides, for his walk, his manner, his bearing, his words, and for his spirit of inward recollection, which condemned all earthly pomp. He did not lack fault-finders; he was mimicked by people of quality and by people of the lowest sort."[116]

He was criticized in the cathedral chapter, and the grand vicar "treated him as a visionary and a fanatic."[117] The parents of the nuns whom he directed (religious of the Congrégation and of the abbeys of Reims), resented his influence over their daughters.[118] Even his charitable efforts were criticized. Père Valentin, his friend, recalled seeing a letter written by "someone distinguished for his character, and other qualities ... whose pen waxed eloquent on his behaviour, his undertakings, his schoolmistresses, and tried to blacken all the good that he did."[119]

It would seem that Roland's unpopularity stemmed from the fact that he was a true *dévot*, and that he was trying to import into Reims the values and ideals that he had learned from Père Bagot and the Aa, and from the austere curé of Saint-Amand in Rouen. His intensely religious personality was antithetical to that of the average *rémois*, who, with Jean Maillefer, held that "we need a little moderation, even in worthy things."[120] The anger that he brought down upon himself is illustrative of a wide resentment felt by the rank and file of Catholics towards this new kind of puritanism.

Another point to be taken is just how small the world of the *dévots* was. Roland, with all his travels in search of self-improvement (and, later, the improvement of his community), was not unique. It has already been noted that in the early years of the century there was considerable mobility and interaction in ecclesiastical society.[121] This activity had not abated. The exchange of preachers for Lent and Advent, the flow of ideas through correspondence and travel, the publication and dissemination of reformist literature such as Démia's *Remonstrances*, all served to link the major centres of Catholic reform. This movement extended even to women. Françoise Duval and Anne Le Coeur were not the only women to travel to Reims to enter the new community; of the original twenty sisters who took vows in 1684, five were "foreigners" from Rouen, Honfleur, Amiens, Paris, and Orléans.[122]

Yet another dimension of interest is the deep difference between the attitude of the *dévots* (and by this we mean not only Roland, but the schoolmistresses and other persons who collaborated in setting up the schools) and that of everybody else towards the question of the charity schools. Roland's difficulties did not all arise from his personality. His decision to found a new community of women earned him a great deal of harassment, above all from the municipal council. For reasons given above, the council bitterly opposed any further religious foundations in the city. It feared the sort of incrementalism that had happened before, where slowly, over time, the new house would take on larger and larger proportions. It also suspected that what had started as a secular community would end up with religious pretensions. It was for this reason that it reacted so sharply to Roland's activities. The possession of a chapel, especially one in which the Sacrament was reserved, was one of the hallmarks of a religious community. So was the title of "Madame" – a title normally reserved for superiors of monasteries – by which

Roland had begun to address the superior of the community, Françoise Duval.[123] Above all, the council feared that control of the new foundation, which as a simple orphanage had been in its hands, would pass to the archbishop.

Had this been the council's only concern, it could have been explained in terms of the city's old struggle against the immense ecclesiastical power of the archbishop. But there was a further element in its opposition to Roland, one that it shared with other members of the upper classes. This was its disapproval of the very principle of the new schools. "All the city combined against him to prevent the establishment of the charity schools, as though it were a crime to undertake it. The clergy, the mendicants, the City Council banded together to work for his overthrow."[124]

This opposition was rooted in social attitudes. Like the merchants and officials in Lyon to whom Démia addressed his *Remonstrances*, the ruling classes of Reims believed that schooling for the working poor was useless and even harmful. The sisters, according to René Bourgeois, "encourage servants in an idleness which is scarcely fitting for housework."[125] The general feeling at the outset was that Roland's enterprise would upset the social balance of the city.

Once the schools were observed in action, however, the council began to change its mind. Bourgeois in his memoirs recorded a conversation with the mayor, Monsieur Dallier. "I asked him if he was not persuaded that the poor need instruction, at least for their children, since they have neither the time nor the capacity to raise them in the elementary doctrines of our faith, and that the parish priests did not apply themselves to this as much as was necessary … and that I myself thought the establishment of these schools to be a good thing." He agreed with Dallier that "in establishing these schools for girls up to a certain age – nine or ten years – the benefit that would come to the public, through the instruction of these children, would be great and fruitful … but that all children above this age should be excluded, and obliged to work … otherwise, the older boys and girls would be rendered lazy and unemployed."[126] People like Bourgeois and Dallier came to accept the schools, but only when they began to believe that these institutions might operate for, rather than against, social control.

Another point of equal interest is the archbishop's relationship with the community. There can be little doubt that Le Tellier treated Roland unkindly. However, immediately after the theologal's death he adopted the community as his own. In light of what is known about Archbishop Colbert's relations with Barré's institute,[127] it seems likely that Le Tellier, also, wanted the congregation under his immediate control; and that the death of Roland gave him this opportunity. Certainly the Soeurs du Saint-Enfant-Jésus became, and remained, the official teaching congregation of the diocese of Reims, and the rule under which they lived, complete with simple vows, was that given to them, in 1683, by Le Tellier.

By the terms of the agreement reached between Roland's executor, Jean-Baptiste de La Salle, and the city council, on 1 August 1678, "all the sisters of the aforesaid community will be secular, and may not be cloistered or veiled ... or make solemn vows at any time or under any pretext whatsoever."[128] This requirement was confirmed in the letters patent, which also made plain that, apart from the house, which, since it had been sold to Roland by a monastery, was already religious property, and the chapel that had been built adjacent to it, the community's property was not to be exempt from taxes. Thus the new community received its definition: it was to belong to the "intermediate state," religious and yet not monastic, which was now beginning to take form in communities across France.

One last dimension remains, almost invisible beneath the political skirmishes which marked this difficult foundation. This is the support that the new congregation received from the people that were going to use it: the women who entered the community, and the parents who sent their children to the schools.

The "Mémoires" claim that "the good reputation gained by the behaviour of these first sisters of Monsieur Roland soon attracted others, and the number increased in a short time, allowing the multiplication of the schools in different quarters of the city, and even in the country."[129] Such stories of success are very familiar in hagiographical writing. In this case, the facts bear it out. In 1675, when the schools opened officially, there were ten schoolmistresses in the community. Roland, outlining his plan for the future, envisaged a community of thirty: twenty to be engaged in teaching – "one mistress being unable to teach more than fifty children" – ten more in the noviciate and working in the house. "In time to come we must count on having a high number of invalids, since nothing ruins the health of the women as much as an occupation of this sort which requires them to talk almost continuously."[130] By 1690, it had reached that number. At the beginning of the eighteenth century, counting its foundations in the countryside, it had grown to forty-two.[131] Within twenty-five years, the growth of the congregation had exceeded its founder's expectations.

At the time of Roland's death in 1678, the sisters were still running the orphanage. But their principal task was that of conducting school in the traditional four quarters: in their house on the rue de Barbâtre, and in the parishes of Saint-Rémi, Saint-Jacques, and Saint-Hilaire, to which they walked after breakfast.[132] The girls in their classrooms numbered around one thousand.[133]

What kind of children went to Roland's schools? There seems to have been no attempt to limit the entry of more affluent students. The school rules simply demanded that all children, rich or poor, should be accepted into the schools "with the same esteem."[134] According to a historian of the Christian Brothers, "In Roland's schools, at the beginning, all the students were more or less verminous."[135] However, they were obviously not as much so as Roland would have wished. "It looks as if in the future we shall have many more scholars," he wrote to his uncle, "the excessive misery presently preventing many of the parents from giving their children the time to go to school."[136]

In comparison to that of the hopitaux-généraux, both in Rouen and in Reims, the pedagogy of the sisters appears to have been light in training in manual work; the children were taught religion, reading, *civilité*, and some arithmetic, with writing added for the advanced students. This, presumably, reflected the desires and ambitions of the parents, and suggests that the wolf was not actually at their door. There were some students who were truly poor, whose books were provided free of charge, and kept by the school.[137] But the free schools of the Soeurs du Saint-Enfant Jésus appear to have found their principal clientèle in a broad range of working people, comfortable and less comfortable, in the city of Reims – "launderers, bakers, wool carders, gardeners, mantle-makers, wig-makers, cobblers, locksmiths, weavers and coopers"[138] whose daughters had, most probably, never gone to school before. The mother house on the rue de Barbâtre was located in the quarter most heavily populated by master weavers, the artisans whose work in the production of wool fabric formed the bulk of the "manufacture" of Reims.[139] It is likely that the children from these tiny workshops attended the free classes of the sisters.

The healthy growth of both community and schools is evidence of the satisfaction felt by ordinary people with their new schoolmistresses. The grudging conversion of the city council has been recorded above. A powerful approbation came from the archbishop in 1683, after the schools had begun to work, and when the products of their discipline and instruction started to appear upon the scene. "We have learned through the experience of several years," wrote Le Tellier, "of the advantage which young girls derive [from the schools], since, when on different occasions we have conferred the sacrament of confirmation upon them, we have found them incomparably more modest and better instructed than they were when first, in the year 1671, we entered into possession of our Archbishopric."[140]

Among the impressions which the new charity schools made upon their society, none was more important than that which carried Roland's friend and executor, Jean-Baptiste de La Salle, into his life's work. In 1679 charity schools for boys, modelled upon the sisters' schools,[141] were opened in Reims, and in 1688 the Institute of Brothers of Christian Schools took shape. At last, schoolteaching by itself, without the benefit of the priesthood, became a fit religious vocation for men. But it should be remembered that they followed a path which women had already trodden.

The appropriation by women of the teaching function, in the sense of public religious instruction, was the high-water mark of their "promotion" under the Old Regime. The eighteenth century saw the slowing-down, almost to a standstill, of the great religious movement which is known as the Catholic Reformation. No new cloistered congregations, and only a handful of secular institutes, appeared after the death of Louis XIV. In the lean years that followed, many communities suffered financial collapse, or were closed for lack of members. Even for the more successful, the byword was consolidation, not expansion.

In a period of contraction there could be no further promotion. The cloistered teaching nuns clung to the rules, and privileges, which they had already won. Most of them, in spite of financial strains, remained faithful to their free schools. The *filles séculières* continued their work without much change, serving in hospitals, orphanages, asylums, and schools. Their status was low: like the parish clergy, but beneath them, they were truly the Church's working class – "proletarians of the faith," as one modern history has called them.[142] There was certainly no question of political power, or of an active voice in the affairs of the Church. "To inspire is not to govern," Abbé Brémond reminds us firmly.[143] Religious women were never to acquire a political influence equivalent to the spiritual influence which they exercised within Catholicism.

This would not have disturbed the sisters of the seventeenth century. None of them – not even the outspoken Mary Ward – had asked for any privilege beyond the privilege of service. In any case, their condition of political subordination should not obscure the reality of their achievement. They now had a presence in the institutional Church far greater than women had ever had before. From mid-seventeenth century, cloistered nuns and *filles séculières* far out-numbered male regulars. The Church, in the words of one historian, had been "feminized."[144] As the right arm of the parish clergy, they remained for many years a force to be reckoned with. In the fields of activity within their mandate they enjoyed an almost unshakeable monopoly, as men of the First and Third Republics were later to discover.

The work which they performed was serious and substantial. "I have insisted," writes Yves Poutet, "on the development ... of a professional life consecrated to Catholic social action."[145] For this reason, the congregations contributed in their own way towards their members' sense of self-worth. Any reader of the annals of religious congregations will know that although their members prac-tised personal humility, they made up for it in *esprit de corps*. The pride that religious women were required to deny in themselves was transferred to their communities – and therefore, by way of a sort of code, to their sex.

"All Christendom is like a great garden ... and all the communities like so many beds in this great garden. Ours, though small, is none-theless one of these little beds which the Gardener has reserved for Himself, to plant in it a quantity of plants and flowers." So wrote Marguerite Bourgeoys.[146] The boast sounds modest to our ears. But given the context of the times, and the lowly social status of the writer, the words were proud indeed. Women could now claim a place in the Church; not only in its prayer life and its charitable activities, but in its apostolate. A citadel which had stood impre-gnable since time immemorial had been entered.

CHAPTER SEVEN

Development of a Feminine Pedagogy

THE TEACHERS: SPIRITUALITY

A leading historian of Catholic education under the Old Regime, Jean de Viguerie, has remarked on the fact that, although in recent years a number of works have appeared on the subject of feminine education, little has yet been done on the groups that developed and dispensed this education. In his mind, this is an unnatural separation. "How can we understand a pedagogy without referring to its source, the spirit of the congregation, and its particular purpose?"[1] The question may also be turned around: can we study the congregations themselves without placing them in the context of their pedagogy? Claude Langlois, in his work on the nuns of the nineteenth century, points out that "the congregations were defined more by the activity that they exercised than by the type of life they adopted."[2] In the same way, the teaching congregations of the seventeenth century can only be understood by reference to the work that they performed and the rationale that developed around it. People are, in part, what their work makes them. Cloistered or uncloistered, the schoolmistresses of the congregations adapted their lives significantly to achieve the priority which they gave to teaching.

For centuries, the ideal of women in religion had been self-perfection through retreat from the world: "to live united to God and removed from creatures by a total separation of mind and heart."[3] The new teaching congregations of the Counter-Reformation also aspired to self-perfection, but through service to others. All of them, in one form or another, shared the purpose laid down by Pierre Fourier for his nuns: "to make their life as holy, fruitful and useful to the public, and as agreeable to God, as they possibly can; and in particular to devote themselves diligently, and wholeheartedy, to the free instruction of girls."[4]

This entailed a different life and a different spirituality. Instead of retreat, the new monasticism must idealize involvement. As Anne de Xainctonge, the foundress of the Ursuline house in Dôle, told her novices, "Having received your life and your strength from God, you can give them back to Him ... only by employing them to make others know, love and adore Him. You must, then, use your ability and natural talents, your religious instruction and your faith, to lead souls to this good Master."[5]

Such involvement, worthy though it was, nevertheless detracted from pure contemplation. From the very outset it was obvious that the demands of the schoolroom would require an alteration of the monastic ideal. To have their effect on "the world," teaching nuns must be sociable and uneccentric in demeanour – "their outward appearance so well composed that there is nothing which can alienate or disgust, or estrange or by its excess intimidate the scholars."[6] To survive the classrooms, which, according to all contemporary accounts, were noisy and dusty places, they must be in sound health, and not worn out by physical mortification. Their prayer life must remain practical. "As for raptures and ecstasies," wrote Mère de Pommereu, "Ursulines do not need them. On the contrary, it seems that if they happened frequently, they would be incompatible with their principal duties which oblige them to continual care of and attention to girls. How would it be to find an Ursuline lifted up from the earth and out of her senses when she was supposed to be teaching catechism or serving the children?"[7]

On the other hand, the women of the Counter-Reformation congregations were determined to make their communities true religious communities. "It is not an association of schoolmistresses that I plan to create," said Anne de Xainctonge, "but a company of Christian virgins vowed to the religious life for the purpose of instructing the young."[8] The Ursulines of Bordeaux were urged to follow their profession "keeping their bodily eyes fixed upon the little creature, and the eyes of their soul upon the Creator for love of whom they do it."[9] The sense of religious calling was at the heart of their new undertakings; they would not even have started without it.

A new religious life, suitable to their purpose, had therefore to be constructed out of the old, by taking some elements from traditional monasticism and abandoning others. Four monastic elements were at odds with the profession of teaching: clausura, Divine Office, the practice of physical mortification, and the traditional religious habit.

Clausura, as has already been indicated, was almost universally imposed upon the communities of the early seventeenth century. It had the effect of reducing their field of action, of containing their apostolic zeal. However, in the transactions which surrounded the process of monastic translation, a significant concession was made to the teaching nuns. In order to enable them to perform their duties, they were allowed to receive day students within the confines of the monastery. The permission was first given in 1607,[10] and repeated in subsequent bulls of erection for all three teaching congregations. The teaching of day students was still considered a daring and dangerous innovation. Therefore the classes were fenced around, literally, with precautions. The students were to enter their classroom by an exterior door, guarded by a servant. Once they were in, and the door locked, the teaching nuns would enter by an interior door. The same procedure would be reversed at the end of classes. There would be no other point of contact between the monastery and its day students. But this small opening allowed the nuns of the Counter-Reformation to exercise their influence on thousands of young girls in the cities and towns of France.

Divine Office was the central act of community worship of a monastery. In strict observance, it was sung in choir in seven parts during the day, and once in the night. The rest of the monastery's life revolved around it. For schoolteachers, however, this practice was virtually impossible, not only because of the rigorous schedule that it involved, but because the singing strained their voices. Most of the new monastic communities asked for, and received, exemption from the duty. Instead, they recited the Little Office of the Virgin, and even here, those nuns engaged in teaching were usually dispensed from the obligation.[11] However, their prayer life remained demanding, as the focus began to shift from public to private prayer, after the example of the Jesuits.

Physical mortifications, of the type practised in reformed monasteries and in the Carmelite convents, were equally damaging to health. The practice of self-mortification died hard. The young women of Mattaincourt invented ingenious penances for themselves.[12] The first novices of Faubourg Saint-Jacques, according to Mère de Pommereu, "slept most of the time on bare boards, and day and night invented a thousand ways to crucify their bodies."[13] In time, however, mortifications came under control of the superiors, and the nuns learned, Jesuit-style, that obedience to the rule was more virtuous than private devotions. "The discipline of the body must not be excessive or indiscreet in the matter of vigils, fasts and other external penances and austerities which often do damage and prevent a greater good," said the rule of the Filles de Notre-Dame.[14]

The same moderation applied to their dress. The coarse clothing and bare feet of the contemplatives were hardly appropriate to the classroom. Even the exaggerated dress and behaviour of *dévotes* was to be avoided, because of the negative effect that it would have on their clientèle. Thus the Ursulines of Dôle were instructed always to keep their faces uncovered, "to show all the world, by their natural and unconstrained modesty, that it is love, as much as their vows, which attaches them indissolubly to God, without the help of walls."[15]

To sum up, the new religious life was designed to be apostolic, to draw the neighbour towards God, through example as well as through teaching. Every act of self-perfection was linked to the effect it would have on others. "For just as the coal which is not hot will not set fire to another coal, as will that which is ablaze: so also will they who are only slightly on fire with the love of God have difficulty ... in enflaming others with divine love."[16]

Differences in outward observance were indicative of a fundamental inner distinction between contemplative and active religious life. The proliferation of new congregations offered a greater choice of lifestyle. Women who desired contemplation could enter the Carmelites, the Visitation, or the reformed monasteries. This left the more outgoing women free to choose the active congregations, which, according to Mère de Pommereu, "create some diversion, since women in general are not capable of continual meditations."[17] On the other hand, the active congregations were advised to choose subjects appropriate to their task: women who were not only pious, but also energetic and healthy. Pierre Fourier described the characteristics of a good schoolmistress: "Sound of body and of mind, with a good nature, good courage and good will, and full of great zeal, to endure the fatigue of this holy exercise."[18] While many entrants fell short of his ideal, there was nevertheless a certain process of natural selection. Women who did not want to teach, or work with children, were less likely to enter communities which required them to take the fourth vow.

The qualities defined in the earlier years of the century – common sense, zeal, robust health – became more pronounced with the evolution of the *filles séculières*. As the maxim "to leave God for God's sake" became the cornerstone of their spirituality, the new generations of schoolmistresses began to shed the tension that had so long existed between monastic practice and the duties of the schoolroom. Their work became their means of perfection. "The sisters of the Institute assure their salvation by their employment," wrote Nicolas Barré.[19] Christ, seeing their devotion to their neighbour, would not fail to advance their own holiness. The prayer life of the sisters remained considerable, but priority was now, without question, given to their apostolate. Barré compared them to servants looking after their master's children, "wholly neglectful of themselves, and putting all their care into cleaning, dressing, and adorning the children."[20] This elevation of what had always been considered hard and somewhat servile work into a holy apostolate was made possible by the "ideology of the school," so central to the Catholic Reformation. Barré was able to draw on social attitudes that had changed profoundly since the days of the early Ursulines.

In an age when every social attitude found expression in religious terms, this promotion of the schoolmistress had to find its grounding somewhere in sacred tradition. The seventeenth century saw the growth of a new popular devotion to the Education of the Virgin. This theme was immensely attractive to religious schoolmistresses, from Alix Le Clerc to Marguerite Bourgeoys, but it also found a response in society as a whole. The tradition that set Mary, in her early years, at study first with her mother, then in the Temple, was elaborated in sermons, in catechisms, and in religious art which may still be seen today. In statues and rood-screens, almost all dating from the post-tridentine period, the child Mary stands at her mother's knee, holding a book (most often, an alphabet). Her posture expresses submission, though frequently a diadem upon her head indicates her role in the salvation of mankind. Her mother, Saint Anne, radiates kindness, firmness, and austerity. Saint Anne is, in fact, the personification of education. But she is not presented as a model of motherhood. She is recognizable, by her dress and by her demeanour, as a religious.[21]

The nun-educator was a new phenomenon. Reconciliation of the two roles was not easy, since it involved the melding of two functions that had hitherto been considered mutually exclusive. But by the end of the century it had been achieved. The ideology of the school, so fervently cultivated in the aftermath of Trent, had made it possible.

THE TEACHERS: PROFESSIONALISM

Of the many thousands of girls who passed through the schools of old-regime France, few, if any, received an education comparable to that of the *collèges* which their brothers attended. The literacy rate among women, as witnessed by the signatures on marriage contracts, remained far lower than that among men. "Nothing," wrote Fénelon, in the last quarter of the century, "is more neglected than the education of girls."[22] Here, in a nutshell, are the three arguments that make the case against the girls' schools of the seventeenth century.

Responsibility for this perceived mediocrity has usually been assigned to the teaching congregations. It has been assumed that both subject matter and teaching method were inferior. The first assumption has recently become the subject of debate, as defenders of the teaching congregations seek to place their syllabus in the context of the times.[23] The second assumption also demands examination. While the intellectual content of seventeenth-century girls' schooling was limited by many circumstances, the care with which the congregations approached their work, and the training which they stipulated for their members, were often exemplary.

A modern historian writes: "The question of educating girls, and in particular of educating poor girls, was raised for the first time in the seventeenth century."[24] For years young ladies had been raised and educated in monasteries, and girls of lesser birth had attended school, either in the occasional classrooms run by schoolmistresses, or, more often, in mixed classes, in defiance of the Church's thunderings against coeducation. But the idea that girls *ought* to attend school was developed in the collective mind of Counter-Reformation society.

The women who initiated this education were untrained for the work; many of them were unschooled, some of them even illiterate. Fourier, for one, had to start by teaching his young schoolmistresses: "he took pains to teach them to read well and correctly, and to make them understand the principles of spelling and the rules of arithmetic ... and gave them a little lesson every day."[25] Even in cases where the women were literate, they had no tradition of female pedagogy on which to draw. And if the records of their various communities do not exaggerate, they faced full classrooms from the very beginning. Thus for the first five Ursulines of Dijon, "the classrooms were soon so full that they could not hold the great number of scholars who turned up," while at Paris, "scarcely six months after the monastery was enclosed they began to bring in little day students ... From the beginning, these were received by the hundred."[26] There was no breathing space, no time in which to develop efficient teaching methods.

However, they had two advantages: their association with the masculine teaching orders, chiefly the Jesuits; and their own commitment to community life. The former gave them a model on which to base their own pedagogy, the latter gave them a permanent structure within which to maintain and develop that pedagogy.

The Jesuit connection may be found almost everywhere. Two Jesuit priests, Bordes and Raymond, initiated the congregation of the Filles de Notre-Dame. Pierre Fourier, himself schooled at the Jesuit college of Pont-à-Mousson, adapted that training to the purposes of the young schoolmistresses of Mattaincourt. Madame de Sainte-Beuve, Mère de Xainctonge, and many other Ursuline foundresses were moved to design their communities as feminine complements to the Society of Jesus. The inspiration even came from beyond the grave. According to Alix Le Clerc, "it was the blessed Father Ignatius who encouraged me to take up the teaching of girls."[27] Over and over again, foundresses felt impelled, like Mary Ward, to "take the same of the Society".[28]

The congregations took of the Society, not its subject matter, which was considered far too sophisticated and profound for girls, but its educational methods. These may be summed up under the headings of discipline and pedagogy.

The sisters faced classrooms filled with girls of all ages, most of them without previous schooling, and, therefore, unbroken to the orderly behaviour that a classroom demands. They had, at first, only the most rudimentary teaching aids. In addition, they taught in common classrooms, filled with scores, sometimes hundreds, of children. A contemporary described the first free classes of the Ursulines of Dôle: "in one room, a great number of girls, old and young, seated on benches ... our sisters take them one after the other, for the subjects assigned to the level to which they belong ... No sister is dispensed from teaching, and as soon as the hour has come, all of them come into this room where they separate into the different benches that make the different classes."[29]

It was imperative to develop methods of managing these crowds. The traditional practice of individual teaching, which left most of the children unattended most of the time, was impracticable with such numbers. The first step was a division of the student population into smaller groups. This division could be by subject. The Filles de Notre-Dame experimented with four rooms, for reading, writing, sewing, and other handwork.[30] However, the division which came to prevail was the division according to ability and knowledge. The Ursulines of Dôle decided upon six grades.[31] Fourier advised three levels: "the little *abécédaires* who are beginning to know their letters ... those who are learning to read out of printed books ... the scholars who read out of registers and other handwritten papers and letters." Each level was divided into benches of ten or twenty students to a mistress.[32] Each mistress had to keep her instruction within the limits assigned to her: "the mistresses will take care not to anticipate each other, but to conform to the rules of each class, and stay within the assigned limits."[33] The *intendante*, or mistress of studies, would review the students' work several times a year, and the girls who had mastered the knowledge pertaining to their bench were promoted to a higher level. This subdivision of the classroom according to levels of achievement, joined in time to the general use of uniform textbooks, laid the foundation for simultaneous instruction, one of the great pedagogical achievements of the century.

Where the pupil-teacher ratio was higher, the women used another Jesuit institution to extend the teacher's control over her students: the *décurie* – a classical military device, borrowed from the Jesuits who in turn had borrowed it from the Calvinists.[34] Each group of ten children had its own *décurionne*, or *dizainière*, who was responsible for assisting with lessons and with discipline. The *dizainières* were simply students who were "wiser and more knowledgeable"[35], and their duties were limited to two- or three-month stints, during which they co-operated with the mistress by ensuring the study and discipline of their group. The *dizainière*, like the *décurion*, was the cornerstone of old-regime schooling. Wherever the ratio of students to teachers was high – as was usually the case in the charity schools – student offices proliferated. Students led the prayers, picked up and distributed the books, drilled their juniors in their recitations, swept the floors.

Also in imitation of the Jesuits, the students were encouraged to engage to compete with each other. "Emulation", in the Jesuit system, was used as the whetstone of the students' minds, "to sharpen and stir up the scholars, awakening them if they are asleep and making them gallop more lightly."[36] The feminine congregations applied the principle with verve. "Each mistress will pair off her pupils two by two, one with the other, those who are most closely matched in knowledge to listen to each other's reading, correct each other, and compete in their prayers, catechisms and lessons."[37] Students competed for academic honours, which often took the form of small prizes, or simply by their position on the benches. For the winners, there was a bench of honour, under a crowned statue of the Blessed Virgin. For lazy or difficult students, there was a bench of penance.[38]

The reverse side of the Jesuits' use of emulation as a spur to good scholastic behaviour was their disapproval of physical punishment or uncontrolled anger in the classroom. The schoolroom was, by long tradition, a violent and rowdy place. "After the Scots there are no greater childbeaters than the schoolmasters of France," Saliat had written in the sixteenth century.[39] Montaigne had recalled with feeling the "cries of children being punished, and of masters drunk with anger."[40] Such excess went counter to the Jesuits' model of self-discipline, and they took pains to avoid it.

This control of emotions was greatly sought after by the women's congregations. Their rules all spoke in the same spirit: "The mistresses will govern themselves in such a way that all their behaviour, their bearing, actions, words and movements will be controlled and composed, a model for their students ... They will not show them any sign of anger, impatience or disdain; they will not call them asses, or beasts, or fools, or bad girls; they will not shout aloud at them, and above all, they will refrain from beating or striking them."[41] A variety of lesser punishments was developed: prayers, to be recited while kneeling, for minor offences, donkeys' ears for poor study, the red tongue for lying. Shame punishments were preferred to physical discipline, which was reserved for extreme cases. "The cane will be used only for serious faults,"[42] and then only with the permission of the *intendante*. This is in striking contrast to the punishments recommended by *L'Escole paroissiale* for boys' schools, which were graded from the cane across the fingers through heavier beatings to prison "in which they will be locked for two, three, four, five, or six hours."[43]

It could be argued that the fact that the nuns whipped at all shows that they could not, or would not, escape the brutal habits of their times. But, in fact, it seems that feminine educators were on the way to developing their own philosophy of discipline, based on a different understanding of the children whom they were to teach. A key text regarding discipline, which can be found repeated in other rules, appears in the Constitutions of the Ursulines of Paris, drawn up in 1623: "In so far as young girls are corrected, some by fear, others by kindness, some by the rod, others by gentle persuasion, some by silence, others simply by a glance, the mistresses of each class will study and remark the nature and inclinations of their scholars as well as their capacity, in order to treat them with prudence and discretion."[44]

Feminine school rules, imitations of their masculine counterparts in so many ways, display one original characteristic: they treated their children as sensitive beings, open to damage. "Fear is like the violent remedies that are used in cases of extreme sickness," wrote Fénelon, "they purge, but they alter temperaments ... a spirit led by fear is always the weaker for it."[45] It is interesting that a manual written for boys' schools in 1709 condemned violence also, but on the grounds that the students were hardened by it.[46] Feminine discipline, initially modelled on that of the Jesuits, developed along its own lines to serve what was perceived as a different, much more vulnerable student population. This helped to make the schoolroom more benign, less violent. "Their teaching is marked with exactitude and gentleness," wrote an admirer. "They can be understood by the youngest and the oldest alike."[47] The sisters brought their own insights to the growing understanding of and interest in "the child" which was a characteristic of the century.

As in the discipline of the new congregations, so in their pedagogy: the Jesuit background is discernible everywhere. "Faire comprendre avant de faire apprendre" – to make a subject understood before it is learned – the principle was central in the *Ratio studiorum*.[48] In close imitation, the women designed a course of studies which demanded that the student fully complete one stage before advancing to the next.

This adaptation of the pedagogy of the *collèges* was all the more inventive because it was applied to schools of very limited academic standards. The teaching nuns lavished their pedagogical care upon relatively elementary courses of studies. Their school rules and manuals described, in detail, even the most basic procedures. What makes their effort doubly significant is that it was through their mediation that the pedagogy of the Jesuits came to pervade the elementary schools of France.[49] The monasteries transmitted their methods to the *filles séculières*.[50] In many cases the *filles séculières* introduced their methods to other schoolmistresses – and masters.[51]

The Catholic pedagogical world was a small place. The *dévot* elite was a close-knit group, held together by travel and by the written word. The women's congregations were developed in an atmosphere of mutual consultation and imitation. Thus Françoise de Bermond, the Provençal Ursuline, came to Paris to instruct Madame de Sainte-Beuve's community in catechetics, and Alix Le Clerc came to the same convent from Lorraine to study its teaching methods. Thus, also, Fourier could come home from the Châlons house marvelling at its techniques, and write: "I should like our sisters from other houses, if possible, to send some of their people to learn this fine method, or to have some sisters from Châlons go around all the houses, to teach the others."[52] The imposition of strict clausura suppressed interaction between monasteries, but the *filles séculières* suffered no such restraints. The Filles de la Charité took lessons from a woman who had trained at the Ursulines;[53] the sisters of Reims received training from "experienced mistresses" of other houses;[54] Démia's schoolmistresses in Lyon brought in one of Barré's sisters to help them set up their seminary;[55] Marguerite Bourgeoys stayed with the Filles de la Croix to learn their system.[56] There is abundant evidence that the congregations drew upon each other's experience in designing and establishing their school rules.

The existence of a set of rules raises the question: were these rules followed? Do written rules reflect actual practice in the interior of seventeenth-century classrooms?

This, of course, can never be answered satisfactorily. But it should be remarked that the creation of the community, and its confirmation by the Church, were strong guarantees for the continuity of its members' work. A community had its own corporate personality, which transcended that of its members. Its rules, once formulated, soon tended to harden, so that further adaptation was difficult. Thus, after a flurry of creative activity at the beginning, literal observance of original teaching methods was very swiftly institutionalized, and the caution would be inscribed: "The mistresses will keep exactly to the customary order of exercises, and may change nothing, without the permission of the Superior and the Mistress-General."[57] Innovation was considered to be disobedience to the rule. An Ursuline who reversed the order of exercises without permission was guilty of a serious fault, which she would have to confess before the community;[58] a Fille de Notre-Dame who wanted to experiment with new methods was sent to another house.[59] In the closed world of the monastery, little could happen without becoming public knowledge. A whole hierarchy of officers stood ready to ensure observance; beyond them, the priests who acted as canonical superiors were available to hear complaints. But the most ardent guardian of custom was the community itself. Changes, even in minute details of the rule, were noted and resented. Rigidity, not laxity, was the tendency of the seventeenth-century institutions.

New members of the community were trained intensively in the practice of their rule, including their school rule. During the first stage of their noviciate, they were taught the subject matter: catechism, reading, writing, arithmetic, spelling, and handwork. They studied manuals, which had frequently been drawn up within the community itself.[60] In the second stage, they practised teaching in the classroom, under the supervision of other mistresses. Even after taking their vows, they might remain for years under the supervision of others. According to Mère de Pommereu, it took seven years to train an Ursuline.[61]

The monasteries' weakness, for which they were taken to task by educational reformers at the end of the century, stemmed not from lack of preparation, but from intellectual isolation. By the will of their ecclesiastical superiors, the religious houses had become autonomous when they became cloistered; the interchange of personnel and of ideas which had marked the early years dried up. Each community secured its own life behind "a rigid and cold barrier."[62] In these circumstances, it would have been difficult to update education systems, even if the nuns had felt the need. Furthermore, as a result of an accumulation of instructions from the bishops, the severity of convent life had been increased,[63] at the very time when life in the world was become more relaxed. It is to these factors, rather than to any lack of dedication and training, that the failures of monastery education should be attributed. "A young girl of quality grows up there in a profound ignorance of the world," Fénelon was to write. "She comes out of the convent like a person who has been raised in the shadows of a deep cave, and who is forced all of a sudden to emerge into broad daylight."[64] It was understandable: given the total isolation implied in clausura, any monastery that lived up to its rule could hardly do otherwise for the boarders who were confined for years within its walls.

The *filles séculières*, by the very nature of their calling, could not hope for extensive preparation. The single *fille dévote* in Montmartre, working alone with her eighty girls,[65] or the three *filles noires*, established in the parish of Saint-Etienne-du-Mont for "lInstruction et lEducation des pauvres filles de la paroisse,"[66] had no time to upgrade their skills. Even in larger communities, like the Magneuses of Reims, numbering five members, the rule was only of the most basic kind, concerned largely with the running of the community.[67] The number of "schools," or rather, classrooms, opened under arrangements like these has not been tallied, but it must be assumed that a great number of girls in seventeenth-century France received their education from schoolmistresses who had little or no formal training.

However, where larger communities of secular schoolmistresses developed, comprehensive school rules and training procedures were laid down. "They ought to have a perfect grasp of their material, in order to teach nothing of which they are not certain, and well informed."[68] Their theoretical training was shorter than that of the monasteries, and their practical training began earlier. "The best way to learn is to teach," wrote Barré.[69] Frequently, as in Rouen, the apprentice schoolmistresses lived at first in a seminary, from which they went out each day to their schools. They worked under supervision until they were considered capable of working alone. Their apprenticeship might take a couple of years. Even when qualified, they were expected to continue to study, "to become capable of advancing in Christian Doctrine, and to learn to write and spell better."[70] Furthermore, the *filles séculières*, like the cloistered nuns, were required to listen to the reading of their rules, including their school rules, once a month. Any infractions of the rule were to be reported to the superior.[71]

They faced other difficulties which the cloistered religious avoided. First, the number of students. For the *filles séculières*, a class of fifty was standard; and there were cases in Montpellier, for instance, in 1685 – where a single mistress was expected to teach a hundred children.[72] Second, distance from the home community, which led to lack of supervision and support. To counter this, the superior of the community was expected to visit the schools at regular intervals "to see and examine how everything is going, and how much the people are being edified."[73]

In the final analysis, the actual quality of teaching remains unknown. But the interest which the larger congregations took in their pedagogy, and the efforts which they took to ensure that their members met certain standards, suggest professionalism, at least in intent. Furthermore, some guarantee of quality was provided by the structures of community life, either within the monastery or in the secular institute. Where community life was strong, its members were more likely to maintain their standards.

In the later years of the century, when the enthusiasm of the Catholic Reformation had begun to fade, many small communities broke up and collapsed. But for those that survived and flourished, there was a new source of moral support: the growing public respect for their institutions. In 1600, schoolmistresses were, socially speaking, only slightly above the servants. In 1700, they were persons of some standing, an arm of the Church – and, indeed, occasionally, of the Crown.[74] They cultivated a pride in their profession. The sisters of Reims knew it well: "Aside from the religious and priests, there is no other profession which finds its state in working at the divine ministry of forming and fostering Jesus Christ in souls, except school masters and mistresses."[75] They felt themselves associated in its dignity. As Marie Barbier, schoolmistress of Montreal, was to write, "It is a sublime employment, worthy of the Apostles; it is the continuation of the work of the Saviour; I have never performed it without fear and confusion."[76]

THE SUBJECTS

Historians of old-regime schooling have remarked on the complexity of its motivation. The desire to save souls through education was born with the Counter-Reformation and remained, though with diminishing intensity, the principal motive. However, the perception of the school as a means of social control never ceased to figure in the plans of seventeenth-century educators.[77] There was a third motive behind the movement of children into the schools. This was the desire of their parents to secure their social promotion. For boys, the lure was obvious: a little Latin and a knowledge of letters might secure them a niche in the expanding world of business and of minor offices.[78] For girls, the material advantage of schooling seems more problematic. Yet the number of parents ready to send their daughters to school suggests that some sort of advantage, social or economic, was to be gained from the effort. "What is astonishing," writes one historian, "is not the relative weakness of feminine literacy, but rather that so many parents insisted in spite of everything on procuring an education for all their children."[79]

However, the demand from parents for girls' schools was weaker than that for boys' schools, and slower to develop. The initial stimulus came from the "supply side": from the rush of young *dévotes* into the congregations. These women were, indeed, responding to a pressing need – but it was their own need, for serious and meritorious occupation in an age when religion impregnated the atmosphere. The success of their free schools ensured their work; but it was, after all, only the public's verdict on what they had already undertaken.

For the women of the Counter-Reformation, the religious motive was absolutely paramount. The profane subjects were simply added to their curriculum as bait, to entice the parents into sending their children to school. "In teaching young girls the things proper to their estate," wrote Anne de Xainctonge, "my desire is to gain their confidence. In teaching them the truths of religion, my purpose is to make them true Christians. Reading, grammar, writing and the other subjects would mean little, if they did not help us to make our pupils better [people], and above all, true Christians."[80]

But what was the teaching of religion? It was much more than a simple imparting of the truths of faith; it was the inculcation of a way of life. For women, whose right to access to sacred learning was, in this male-dominated age, a matter of dispute, this was doubly true. Doctrine as a science, with all its subtleties, was not altogether appropriate to the female sex. The purpose behind the education of girls was "above all, to engrave the fear of God in their souls, and to form them in the exercises suitable to their sex."[81] Thus for the one subject – catechism – which dealt with Christian doctrine, several others were directly related to the behaviour of the children as Christians and as citizens.

The teaching of catechism was approached with great diffidence. There was some initial uncertainty as to how women could teach it without overreaching themselves. Mademoiselle Le Gras, the exponent of extreme simplicity, maintained that it could only be taught in the most rudimentary way: "It would be very dangerous for our company if we tried to speak in a learned way, not only for our own sake (inclined as we are to vanity), but also for fear of saying things that are in error."[82] However, few others were prepared to go so far. The approach that was recommended most often was a combination of humility and intensive preparation. "The sisters will take care not to deal with lofty and subtle questions," wrote Barré, while at the same time prescribing an hour's preparation each night for the lessons of the following day.[83]

At a time when new versions of the catechism abounded, the teaching congregations chose theirs carefully. The Ursulines were among the first catechists to use the Bellarmine catechism, which was specifically designed for children. However, they later drew up their own catechism, so as to avoid, as much as possible, material considered unsuitable for girls – in other words, the sixth commandment.[84] Mademoiselle Le Gras, also, wrote out a catechetical model, to reduce the difficult formulae of faith to something comprehensible to the children of the charity schools.[85]

The teaching of catechism was a difficult exercise. "Let the tender minds of these young girls not be overloaded, or wearied, or fed up with these good foods," warned Pierre Fourier.[86] But in spite of a host of downward revisions, the content of Christian doctrine remained intractably difficult to explain. "The great mysteries," which must be taught to the faithful, were "the unity and greatness of God, the adorable Trinity, the Incarnation of the Word, the divine Eucharist, the Sacraments, the Commandments of God, etc ..."[87] Between the extreme simplicity of the "profane" syllabus and the complicated, abstract terms and concepts of the catechism, writes one historian, there was an "abyss."[88] The obvious recourse was to teach by rote. But serious catechists were warned against this temptation. The preferred solution was to combine memorization with informal questioning. By the end of the century the method was firmly set. After the common recitation of questions and answers, the schoolmistress was trained to ask "subquestions." "She must give more time to questions and answers if they are so complicated and obscure that the children and the uninstructed adults cannot grasp or understand their meaning."[89] The catechism lesson was to end with a summing up of one principal idea, and an edifying story to be taken home and repeated to parents.

More attention was devoted in the manuals to catechism than to any other subject. However, the exhaustive detail, and the insistence on strict adherence to the methods laid down, appears to have had the effect of stifling the teachers' creativity. The search for uniformity, which characterized the period, had the effect of fixing all teaching of catechism into an immutable form – one which has lasted till recent times.[90] The feminine congregations shared in this general experience.

The pedagogy of Christian living covered the entire school day, and subsumed every subject taught. Much time was devoted directly to behaviour training: to "Christian duties, hatred of sin, love of virtue, and *civilité* and good manners."[91] Although the sisters drew heavily upon masculine teaching traditions, they also developed new approaches, to allow for the particularities of their sex.

Most girls who went to school in the seventeenth century were directed towards motherhood and home management. Only the boarders of the Benedictine and Cistercian monasteries and of the Visitation were guided towards the cloister. The teaching congregations specifically proscribed training for the religious life. The *Annales des Ursulines* commented: "Since we do not take girls for the express purpose of turning them into religious, it will no longer be necessary to teach them the ceremonies of the choir or other monastic exercises."[92] The reasoning behind this was made clear in their mandate. Christian motherhood was generally seen as the means to convert the world. "Young girls will reform their families, their families will reform their provinces, their provinces will reform the world."[93]

To fulfil their mission, Christian girls had first to learn to be devout: "since they will be more pleasing to Our Lord, and more useful to themselves if they are truly devout and virtuous, than if they are clever."[94] The youngest children were first taught their prayers, and how to make the sign of the cross, "making sure that they form it slowly and with attention."[95] From that time on, from the moment of their entry in the morning, every school day included exercise in prayers, in examination of conscience, in attending mass with reverence and decorum. Indeed, the grand processions of day students, two by two, through the streets to the church, became a form of theatre by which these young recruits to the *dévot* world showed themselves to the public.

Modest and dignified behaviour was intimately tied to the practice of religion:

The mistresses will teach their little ones to show modesty ... They will train them in the careful and perpetual control of their eyes, in the movement of hands, head, and body; in how to speak, how to walk, how to behave in church, and at school, and at home; how to eat at table, and walk through the town, and speak to people; how to ask questions, or give a response, or write a letter.[96]

Religion, the study of salvation, merged imperceptibly into *civilité*, the study of one's place in the world. And the place of women was within the barriers of their own modesty and *pudeur*, or feminine shame.

The accent on horror of sin, "particularly of those [sins] which are contrary to purity," was more marked in feminine than in masculine pedagogy.[97] Fourier, and others after him, saw the innocence of early childhood as a gift which could be preserved by constant protection. A girl, if shielded from bad influences, could grow up in ignorance of all sins of impurity. This principle, added to the nuns' natural reserve, made direct reference to the sin of impurity almost unthinkable. Sexual reticence was pushed to such lengths that some religious were reluctant to discuss the details of the Incarnation, or to mention the word "marriage."[98] They taught purity mostly through indirect reference. The usages of the sisters of Reims are typical: "It is enough to say, that displeases God, that is bad, we should avoid it more than death itself. And when the children go on to ask if it is a mortal sin? we must answer that a good Christian who loves God with all her heart should not ask this question, and that the very word is displeasing to God."[99]

But if the schoolmistresses did not talk directly about impurity, they did not hesitate to attack the occasions of sin. Their students were instructed not to sing worldly songs, or to dance. They were to dress modestly, "never to have bare throat or arms, like worldly women and prostitutes,"[100] to talk "like Christians," and to avoid walks, talks, and games with boys.[101] They were to have their own beds if possible; certainly they were no longer to sleep with their parents or brothers.[102] In a number of ways, they learned the distrust of the body which was so much a feature of the seventeenth century.

Pudeur went far beyond physical modesty. It represented the feminine identity as it was perceived in the seventeenth century, in all its weakness and limitation. Thus Fénelon could write: "in their sex there ought to be a *pudeur* towards knowledge, almost as delicate as that which inspires the horror of vice,"[103] and Madame de Maintenon could tell her students: "it befits the modesty of a girl or a woman to appear ignorant of things, even when she knows them."[104] To seek learning for its own sake was unfeminine, and dangerous.

Dévotes of the seventeenth century lived within this definition of their nature. Their own writings are full of self-deprecation, and allusions to their natural weakness. Their pedagogy remained humble and unassuming, an acknowledgment of the limitations of their sex. It may be argued that this was the price which they were required to pay for the very real advances which they had been allowed to make in their own education and that of others.

In the small repertoire of "profane" subjects taught in girls' schools, reading was by far the most important. There was no *petite école* that did not claim to teach its pupils how to read. This was because its profanity was more apparent than real. In fact, reading was "an instrument of salvation,"[105] since it allowed access to the word of God; therefore it was the duty of Christian educators to make it available to all children.

It was the pedagogy of reading, more than anything else, that demanded a new organization of the classroom. The first *congrégées*, like the Ursulines of Dôle cited above, still gave their reading instruction individually. But the numbers of children to be taught made a more orderly system imperative. The teacher had to be able to lead all her children together – hence the importance of the division of classes into smaller groups of equal ability. The problem of what to read came next. Credit for the invention of the blackboard is generally given to Pierre Fourier, who in his constitutions prescribed for each class "a slate, or plank, or board, hung in a high place in the schoolroom, so that all the pupils there can easily see it."[106] This blackboard, and other variations such as large printed cards, were particularly valuable for beginners. Here are Barré's instructions on their use:

As a lesson for the children of the third class, the mistress will show them a large sheet on which all the letters are printed in big characters. She will name them, three or four at a time, showing the differences: for instance that an M has three legs while an N only has two; that the U is made like the N except that the U is open at the top and the N is open at the bottom; and likewise with the other letters.[107]

The other learning tool which made simultaneous instruction possible was the cheap book. By mid-century at least, children were expected to have a standard book purchased for them by their parents or, if they were poor, provided by the school.

All the children having the same book [the Ursuline rule directed] and each one sitting alone and in order, the Mistress will make the sign of the Cross ... then she will spell out five or six lines, and afterwards read a page or two, pronouncing well, and making the pauses and accents; during this they will all look at their own books, and in a low voice will follow what the Mistress is reading.[108]

The beginners' reading was in Latin, the language of the Church. They first learned single letters, then syllables, which the mistress indicated with a pointer. The younger children were then left in the care of the second mistress, or the *dizainières*, to practice their reading.

The intermediate and senior classes were taught to read in French. In order to expand their reading skills, it was the custom to ask the older students to bring in family papers: marriage contracts, inventories, land titles, account books. "Require the pupil to pronounce this old-fashioned French properly and with a good accent; do not allow the letters to be guessed at, or the lesson recited by rote and by heart."[109]

Instructions such as these would seem to imply that for many girls, in many schools, proficiency in reading was perfectly attainable. Whether, in the future, they read the spiritual works for which they had been instructed or the harmful books – "tales of fictitious events, with profane love mixed in" – which Fénelon so strongly deplored,[110] they nevertheless joined the growing population of readers which was one of the features of the seventeenth century. The vast majority of the students of the *petites écoles*, however, did not reach the higher classes. They stayed at school for two or three years at the most, leaving when they had made their first communion, somewhere between the ages of ten and twelve. They then moved back into a world which was still largely illiterate, and where such reading skills as they had learned might be of little use.

It is difficult to judge, then, what effect the reading classes of the charitable schoolmistresses had upon the women of their time. A historian of literacy has pointed out that for the common people the seventeenth and eighteenth centuries were a period of transition between an oral and a written culture.[111] The only traces which are left of this advancing literacy are signatures in the marriage registers. Women's signatures, while rising steadily in numbers, always remained significantly fewer than men's. But this simply tells us whether they could write. Of the many women who learned how to read, but not to write, no satisfactory estimate can be made.

If reading was the instrument of salvation, writing was a useful skill, a saleable commodity. The two disciplines had not yet undergone the bonding that would one day make them two parts of the same learning process. They were seen as two unrelated skills, required for different purposes. This dissociation, according to the above historian, was "an essential phase in the passage of civilization from the oral to the written culture."[112]

Many *petites écoles*, including those that catered to the poor, wrote into their syllabus the phrase "to teach to read and write." At the best, they must only have meant that writing would be made available to exceptional students. In existing pedagogical practice, a student could progress to writing only after mastering the skill of reading. The *abécédaires* of the lowest classes were never allowed to put pen to paper.

Writing required additional tools and facilities. The students' parents were normally required to supply the tools: "a little lap desk without a lock ... a knife, some paper, an inkwell and some powder."[113] Sometimes writing students were expected to pay an extra fee. The school had to supply tables, which were over and above the benches on which the students otherwise sat. The handling of the materials was the subject of detailed instruction. The students had to learn to sharpen their quill pens for each copy that they were going to make, to keep their paper clean and neat, to powder their new work with sand or sawdust in order to keep it from smudging. The ink, which was often made by the teacher, had to be kept from drying out, in ink-wells of horn or lead. It has been pointed out that writing as a universal discipline had to await the development of technology, in the form of slates, pencils, and steel pens.[114]

In ideal circumstances, the teaching of writing was work for an expert. The school rule of the Paris Ursulines called for one or two writing mistresses, in addition to the regular class mistresses, to teach the day school.[115] The writing mistress was required, first, to show her students how to hold their pens, then to form letters, then elisions, then whole lines; "she should teach them to be tidy, not to blotch their papers with ink, or stain their clothes ... Above all, she should take care to make them sit straight while writing, and in the future allow less writing time to those whose posture is being damaged."[116] In the schools of the Congrégation, other members of the community assisted by writing onto the students' papers the examples which they would be expected to copy the next day.[117]

In the many charity schools where ideal circumstances seldom prevailed, other arrangements had to be made. The class mistresses left the students to write their lines from examples, then corrected their work afterwards.[118] Sometimes the more advanced students were called upon to correct the beginners. In some schools a special period was set aside for writing instruction, in the hour after lunch before the younger children returned.[119]

Once the students had mastered the many techniques of writing, they were introduced to *orthographe*, or spelling, in French: a subject which, as Pierre Fourier warned, was full of discrepancies. After practice in dictation, from some "good author, not too far removed from the most common form," they were tested by a practical application of their skill: "For spelling they will sometimes be given receipts acknowledging merchandise sold or work performed, or for money lent, and for the various everyday affairs which need to be recorded for greater assurance."[120] Finally, the best students were encouraged to compose their own small works.

It is obvious, from the instructions in the school rules and from the furnishings of the classrooms, that writing was not considered a subject for universal use. The huge classes of sixty, even eighty students, crowded along their benches, could not have been accommodated by their teachers, even if it had been considered necessary. The difficulties were simply too great; furthermore, the needs were small. Writing remained a privileged subject, available only for those who required it in their calling.

It is remarkable that it was offered at all in the girls' schools of the day. There was a bundle of overlapping prejudices against women who could write. For the upper classes, writing, in so far as it was a trade, still carried a taint of servility. "To be a writer is to lose half of one's nobility," wrote Mademoiselle de Scudéry.[121] Among the writing professionals, there was no desire to see women invading their profession. "This art belongs to the masculine sex," protested the master scribes of Rouen.[122] Some moralists saw it as a dangerous skill, which would allow women to carry on underhand liaisons. But the chief argument against writing seems to have been that it undermined the existing order. The later seventeenth and the eighteenth century saw a strong resurgence of the opinion that education should be tailored to the station in life of the students. "We should exclude from writing those who by the workings of Providence have been born to labour on the land."[123] What applied to the lower classes applied also to women: they should not exceed the limits of their condition. A century later, Restif de la Bretonne stated the case succinctly. "Writing and even reading ought to be forbidden to all women. This would be the way to confine their ideas, and to enclose them in the useful work of the household, and also to inspire them with respect for the first sex, which would be instructed in these same skills with all the more care since the second sex is being neglected."[124]

It has been suggested that the Church of old-regime France became the accomplice in a general downgrading of the education of women. There are cases of synodal regulations and episcopal ordinances specifically forbidding girls' schools to teach writing.[125] This, however, was a development for the future. Among the feminine educators of the seventeenth century, and their masculine mentors, very few showed any reluctance in principle to teaching girls to write. This may have been a sign of their own confidence in schooling, as a means of saving and regenerating the world. It may also have been a response to the desires of the parents. The schools were bargaining with society: in return for the religious instruction that they wanted to disseminate, they had to offer the training that parents found useful. For a small but growing segment of the population, the schools offered the possibility of social ascension.

Confirmation of this effect is strongest when it comes from a hostile source. Therefore the remarks which René Bourgeois of Reims – himself no friend to the charity schools – made with reference to Roland's schoolmistresses are instructive: "Their method is far from the action in which girls should be nourished and raised ... they encourage the servant class in an idleness which is scarcely fitting for domestic life."[126] In similar vein, a traveller visiting Canada in 1752–53 taxed the Congrégation of Montreal with spreading "a slow poison ... in so far as an educated girl acts the lady, and is affected, and wants to be established in the city and to marry a businessman; and considers as beneath her the estate into which she was born."[127] In some minds at least, the schoolmistresses were making a poor job of social control.

Usually only the senior students, who had mastered the skills of reading in Latin and in French, were given training in arithmetic. In most schools, its small share in the school curriculum (approximately two half-hours per week) indicates its minor importance. Children were first taught arithmetic through the use of *jettons* or counters. Then they were taught to calculate on paper: "[The mistress] will teach them the nine arabic numbers, as well as the roman numerals, and will then make them count to a thousand." Next came the practical training: "She will make them calculate the cost of the things that they have bought – for example, fifteen ells of lace at thirty-five sols an ell – then she will make them add up a total sum, and pay it in different sorts of coin."[128] Here, obviously, was training for home management. However, many girls who were destined, like Jean Maillefer's mother, to work in their family businesses,[129] must have profited from these classes. Training in home management was also training for the workshop.

Next to reading, the most important subject in the "profane" syllabus was handwork. If the rules are to be believed, there was not a girl, from the richest to the poorest, who did not learn at school to work at "whatever handwork is appropriate to her state, to avoid the evils of idleness."[130] Handwork was part of the essence of femininity. The distaff was its symbol. "The strong woman spins," wrote Fénelon, "she stays in her house, she is silent, she believes, and she obeys."[131]

Handwork varied from one institute to the next, with the purpose of the school and the character of its clientèle. For the boarders of Faubourg Saint-Jacques, there were "flowers in tapestry, embroidery with gold and silver, bobbin lace, French sewing, English sewing etc. etc."[132] But they were also taught "to repair whatever has become unstitched or torn, and to mend their linen."[133] The students of Dôle learned embroidery (as well as drawing, and "various accomplishments"). But they also learned dressmaking.[134] The students of Pierre Fourier's Congrégation were taught "to sew, to make bobbin lace and needle lace ... cutwork and shadow stitch and various other similar works."[135] Both here and in Dôle, the lowest class was exempted from sewing, the reason given by Mère de Xainctonge being that "experience has shown that when these little folk apply their minds to manual work before being able to recognize and assemble their letters, it is extraordinarily difficult to teach them to read."[136] In these schools, it seems, reading was more important than handwork; but it is interesting that the children found it less congenial.

The better schools were anxious not to take their students' handwork to a professional level. "You will be content to teach ordinary handwork, all of it of a sort to be easy and suitable and useful to poor and rich alike. You will not teach them other works that are rare and complicated and over large," wrote Fourier.[137] "Fancy" work was inappropriate for modest young women of good family. Such expertise was left to working women, or to religious communities in financial need.

Where the size of the community allowed, handwork was taught by a specialist. It was sometimes taught in conjunction with arithmetic and spelling, which required individual attention. Thus the girls who were not working on their books were able to work on their sewing. Ideally, a special room was reserved for the work. The convent of Dôle built such a classroom in the late seventeenth century: "longer than it is wide, lit along one side only, by windows which are not elbow-high, but lower, in order to have more light."[138]

For the mistresses in the *petites écoles* of Barré and Roland, working with their crowded benches of girls, handwork seems to have been reserved for spare time, when other work was done: "[The students] who do not write will do handwork after their reading; if however those who do write are diligent enough to finish early, they will do handwork to avoid idleness."[139] The brevity of the rules on this subject seems to suggest that handwork was not a priority in these *petites écoles*: an indication, perhaps, of the somewhat different expectations of parents.

But handwork reigned supreme in the many pauper schools and workshops of France. Here reading was at best a minor concern; for older girls it was often forgotten altogether. The apprentices worked in silence, sewing, knitting stockings, and lacemaking, to a background of spiritual instructions and improving readings, with occasional group singing, "to refresh and recreate their spirit."[140] Sometimes, but not always, they were permitted to keep the proceeds from their work. In these austere institutions, the religious educators succeeded finally in meeting the expectations of the ruling elite, by creating a skilled and disciplined workforce with no pretensions to book-learning.

Training in the manual skills was a valuable part of seventeenth-century female education. Sewing was a skill as writing was a skill. In terms of its application to the everyday life of women, it was far the more useful of the two, and no educator of the time would have dreamed of eliminating it. But it was also indicative of the restrictions which society placed on women. "The knowledge taught to women, like that taught to men, should be limited to what is relevant to their functions," wrote Fénelon.[141] And their functions were largely domestic. The horizons of female education were limited by a social diktat which allowed no scope for radical change.

How, in the end, should we assess the seventeenth century's efforts to educate its girls? In size and scope they were impressive. No overall estimate has yet been made of the number of women who had found their way into schoolteaching by the end of the century, though the statistics of one congregation for the year 1700 – between ten and twelve thousand Ursulines in three hundred and twenty monasteries[142] – can serve as an indication. What is known for certain is that by that time there was hardly a town, however small, without at least one school for girls. In 1700, girls in cities and towns across the country were expected to go to school, whereas in 1600 very few parents had even dreamed of the idea. What had been a luxury of doubtful value had now become a social necessity.

What was the quality of their schooling? For Fénelon, with his upper-class world view, it was vapid, frivolous, and excessively pious. For modern observers, with their upwardly mobile world view, it was limiting, oppressive, and certainly excessively pious. But in fact, at its best – a best which did not necessarily translate into "most expensive" – it was what education still is: a training for the real world in which its students had to live.

The religious schoolmistresses of the seventeenth century were the product of their times. They exemplified the mind of the Catholic Reformation: its emphasis on order and obedience, its spirituality – and also its activism. Within their limited sphere they participated in significant social change. Though the intellectual content of their teaching remained slight, they contributed towards the rationalization of the classroom which was essential to the development of modern teaching techniques. They also assisted in the modernization of the attitudes which adults held towards children. Finally, they joined with other religious elites, both Catholic and Protestant, in promoting schooling as the means of regenerating society. For these reasons they left their own considerable mark on modern pedagogy.

CHAPTER EIGHT

The Making of Communities

From the very beginning of its involvement in feminine education, the reformed Catholic church laid down two basic principles: that girls should be taught only by women, and that teachers should be unmarried. "It is advisable," wrote Pierre Fourier in 1598, "that these be persons free of the servitude of marriage and unencumbered by all other cares which might hinder the work of teaching."[1] Celibacy, whether temporary or permanent, was a universal condition for teaching in the schools of the *dévots*.

This raised the question of how these celibate women should live. In some cases they continued to live at home, as the first Ursulines did in Brescia. But the preferred solution was a community. "It is not easy to teach satisfactorily, with good order and real benefit to the scholars, if there are not several mistresses together, because one by herself cannot serve everybody in a school where there are many girls with different capacities, and at the same time take part in the housework."[2] Community life was as practical for reasons of security and support as it was compatible with the religious practices to which most of the women wished to commit themselves.

The building of community life was therefore a primary concern for the new religious schoolmistresses. Just as their outward service was important to secure acceptance in society, their private life was important for their own survival. It required at least a minimum of material furnishings and of financial stability; it also required a certain amount of internal regulation, to ensure the mutual co-operation of members. And because this was the seventeenth century, the *siècle sacral*, it had to have a religious justification. The making of a congregation, in the words of Jean de Viguerie, was "a work in itself ... a holy enterprise."[3]

This chapter will examine the various aspects of community-building, both psychological and material. On the psychological side, the members had to provide themselves with a framework of rules inside which to live together; and – equally important – a spiritual rationale for their new existence. On the material side, they had to see to the procurement of revenues, and to the maintenance of their houses. This was as imperative for the communities of the Counter-Reformation, created for the most part before 1640, as it was for the secular institutes of the Catholic Reformation, which began to take firm shape in the 1640s, and continued to evolve throughout the century.

In the course of the three centuries since Trent, the Catholic church has succeeded in establishing a harmony between the contemplative and the active religious life. The harmony was consecrated, in the twentieth century, by the adoption of Thérèse, the little Carmelite of Lisieux, as patroness of the missions. By this time the active orders found it less painful to acknowledge the contemplative life as a higher, more perfect form of religious life.

This only happened, however, after the day had been carried, in numerical terms, by the active orders. Throughout the nineteenth and twentieth centuries, the active congregations grew while the contemplative orders did not. By 1969, only 10 per cent of all female religious in France were contemplatives.[4] In the Old Regime the order was reversed: the *congréganistes* were always in the minority.[5] In the seventeenth century they were still newcomers, in a society that was suspicious of change. In consequence, they had to build defences, against attacks on their legitimacy, against the draining away of their best subjects into "real" religious life. The quarrel between the active and the contemplative orders was continuous and, sometimes, bitter.

As has been seen, resistance to change was particularly strong in France, where the continuing power struggle against the Protestants prolonged the siege mentality of the sixteenth century well into the seventeenth. The first active congregations aroused sharp controversy when they sought dispensation from formal vows and strict clausura. The Council of Trent had forbidden religious women to leave the grounds of their monastery without express approval from their bishop.[6] Many sincere reformers, like Archbishop Denis de Marquemont of Lyon, felt that the entire reform program would be jeopardized if exceptions were made.

Novelty was heresy. Innovation in feminine religious life was scandalous. Long before it was confirmed by the papacy's official condemnation of Mary Ward's institute (1630–31), this attitude reigned supreme, both in the Church and in society at large. Monsignor Ingoli, head of the Congregation *Propaganda Fidei*, was only driving the point home when, in 1629, in his correspondence over the suppression of the English Ladies, he wrote, "It matters little what the times demand, the Canon Law of the Church will not allow women to live in community, unless they become religious, and as this entails enclosure, then all congregations that refuse the enclosure must be suppressed."[7] In most quarters, the Church's need to rechristianize its people was not considered sufficient cause for any change in the monastic discipline of women.

It was therefore necessary, wherever innovation was attempted, to give it legitimacy by showing that it was, in fact, a return to old tradition. This could be done either by appealing to precedents in Church history or – even better – by pointing to a scriptural model. An extensive polemic had to be developed to protect the new congregations against their critics.

The reformers argued that history showed that the law on clausura could be applied in mitigated form. "Clausura does not consist in an unchangeable, indivisible form," wrote Fourier; "it is capable of being more, or of being less."[8] François de Sales insisted that strict clausura was a recent phenomenon in the Church's life, and that many holy congregations had flourished before it came into effect. His argument received confirmation from the great Cardinal Bellarmine: "Before Boniface VIII, there were religious who were not confined to their monasteries in the sense that they could not go out when it was necessary ... Solemn vows and strict clausura only became Church law under Boniface VIII."[9]

The event referred to by Bellarmine – the decree of Boniface VIII in 1298, enforcing strict clausura – became a sort of watershed in the eyes of the protagonists of change. They appealed beyond the Church of recent history to the Church of earlier times. "I have no thought of making innovations," wrote Anne de Xainctonge; "... however, as early as the first centuries of Christianity, we find deaconesses entrusted with various outside ministries. It was they who took care of the women and young girls, and undertook to instruct them in preparation for baptism ... So it is not an innovation, but the resurrection of a usage which had its justification then, and does so again today."[10]

This appeal to the example of the deaconesses and the apostolic women of the early Church remained one of the favourite arguments of proponents of the active religious life. It reinforced the position they had already taken. Thus the Filles de la Croix, the first religious community of women to live under simple vows in France, in a prospectus describing the work that they did "for the poor of their sex in all their spiritual needs," added: "They have been all the more strengthened in this worthy course since they have learned that in other times the Church employed the widows and unmarried women who gave themselves to its service, and who on this account were called *Deaconesses* ... as is seen in the fourth Council of Carthage and in many others."[11]

But the deaconesses of the early Church, while they served as a useful precedent, did not give the new congregations much to work with. The faithful of the seventeenth century needed models whom they might imitate, patrons to whom they might pray. For this they went to the Gospel and to tradition. A whole new cluster of devotions appeared in the seventeenth century, most of them developed by various religious orders.[12] Some of these devotions were to saints and angels, others were to the various "states" of Christ. Thus the "mixed life" of Jesus – his life of contemplation and preaching – was the principal model for the Jesuits; Mary Magdalen, "the humble and fervent disciple of Jesus, sitting constantly at his feets, attentive to his word"[13], was the special patroness of the Carmelites; Martha became the patroness of *hospitalières* and of other cloistered nuns who served the poor.[14] Teachers invoked the guardian angels, whose task so perfectly prefigured their own. Thus Anne de Xainctonge pointed to their example, comparing them favourably to the cherubim, whose only function was to contemplate God, and concluding: "Since this good Master has destined us to perform the work of guardian angels in our classrooms, let us follow the example of the angels of Heaven."[15]

But the principal patroness and model of the congregations was the Virgin. Almost every monastery and institute adopted her in a special way, sometimes electing her as abbess or superior of the community, always pointing to her as an example of the perfect religious. Many of the women's communities of France could have claimed, with the sisters of the Congrégation of Montreal, that "we have no other Constitutions but the life of the most blessed Virgin."[16]

As Charles Flachaire has demonstrated, the image of the Virgin changed in the course of the seventeenth century, from the "little princess," the "dear little mistress" of the Jesuits, for whose honour they were ready to do battle, to the personification of virginal purity, "clothed in a majesty both reasoned and severe"[17] to whom religious men and women could relate. To the Jansenists she was Jansenist, to the Carmelites, Carmelite; to the Sulpicians, the model for the clergy and the queen of the missions.[18] It is interesting, therefore, to see the way in which the active feminine congregations adopted her as their own, and endowed her with the special qualities that pertained to their vocation.

The devotion to the Education of the Virgin has already been mentioned.[19] This was part of a larger Catholic tradition which had built up around the early years of Mary: her birth to the aged Saint Anne, her girlhood as a consecrated virgin in the Temple of Jerusalem, and the series of miraculous events which led up to her marriage to Saint Joseph. Though without foundation in scripture, the tradition was immensely popular, as paintings and statues in numberless churches attest.

The tradition was solidified in the Counter-Reformation. The feast of the Presentation of the Virgin became the patronal feast of Saint-Sulpice, and by extension, of the clergy. It was treated as doctrine in catechisms. "How long after her birth did the most Holy Virgin remain in the house of her father and mother?" children were asked; "At the end of three years where did she go?" And they answered, "To the Temple of Jerusalem, to offer and consecrate herself entirely to God, with many other holy virgins, who lived together in the Temple."[20] The tradition was incorporated into the faith and the spirituality of Catholics.

No one found it more inspiring than the new *dévot* schoolmistresses, because it helped to authorize the lives that they were establishing for themselves. They concentrated on two themes: Mary's consecrated life in the temple, and the work that she did there, instructing young girls. Depending on the emphasis of their own lives, they stressed either the first or the second theme. Thus Alix Le Clerc, whose natural bent was towards the cloister, wrote: "The blessed Virgin in the Temple worked like the other girls, and like them performed the common duties; but at certain times she retired to devote herself more particularly to prayer, and to the contemplation of divine things – in which she is the model for the exercises of the sisters of the Congregation."[21] On the other hand Marguerite Bourgeoys, the *fille de paroisse* for whom the Virgin was the model for an active, uncloistered life, drew a different picture: "All the time that she was in the Temple, which was the school for girls, she was an edification for all the others, and by her instructions and by her actions, doing the work of a servant, she served her companions in every way she could, and taught them many kinds of worthwhile skills."[22] The two women, both schoolmistresses, used the same devotion to justify their different interpretations of the active life.

The mystery *par excellence* of the active congregations was the mystery of the Visitation. "Mary set out ... and went as quickly as she could to a town in the hill country of Judah." This event in the Gospel of Luke, which had attracted little devotion in the past, came into its own in the seventeenth century. François de Sales introduced it as the perfect model for his new community, in which he hoped to combine the corporal acts of mercy with the contemplative life: "In this mystery the most glorious Virgin performed that solemn act of love for her neighbour ... but yet composed the canticle of the Magnificat, the sweetest, noblest, most spiritual and most contemplative [song] ever written."[23] It is significant that Archbishop de Marquemont, when he moved to cloister the congregation, pressed for a new title, that of the Presentation of the Virgin, "to which the offering of the sisters can be more closely related."[24] The implications of the Visitation were clear, both for the proponents and the opponents of the feminine active life.

The former won their case by degrees. It was difficult to dissociate women from the action of the greatest woman of all. Vincent de Paul readily invoked the Visitation for his women's *charités*: "They will honour the visit of the Blessed Virgin who went to visit her cousin cheerfully and promptly, while thinking some good thought."[25] But the implications of the new devotion went even deeper. Throughout the Catholic community, the Visitation became a symbol of the missionary mandate of the Church. Jean-Jacques Olier, the respected founder of Saint-Sulpice, wrote: "It is from the mystery of the Visitation that apostolic men and missionaries ought to draw the graces of their sublime vocation. From the moment that she conceived and formed Him in her womb, she, first of all, went out at once to announce Him, and thus did what the Apostles later did by her example."[26]

If the Virgin was a missionary, why could other women not be missionaries too? Where François de Sales had placed Mary's action at the service of her contemplation, and Vincent de Paul had used the same model to sanctify purely charitable activity, others invoked the Visitation as a sanction for a feminine apostolate. This was the meaning of Marguerite Bourgeoys's words, already quoted: "Monsieur Gendret once said to me that Our Lord had left three states in which women could follow and serve the Church: that [the state] of Saint Mary Magdalen was observed by the Carmelites and other recluses, and that of Saint Martha by the cloistered religious who serve their neighbour; but that the outgoing life of the Blessed Virgin was not honoured as it should be, and that even without veil and wimple one could be a true religious."[27]

The idea that women might participate in the apostolate, which was so thoroughly condemned within the Church on the authority of Saint Paul, was made respectable on the authority of the Blessed Virgin.

The feminine apostolate received further consecration from the model of Mary, Queen of Apostles. According to scripture, Mary was present in the upper room in the days before Pentecost.[28] In the growing marian devotion which marked the seventeenth century, this presence became central: Mary ruled the apostles, and gave them their orders to preach the gospel. "It is true that outwardly Saint Peter, being the image of Jesus Christ, had power over her; but inwardly he submitted to the most Blessed Virgin," wrote Olier.[29] The primacy of Mary in the early Church became an article of faith, which Christians could see expressed through the medium of devotional art.

Mary's participation in the work of the early Church was usually linked to the work of lesser women who, according to tradition, had assisted the apostles, the "devout, holy and fervent women, young and old, who lived in their time, and assisted them in the conquest of souls, by their prayers and good example, by their austerities, and by their great works."[30] Whereas her example on its own might arguably have been beyond the power of mere women to imitate, the holy women provided a link between the supernatural and the natural. They were not simply subjects for meditation; they were exhortations to action. Among the *dévots*, contemplation was nothing if not a call to imitation. Thus the logic of seventeenth-century piety allowed women gradually to claim new areas of activity. "We go on missions to contribute to the education of children, because the Blessed Virgin, by visiting Elizabeth, contributed to the sanctification of Saint John the Baptist," wrote Marguerite Bourgeoys in the 1690s.[31] By this time, her claim to a missionary role was no longer beyond the realm of reason. The feminine active religious life was no longer looked upon as something outside divine law.

However, it was still seen as an inferior state, less perfect than the contemplative life. "We are asked why we would rather be wanderers than be cloistered," Soeur Bourgeoys wrote, "... and why we do not take solemn vows which lead to great perfection, the reason why women are moved to embrace religion; which is more honourable."[32] The *filles séculières* were constantly forced to defend themselves against this imputation of inferiority. "The religious state is certainly holy," Monsieur Vincent protested, "but it doesn't follow that only those who embrace it are sanctified."[33] However, custom ruled otherwise. The formal religious state carried with it not only respect, but spiritual advantage, in the form of indulgences. Ineligibility for indulgences was a serious matter, as Mademoiselle Le

Gras decided, when she petitioned the pope to grant a special indulgence to all the sisters who persevered in the company until
death. But in general, the merit of the secular institutes remained
hidden and unrecognized.

That the *filles séculières* found this hard to accept may be deduced,
both from the defensiveness of the literature, and from the problems
that the institutes had in keeping their members from entering formal religious life in search of true perfection. Vincent de Paul actually
discouraged his sisters from associating with religious: "As for the
grandeur of religious, leave it alone; treat them with great esteem
but do not seek their company, not because it is not good and highly
excellent, but because the communication of their particular spirit
is not right for you."[34]

Barré was even more emphatic:

When a mistress of the Charity Schools is tempted to leave her work to
enter a religious house, let her take care what she is doing. She is abandoning
a state that is more evangelical, more arduous, more poor, more despised
in the world, for another more comfortable, more honourable, but which
is useful only for herself ... In wishing to shut herself into a monastery,
she is like a cowardly soldier who wants always to be in garrison, never
out marching on campaign. She is leaving the spiritual war which she joined
for God and for Jesus, in order to rest and to live at ease, in a safe place,
unconcerned for the interests and the glory of her King."[35]

By means of preaching like this, an ideology was gradually developed which gave spiritual respectability to the active life. That
this was a long and painful process can be seen from the fact that
the fight, which began in the early 1600s, was still being joined in
the latter part of the century. Madame de Miramion, reflecting in
1678 on her own continuing attraction to the contemplative life,
concluded: "It still remains to make a sacrifice of all your time, to
be employed as He wishes, and not as you wish ... Whoever is called
to retreat, let him stay there; whoever is called to action, let him
act. The saints have eternity for contemplation, while for those who
are called, this life is given for work."[36]

The status of a community was reflected in the vows which its
members took upon entrance. Vows as such were of universal application; any adult could take them, and for any number of purposes. Vows of this sort were simple, private vows. Entrance into
a recognized religious order, however, was conditional upon the

taking of solemn vows. The aspirant made a public commitment, in front of witnesses and to an ecclesiastical superior, by which he or she officially "died to the world," and entered the religious state. These vows sprang from a medieval view of Church, according to which "everything was regulated according to the needs of the diocese, not the spiritual destiny of the person."[37] They were not so much a private affair of conscience as a social commitment made to, and received by, the Catholic community.

The founders of the new congregations recognized that solemn vows would lead directly to clausura. On the other hand, the absence of vows of any sort would strip their communities of all semblance of stability. They decided to follow the example of the new masculine orders, notably the Jesuits, and take simple vows of poverty, chastity, and obedience. These vows were perfectly valid. "Before God," wrote Cardinal Bellarmine to François de Sales, "simple vows are no less binding, and of no less merit, than solemn vows."[38] However, they did not entail the formal change of state, and the "civil death" so precious in the eyes of the seventeenth century. This made them unacceptable to the jurists of the Gallican church. In the face of opposition, and fearful of suppression, the early congregations gave up their innovations, and submitted to solemn vows with all their implications.

The novice, then, kneeling in the middle of the choir, and having at her sides the superior and the assistant, will say in an intelligible voice: I N... ask for the love of Our Lord God, to be received by holy Profession into the Congregation ... to devote myself within it all my life to the divine service, through obedience, chastity and poverty.

Having received her black veil, she rose and sang the verse, "Haec requies mea in saeculum saeculi" – "Here is my rest for all time." Then, prostrate before the grille, she was covered with a funeral pall while the Office of the Dead was recited.[39] Her commitment to her monastery was complete, and permanent.

The first *filles séculières*, the Filles de la Croix and the Filles de la Charité, took simple vows. But the juxtaposition of vows and community life soon raised questions as to what their actual status was. It seemed at the time to be without precedent.[40] Vincent de Paul, who as superior of the Visitation convent of rue Saint-Antoine was well acquainted with the history of that congregation, was determined that his *filles* would not be tempted, or coerced, into religion. "The Filles de la Charité cannot be said to be religious because to be religious it is necessary to be cloistered. The Filles de la Charité can never be religious; woe to anyone who talks of making them religious."[41] His purpose was to keep all the appearances of secularity, while giving his company the substance of religious life. He circumvented canon law, by ordering that individual sisters, on the private advice of their confessors, could take simple vows – the vows that any lay person was entitled to take – not *before* their superiors (and therefore in a stance that recalled solemn profession), but *in the hearing of* their superiors.[42]

There was no question in Monsieur Vincent's mind that his sisters were to be religious in all but name. There were other like-minded communities, in which the simple vows of poverty, chastity, and obedience were taken with considerable ceremony; sometimes a fourth vow of stability was added, to give the other vows permanence.[43] But this marked "religious" dimension is not found in all communities of *filles séculières*. Indeed, the basic arrangement, practised by many small communities, was simply a notarized agreement between the entrant and the superiors, the former promising to observe the rules of the house, the latter promising to feed and maintain her.[44] Between the one extreme and the other there was a wide variety of practices. In some cases, as for instance the Filles de Sainte-Geneviève, there was no vow of poverty; in others, no vow of obedience. Many communities made only promises. Among these were Barré's sisters, who were asked only to "live in community, without taking vows, or observing clausura, under the direction of their superior, whom they are obliged to obey in the truth of pure and holy love."[45]

This term, "pure love," became the codeword for a new relationship between the communities and their members. Although the *filles séculières* varied in the degree of their secularity, all shared one characteristic: they rejected the principle of perpetual commitment which the religious "state" implied. The member who failed to fit into the institute, even though she had been formally admitted, would not be obliged to stay. "She will be put out": this was the community's ultimate punishment.[46] It was not forced to maintain an unwilling subject. "We do not want any prison among us, or any chains other than those of pure love," the sisters of Montreal told their bishop.[47]

As with individuals, so with institutes: the "monastic temptation" was always very real. Communities could be upgraded, so to speak, and accepted into recognized religious orders. The founders were only too aware of this. Precautions were frequently written into their constitutions, to guard against such an eventuality. Many acts of foundation stipulated that if the community came to be cloistered, all moneys should pass to another institute. The frequency of defensive strategies such as these provide more evidence of the precarious state of the *filles séculières* vis-à-vis the cloister, and the attraction which *dévotes* of the seventeenth century continued to feel for the contemplative life.

However, the active communities never lacked for supporters. Not all women longed for "flight from the world." Many, active by nature, found their vocation in action. "It was God alone that made me know that I did not have to make myself invisible to glorify Him, and that I could be His without burying myself behind the grilles of a cloister," wrote Anne de Xainctonge.[48] Desirée d'Antoine confessed to her Ursuline companions that in the work of preparing penitents for confession "she felt more filled with God than she did while praying."[49] The Marquise de Portes, a friend of Olier, also received a sign that she was not meant for the cloister; "she feels an inward desire which moves her to the service of her neighbour."[50] Many women were sincerely happy in the active life, for all its hardship and social inferiority; indeed, they even managed to feel guilty about their happiness. When some schoolmistresses admitted that they often found an inspiration in their classrooms that they did not find in prayer, Barré allayed their scruples: "It is here that He visits them and enriches them with His favours, to make them understand it is here that He wants them."[51] Perhaps the most touching testimonial of the pleasure that could be felt in active service came in the confession of a Fille de la Charité on her deathbed: "I had too much satisfaction when I went into the villages to see those good folk; I was almost flying, so much joy did I feel in serving them."[52]

Once they had adopted the status and rule of established "religion" in the early years of the seventeenth century, the new congregations at once adopted the monastic structures that went with it. All female monasteries were considered as minors, "in a state of wardship,"[53] subject to the control of a canonical superior. In the case of most of the new congregations this was the bishop, or his delegate. The canonical superior had final responsibility for the community's spiritual and temporal well-being. A visitor, chosen from either the secular or the regular clergy, made periodic inspections to verify the regularity of the monastery. Regular confessors were also appointed to the community, though the nuns' right to confess, at intervals, to another priest were respected. This was in accordance with the ruling of the Council of Trent, and it made it more difficult for individual confessors to gain complete control of the religious.[54]

The day-to-day government of the monastery was the responsibility of the superior, or prioress, elected by the community for a three-year term. She had extensive powers over every aspect of the monastery's life. She was assisted by a group of officers, some of whom she nominated, others of whom were elected. These officers met in council to oversee the finances and to decide matters of policy. The council's function was advisory rather than deliberative: the superior's decisions were almost always ratified. The community as a whole expressed itself only through the election of the superior and the officers – and at that, only the senior choir nuns known as *vocales* were allowed to vote. The novices, the young *professes*, and the lay sisters were without a voice. Religious communities, like the rest of society, were defined by a strict hierarchy.[55]

For a short time at the beginning, this hierarchy was less rigid. The first nuns took a part in the original work of creating their community life. The correspondence of the founders is full of suggestions from the members, many of which were later incorporated into the rules. Sometimes the input even of junior members was actively sought. Thus the Canonesses of Saint Augustine of Dieppe, in 1627, submitted various points of the rule to discussion by the novices, to know "what they liked better, or rather what they found to be the more perfect."[56] The same process took place at Faubourg Saint-Jacques.[57] A great many of the monastery's customs came first from suggestions from the nuns themselves.

However, within a few years of foundation, when the constitutions had been definitively drawn up and approved, no major redirection of the community's life was possible, either by the nuns themselves, their superiors, or even the bishops. The rule, as constituted, fixed the life of the community, down to the smallest actions of everyday life.

The rule was the community's charter. Its general statements on poverty, prayer, chastity, humility, obedience, and fraternal correction formed a framework on which their more elaborate and up-to-date *règlements* could be built. Every event in the community's life was subject to regulation, from the admission of novices to the burial of the dead. Every nun was expected to learn her rule by heart, and to hear it read at regular intervals. Even the minutest details were the subject of general knowledge.

The rule protected the community by providing an authoritive answer to all challenges, either from without or from within. Nuns could appeal to their rule, if need arose, even against the ordinary. Thus the Ursulines of Nantes challenged the bishop's right to impose a superior on them without an election: "We wish to live and die in the obedience of our Rules, Bull, and Apostolic Constitutions."[58] However, the disadvantage of so permanent an authority was that it encouraged scrupulosity. The ideal of perfection was too often confused with a literal observance of the rule.[59] Once fixed in writing, the life of the monastery ceased to change and grow. To take one example: the rule of the Ursulines of Paris, after undergoing a thirty-year period of trial and adaptation, was fixed in its final form in 1640, and then remained unchanged until the Revolution.[60]

The imposition of monasticism entailed the imposition of a monastic economy. The house had henceforth to be complete in itself. A whole gamut of minor offices was necessary, to assist the community's physical and spiritual functions. "Superior, assistant, mistress of novices, intendante, prefect, mistress of day students and of boarders, bursar, choir mistress, sacristan, portress, table servants, baker, mistresses of the workroom, the cloakroom, the linen room, the infirmary; apothecary, the reader for the refectory, the person who corrects the faults which are made in the reading in the refectory, keeper of the stores, gardener, librarian, chaperone of the parlour ..."; these offices, and others, many of which required assistants, absorbed much of the personnel of the monastery. "Care will be taken that the monastery has all the officers that it needs, for on them depends good government," wrote Fourier.[61] In addition to the choir nuns, each community admitted a number of lay sisters to do the heavy work, and one or two *tourières* to perform the outside errands. About half the members of an average monastery had occupations other than teaching.

This considerable population was dependent on the monastery for its support. From the moment of profession, a nun and her community were committed to each other for life. Monasteries had, therefore, to anticipate periods of support for members who were no longer productive. It was essential for a well-run house to secure its sources of income. These fell under three headings: gifts and endowments; earnings; dowries.

At the inception of every religious community there was a temporal founder (or in the case of a feminine community, more commonly a foundress). This person presided over the community's birth – frequently a difficult and lengthy process. To give one example: Madame d'Aclainville, foundress of the Ursuline monastery in Rouen, obtained for it a papal bull, letters patent, episcopal approbation, municipal approbation, and a decree from the Parlement of Normandie. She then went to Paris for three nuns to begin the establishment. Finally, she made a donation of eight thousand livres in capital and two hundred livres in *rentes*.[62] The reward for this effort was the title of foundress, and the privileges that went with it.

Foundations often came with difficult conditions attached, for which the nuns paid heavily through the years. Frequently the founders reserved the right to nominate persons to the community. Thus the Ursulines of Boulogne were bequeathed a property on condition that two poor girls be received and educated in perpetuity.[63] The Ursulines of Le Havre received a donation of six thousand livres from Denis Barbey, "on condition that his daughter Marguerite will be considered as foundress, and received and maintained her whole life long, if she wishes to be professed."[64] The official of Toul offered the nuns of the Congrégation a new foundation at Neufchâtel, on condition that they admit into their community his niece, who was a cripple.[65]

Foundations were usually exhausted fairly rapidly. Further gifts, from the same or other donors, were quickly ploughed back into the temporal, in the form of new buildings or acquisitions of land, or embellishments to the chapel. The beauty of their chapels was a matter for subtle competition between communities, and no one was anxious to fall behind; "which may give seculars cause to think that we do not have great care for the service of God."[66] On the other hand, there were quarters to be built for the novices, and new facilities for the boarders; these, also, were needed to create a favourable impression among supporters. Many monasteries undertook, and completed, ambitious building programs during the seventeenth century.

The day-to-day running of the house, therefore, usually depended on other resources. By the terms of their contracts with the municipalities, the teaching congregations were forbidden to beg. They were also required to provide free schooling, an obligation to which they were usually firmly held by the municipalities. "The religious were established here solely for the good of the city," ran a declaration in Montbrison at the time of the Revolution, "which is to say for the free instruction and education of poor girls."[67] There was little, or more often no, opportunity for revenue from that direction. The nuns earned money in two ways: by handwork of various kinds, and by taking in boarders.

Handwork consisted mainly of needlework, lace, and weaving. A community, especially if it had spare hands, could raise substantial sums in this way. There is an instance of one Ursuline convent which was able to earn fifteen thousand livres with a single consignment. Some nuns, like the Ursulines of Besançon, specialized in banners, scapulars, and other embroideries for the cathedral.[68] Others made sweets and preserves. But where the community was already insufficient for its teaching load, these incidental activities were impossible. "Produced by the work of the religious – nothing," reported the Ursulines of Boulogne, in a financial statement. "Our institute obliges us to instruct and educate young girls both day students and boarders ... and this keeps us so busy that it is all we can do to perform the indispensable duties of the community."[69]

Boarders could be older women, retired to the monastery to end their days, or involuntary guests, incarcerated for religious, political, or moral reasons. However, for the most part they were young girls between the ages of five and eighteen, for whom the monastery was a school. Their *pension* varied with the social quality of the monastery. Thus the Ursulines in the little convent of Maringues charged one hundred livres per year, while the Ursulines of Paris charged two hundred and forty livres.[70] The number of boarders was seldom higher than thirty or forty, and often as few as three or four. Thus while they certainly constituted an important source of revenue, it was not enough in itself to support the monastery.

The principal source of income on which the religious communities depended was the dowries of their members. These, like the price of the *pensions*, varied with the social quality of the monastery. In 1662, the average dowry required by the monastery of Faubourg Saint-Jacques was ten thousand livres.[71] This was two thousand livres less than was asked at the Visitation of the rue Saint-Antoine,[72] but a great deal more than the average for Ursulines across the country, which ranged between twelve hundred and twenty-five hundred livres.[73]

The normal practice, if there was no immediate use for the dowry, was to invest it, either in property within the city, or in land, or – as was most often the case – in *constitutions de rente*. These last were, in actual fact, disguised loans: the seller advanced a lump sum to the purchaser, in return for which he received regular interest.[74] Thus many monasteries became bankers for their neighbourhood, and some – depending on the success of their dealings – became rich. However, a decision to build onto the cloister, or to buy another property, could quickly turn the lender into a borrower. Communities moved regularly between the one and the other activity.

The dependence of the new communities on the money market rather than on land led them into straitened circumstances as the century progressed. By mid-century, inflation was beginning to affect their income. In 1661, in the monastery of Faubourg Saint-Jacques, the building of a new dormitory wing, long anticipated, had to be delayed "because of the extraordinary price which grain has reached."[75] After 1689, the bursar was forced to borrow from time to time on the latest dowries, in order to pay the food bills.[76] Other houses, less well endowed or less prudently managed, went into debt, while some closed altogether. The monasteries' difficulties were aggravated by the government's search for revenues: first, by the reduction in the *rentes* paid by the Treasury,[77] then by its inclusion of the teaching congregations in corporations liable to the payment of *aides*, then by its demands for back payment for the rights of mortmain, which religious houses had usually taken for granted. In 1691, the back payment due from the monastery of Faubourg Saint-Jacques was assessed at twenty-six thousand livres, while that of smaller houses was assessed accordingly.[78] The instability of money, and the raids of the government on what they had long believed to be their exemptions, threw many communities into permanent financial embarrassment.

At the beginning of the eighteenth century, there were some two thousand feminine monasteries in France. Around five hundred of these were miserably poor.[79] Various reasons have been cited for their distress: the incompetence of superiors, the carelessness of bishops, the exigencies of royal fiscal policy. However, it may also be suggested that the economic structures of monasteries did not accord well with new realities. They had been founded and furnished during a period of indulgence, mostly under the regency of Marie de Medici, the reign of Louis XIII, and the regency of Anne of Austria. From the 1660s on they found themselves facing growing pressure from the royal government and the parlements, which now saw them more as burdens on the economy than as assets to society and bridges to heaven. At the same time, private charity began to dry up. The elites began to turn away from the foundations that they had once so enthusiastically espoused. Families were losing their commitment to the monasteries. And where they no longer gave their sons and daughters, they no longer gave their money.[80] Unlike the older monasteries, the new houses had not, for the most part, sufficient landholdings to act as a cushion against hard times. The maintenance and improvement of their buildings depended on donations which were now much less generous than before. However, their costs were permanently built in; their nuns and boarders had to be fed, their buildings maintained. From the time that the bursar began to borrow on the latest dowry to pay the butcher, they were in danger.

Perceptions were changing. The age of mysticism had passed, the age of moralism had begun.[81] For a public increasingly concerned with social welfare, and decreasingly impressed by the utility of *la vie parfaite*, monasteries did not offer good value. "The nuns of the Congregation number almost sixty, and they run one school; we don't need as many as that to run four," wrote Roland, comparing the work of his sisters in Reims to that of the local monastery.[82] Vincent de Paul had made the same observation regarding the cloistered *hospitalières* of Paris: the Filles de la Place Royale numbered forty religious to twenty-five sickbeds, the other *hospitalières* twenty-six to sixteen – whereas a handful of Filles de la Charité working in a parish were caring for up to sixty patients at a time.[83]

The monasteries' hard times paralleled the rise of the *filles séculières*. The basic difference in the nature of their community, and the terms of their recruitment, made the latter more congenial to the mind of the times of Louis XIV, and therefore more attractive to charitable donors.

The *filles séculières* were organized in a number of different ways. In some cases their institute was "founded," which meant that their house and their income were assured to them, in return for the performance of certain recognized duties. In other cases, they remained clear of permanent commitment, reserving their right to enter and leave employment as the conditions warranted. The most famous exercise of this right took place in 1694, when the group of Dames de Saint-Maur who were invited to establish the school at Saint-Cyr withdrew to avoid submitting to clausura.[84]

As a community grew, it became necessary to maintain at least a mother house, where young sisters could be trained and old sisters retire. But the bulk of their work was done elsewhere – either within the neighbourhood or across the country. Therefore the communities remained simple in their structures. A superior, who was sometimes elected, sometimes appointed by the trustees, governed the community with the same moral authority as did the prioresses of the monasteries. No seventeenth-century community could have conceived of a life without obedience to authority. "A community is nothing but a Tower of Babel if obedience does not rule and order all things."[85] Even in the two-member communities of the Filles de la Charité, one sister was named as superior over the other.[86] However, a new stress was laid on the equality of the sisters: "thus the Superior, after her resignation, can be employed in any of the offices of the house according to her capacity."[87] A swift rotation was often recommended: "by this means Superiors, having become inferiors, can hope to become superior in virtue and therefore in truth."[88]

The number of officers was kept to a minimum. Two assistants, a sacristan, a portress, and a cook were as much as was necessary for these small working houses; and indeed, many communities had to do with less. Where there were fewer than four members, the superior kept the accounts herself.[89] All the sisters, including the superior, were expected to help with the chores.[90] The stately order of the monastery was exchanged for mundane efficiency, because the women knew that their main work was elsewhere.

Some of the houses were provided from the outset with the revenues to support their work. These funds could be administered, in the tradition of the *hôpitaux-généraux* from which many communities took their start, by a board of trustees.[91] They could also be administered by the sisters themselves, as in the case of the communities in Reims and Montreal.[92] It should be remarked that the passage of time, and the proliferation of communities, had succeeded in allaying early fears about feminine incompetence in money matters. By the latter part of the century, both cloistered nuns and *filles séculières* could be found managing their own communities' affairs.

Many other *filles séculières* were salaried workers. The members were sent out to work for an agreed payment, to be made to the institute by the local hospital, parish, or municipality that had requested them. Arrangements varied from case to case. Sometimes payment was provided through an individual foundation, which could be very small. In the village of Saint-Saturnin près d'Aumâle, for instance, a foundation of fifty livres' *rente* for one sister was set up in 1698. Since the sisters normally came in pairs, at least, this left the rest of the money to be raised in some other way – how, the records do not tell us.[93] Larger corporations often settled for annual payments. The city of Toulouse paid its Dames de Saint-Maur a generous "hundred and eighty livres each and a hundred livres for their servant."[94] The usual salary was one hundred and fifty livres, plus board and lodging. The three schoolmistresses who were established in Bonnétable, in 1690, were provided with a vegetable garden, bread, meat, and wood, in addition to their pay. For this they taught two hundred children on a regular basis (three hundred during Lent and before First Communion), and visited the sick.[95] This was a bargain, as many charitable donors must have seen. Schoolmistresses cost considerably less than schoolmasters, who could usually expect upwards of two hundred livres.[96] The Filles de la Charité went into the hospitals on contract, or, if they worked in the parishes, were paid by the local ladies' *charités*, first for the care of the sick and, second, for the conduct of a class for poor girls. They were never well paid. In their spare time, they did handwork and spinning, to raise money for the institute.[97]

The original goal of the founders of the monastic congregations had been to choose their membership without reference to money. "It is not gold and silver that make good monasteries," Anne de Vesvres had written, "but the virtues which the members bring and which they practise."[98] François de Sales had looked forward to a day when monastic revenues could be limited, "so that even in this matter moderation will be followed, and there will be no superfluity of goods in the congregation."[99] Jacquette de Chesnel, first superior of the Filles de Notre-Dame at La Flèche, desired the same thing for the same reason: "She said that if the house was sufficiently endowed for the food and board of the nuns, she would not take a dowry for the women who entered religion, but only pensions, considering that great temporal wealth ruins religious houses, and there is as much to fear from seeing them too rich as too poor."[100]

However, the financial equilibrium which the founders anticipated did not materialize, and considerations of dowry came more and more to dominate the choice of novices. The reception of a new postulant was preceded by a bargaining session between her family and the bursar of the monastery, in which the latter's hand was strengthened as vacancies in the community filled up and the waiting list of aspirants grew. Some women of modest means were still accepted as choir nuns, but these became ever more the exception. In fact, women of good family and little fortune were often forced to enter as lay sisters, like the novice in the Visitation for whom "a numerous family did not permit Monsieur her father to give her a dowry sufficient for any rank but that of domestic sister."[101]

In fact, dowries tended to increase in size as time passed. This caused considerable resentment; the public, from the 1630s onwards, was ever more of the opinion that the religious orders were devouring too many private fortunes. An infamous case involving a sixteen-year-old heiress, Marie de Castelnau, whose dowry was set at thirty thousand livres by the Ursulines of Faubourg Saint-Jacques, confirmed all the worst suspicions, and inspired the Parlement of Paris to order the elimination of all dowries in favour of life pensions.[102] However, dowries continued to be negotiated. In 1693, a royal proclamation ordered congregations to limit themselves to life pensions of three hundred and fifty to five hundred livres, plus initial payments of twelve hundred to two thousand livres. The congregations evaded the law, by no longer passing formal contracts.[103] Dowries were too important to the monastic economy to be foregone.

Dowries served a social, as well as a financial, purpose. They provided the means by which aspirants could be sorted out according to rank and income. In seventeenth-century France, the women's monasteries were an integral part of the social fabric. Depending on their location, they became the preserve of whatever families constituted the dominant society: noble and bourgeois-merchant in cities like Rouen, "nobles et nobles hommes" in Blois,[104] *noblesse de robe* in parlementary cities like Rennes.[105] The monasteries offered an honourable "state" for their daughters. In return, the families formed an extensive support system, on which the monasteries could draw for all their needs.[106]

The close relationship between the monastery and the pious family provides a key to the rise and decline of monastic vocations. Throughout most of the seventeenth century, after the initial phase of foundation was over, the majority of entrants into the feminine religious life were young girls. They were frequently fresh out of school – as often as not, the *pensionnats* of the very monasteries which they were now entering. This was perfectly legal as long as they had reached sixteen, when, according to canon and civil law, they were capable of making their profession. But the monasteries interpreted the law liberally, and many girls were professed before the canonical age. "These poor children are pushed into these perpetual prisons," wrote Oudart Coquault. "They are put in at ten, eleven, and twelve years, clothed at thirteen or fourteen, and professed at fifteen at the latest. More than four years later they still don't know what they have done; it is at twenty-two, twenty-three, twenty-four and twentyfive that they begin to realize what sex they belong to."[107]

Even sixteen seemed to many contemporaries an early age for so final a decision. Only too clearly, the interests of the girls themselves were confounded with the piety, or the self-interest, or both, of their families. This is not to say that they were physically forced into religious life. The Council of Trent had condemned forced vocations, and the Church guarded against them by ruling that novices must be questioned by a representative of the bishop before profession. But no last-minute precautions could neutralize the effects of a conditioning that often began in early childhood. "One goes," wrote Jean Cordier in 1643, "to the clothing of a girl who has been trained to respond according to the wishes of her father and mother, not her own wishes. They dress her like a little goddess ... They assemble her relatives, they ask her, My daughter, do you wish to be a religious? Her conscience says no but her mouth, betraying her heart, says yes. They throw her into religion as though into the arms of an Idol."[108] According to Vincent de Paul, this made for insipid, unmotivated religious. "They do not have a true vocation, since they were put there by their parents, and stay there out of human respect."[109]

Family pressure must help to explain the huge burgeoning of feminine vocations in the first four decades of the seventeenth century, and the falling-away which occurred thereafter. This pattern is revealed in the monastic books of profession. It appears that the number of vocations peaked in the 1620s and 1630s, while, at the same time, the average age of entrants dropped, from twenty-four in the earliest years to under eighteen. Indeed, from the mid 1620s to the early 1670s, more than half the entrants were aged seventeen or less; approximately one-quarter were fifteen or under.[110] These were for the most part boarders, moving straight into religious life within the walls of the only home that they had known for most of their lives.

The same study shows that by the end of the 1660s the number of entrants into religion was in decline. This supports the thesis of Jean de Viguerie, that the phase of positive promotion of religious vocations by families ended in the 1660s; that from now on, families were more likely to oppose than to encourage religious vocations.[111] At the same time, the average age of entrants was rising.[112] Most families of quality turned against schoolgirl vocations; and with that the rush into the monasteries came to an end.

The secular institutes recruited, for the most part, from a different population. "Most of them are daughters of peasant farmers or of artisans," said Vincent de Paul of the Filles de la Charité, "and if there is some noble blood, it is rare."[113] In fact, the *filles séculières* seem to have included women from all walks of life. But even though they often accepted a dowry, the institutes did not depend on it for their choice of subjects. The humble working life of their members was a source of strength to them, because it freed them from the tyranny of heavy expenses. Superiors were able, if they wished, to dispense with dowry requirements. "When the women have a true vocation and are suitable for the community, they bring their own dowry and call down the grace of God upon the house," wrote Marguerite Bourgeoys.[114]

Because the women worked for their living, they did not require preliminary funding. "They have to bring something to wear for the start, as well as their linen and small clothes, and some money to take them home, in case they cannot get used to the lifestyle of this little company," Vincent de Paul wrote for the benefit of new postulants.[115] Criteria as modest as this imprinted an essentially humble character upon the communities that set them. Indeed, the problem that the secular institutes faced was one of preventing women from entering their communities simply as an escape from poverty, or, as Mademoiselle Le Gras suspected, so that they might see a bit of the world.[116] Hard work and austere living conditions were seen as the best cure for that. But the point must be made that the *filles séculières*, for all the rigours of their lives, were often no worse off than they would have been "in the world."[117]

The *filles séculières* differed from cloistered nuns in another important respect: they were mobile – a sure sign of the modest social standing of their profession. They were free to go "out of doors" in the performance of their work. In spite of the proven usefulness of this freedom, it remained a sensitive subject throughout the century. Society questioned the regularity, and even the moral character, of religious women who were not enclosed. "We are asked why we would rather be wanderers than cloistered, the cloister being the conservation of our sex," wrote Marguerite Bourgeoys.[118] The secular institutes took defensive action, by circumscribing the women's outdoor activity with every possible precaution. The sisters were never to go out without the superior's permission. They were not to visit, or eat with, family and friends. Wherever possible, they were to travel in twos. Their bearing was carefully prescribed: "In the streets, they will walk modestly with their eyes cast down, and they will not stop to talk to anybody, particularly of the other sex, unless there is serious need; and at that, they must cut the conversation short and go quickly on their way."[119] Because their life "exposed them to many occasions of sin," postulants were not usually accepted under the age of eighteen. As Vincent de Paul pointed out, "when a religious would like to commit sin, the grille is closed"; for the *filles*, however, their only grille was the fear of God, their only cloister the city streets.[120]

Some of the *filles séculières* took their mobility further, and travelled to postings across the country. "They are so entirely dependent on their Superior, that they are ready at the slightest word to change places without resistance, and to go everywhere in complete indifference," wrote Barré.[121] In seventeenth-century minds, this "indifference" was heroic. The rule of stability which bound religious to their monasteries, and which seems inhibiting to the modern mind, was, in fact, a comfort that many women were loath to abandon. Monastic communities were close-knit, intensely loyal, and unused to the idea of separation. Thus the Ursulines' annals describe the distress of the Paris community when Mère Saint-Dominique was sent away to head the new convent of Rouen: "The religious, almost all of whom she had guided in the noviciate, dissolved into tears; the boarders, whose Mistress-General she was, uttered loud cries, all of them regretting her as much as if they had personally lost their own mother."[122] Furthermore, even where the nuns themselves were prepared to move for the purpose of founding a new house, their families often resisted the idea strenuously.

The communities of *filles séculières* which expanded beyond a single house still tended to remain within narrow regional bounds. The foundations of the late seventeenth and early eighteenth centuries, in fact, were often diocesan, with the bishops taking a leading part in the work of creation. However, the few secular institutes that developed a wider base were able to achieve the autonomy and unity that had been denied to all women's congregations at the beginning of the century. The originality of Barré's *maîtresses charitables*, and of the Filles de la Charité, was that they transcended diocesan boundaries. The members were directed from the centre, and were ultimately responsible to the centre. "When the sisters are requested somewhere, the people who ask for them are free to send them away when they wish. Since they are not founded, and do not wish to be founded, the parties are left free and under no obligation on either side," wrote Barré.[123] These larger institutes, few in number, were the forerunners of the active congregations, with their internal government and superiors-general, which became so successful in the nineteenth century.

At a time when sumptuary laws were still in vigour, it is not surprising that the dress worn by different communities helped to define their social and religious status. The monastic teaching communities had, from the outset, given up the extremes of religious dress, as unsuitable for their work with secular persons.[124] However, their dress, though modified, remained very much the religious habit, complete with veil and wimple, worn over the cropped hair that symbolized their death to the world.

The *filles séculières* followed three basic rules: they dressed modestly, avoiding all extremes; they dressed to suit their station in life; and they avoided the marks of "religion," notably the veil.

At the lower end of the social scale were the Filles de la Charité, designed by their founders to remain humble, both in their recruitment and in their work. "God in His goodness has been pleased first and foremost to call village women to make up your company," Vincent de Paul told them. To those who were not villagers by birth, he recommended that they become so by imitation.[125] Therefore they dressed as did country women of the Paris basin, in coarse grey serge, with a white linen turban. The costume, and especially the headwear, caused embarrassment to some of the sisters, but Monsieur Vincent remained adamant. The humble dress was symbolic of their vocation of service. "Say that you wish to wear the crown that God first prepared for the Filles de Sainte-Marie," he said, in direct reference to the nuns of the Visitation, who by accepting clausura gave up their work among the sick and poor.[126] Only later, at the end of the century, did the Filles de la Charité adopt the starched cornets by which they became known to the world.

Grey, or brown, was the colour commonly worn by lower-class women. It was also the colour associated with women who worked for the *hôpitaux-généraux*. The first *soeurs Barré* of Rouen, though drawn largely from the middle classes,[127] have left a portrait of one of their sisters in working women's dress. In general, however, schoolmistresses were dressed as *bourgeoises* and as widows: in black, with a coif enclosing their hair,[128] and tying under the chin, and a large black kerchief, also knotted under the chin, covering head and neck. Only common materials were allowed, in dresses, stockings, gloves, and shoes, so that the modesty of their station in life should be emphasized. Even the colour of their underskirts conveyed a message: "A schoolmistress of the Saint-Enfant Jésus is more appreciated with a good grey petticoat under her dress, than with a black petticoat which always gives a higher air."[129]

One exception to this bourgeois pattern may be found in the dress of the Dames de Saint-Maur who were employed in Saint-Cyr. For them Madame de Maintenon designed a special dress, decent but rich enough to fit the noble circumstances in which they were living. In other situations, their dress was designed to testify clearly to the social station of the *filles séculières*. It was also meant to convey the spirit of modest and sensible piety which they held to be characteristic of their institutes. But, like the life itself, it lacked grandeur – and herein lay a problem.

"The contemplative is like Rachel, beautiful but sterile," wrote Barré. "Leah who was ugly, but fertile, is the true symbol of the active life."[130] In this telling defence by their most ardent supporter, the dilemma of the *filles séculières* is revealed. They had won the blessing of their society, especially of the governing elites, because of their usefulness. But their institutes were essentially unglamorous and unaristocratic, at a time when appearance and rank counted for a great deal.

The vow of poverty which was universally taken in the monasteries had not eliminated class differences. Indeed, according to Mère Juchereau of the Hôtel-Dieu of Quebec, the nuns of France were "more intoxicated by their rank than the most worldly of worldly women."[131] Marguerite Bourgeoys defined the chasm that divided the two types of life. The contemplative life was "austere," "in the deserts." (This was a clear allusion to the image of Mary Magdalen living as a hermit in her later years, and hence to the Carmelites, whose patron she was.) But it was also the portion of the rich. The "little life" of hard work and simplicity was "fitted to the condition of a poor woman."[132] The poverty which it involved was not the sort of poverty that attracted the rich. Women of quality might be capable of submitting to the rigours of contemplative rule, and sleeping on boards, and wearing hair shirts, but they could not go out alone. They could not do servile work. According to Vincent de Paul, that was why God chose poor women for the company: "If He had taken rich women, would they have done what these do? Would they have aided the sick with the most menial and arduous services?"[133] Though some women of high birth joined the secular institutes, they did so in defiance of the natural order of things. Most filles séculières came from more modest levels of society; and for this reason they had to battle against their own, and others', sense that they were inferior to "real" nuns.

The making of communities was a gradual process, involving the ideas and efforts, and trials and errors, of a number of people. At the forefront were the founders, men like Fourier, Vincent de Paul, and Nicolas Barré. They contributed leadership, ideas, spiritual motivation, and tactical skill. But the inspired founder, with his perfect blueprint for a new congregation, exists only in hagiography. There is ample evidence of the input of ordinary members, especially in the early years. Who made your community? Vincent de Paul once asked his sisters; "Not Mademoiselle Le Gras; she never thought of it. As for me, alas! I didn't dream of it."[134] He attributed the creation, after God, to Marguerite Naseau, the "poor cowherd without instruction" who became the first fille de la Charité. In fact, this congregation, and the others, were built through the joint efforts of the founders and the members. Even while it was in progress, however, their work was immediately subject to the wishes of the local hierarchy, to whom they owed obedience. It was also under the influence of the benefactors, who, because they paid the piper, were also able to call the tune. Arching over everything else was the influence of "the world," according to whose wishes and prejudices communities ultimately stood or fell.

The growth of the congregations could not have taken place without the changes which placed religious life at the service of the public. Society's growing demand for services – with schooling in the forefront – and the Church's determination to provide those services as a part of its mandate gave women their chance to become an indispensable part of the system. The congregations of the seventeenth century were shaped to the purposes of a particular society, and they reflected that society faithfully.

But society's contribution was supportive, not creative. The physical capability to take over such a role, and the psychological motivation to do it well, came from the women themselves. The institution which endowed them with this capability and this motivation was the religious community.

Conclusion

In 1631, a bull of suppression condemned, abolished, and cut off the Institute of the English Ladies, giving as reason that "they went freely everywhere, without submitting to the laws of clausura, under the pretext of working for the salvation of souls."[1] By 1700, in France and in New France, as well as in other parts of the Catholic world, women doing exactly this had become part of the Church's structure. The tridentine reform had rejected the "intermediate state" between religious and secular.[2] Now it was here, in fact if not yet in canon law. A new form of religious life had been created.

That this was a radical change in the Church's structure is self-evident. An enormous expansion of the Church's activity took place, into fields of charity and hospital care and education, because there were now personnel to implement it. The importance of this charitable mandate to the French church of the Old Regime can be understood best by seeing how hard, in the early days of the Revolution, it fought to hold onto it.

Furthermore, the new "active life" congregations were only the most visible part of a changing situation. The Gallican church had been opened up, to admit women to its professional ranks in numbers never known before. Not only in the active religious life, but in the contemplative life, women now outnumbered men. The Church had been "feminized." This fact, long considered to be of no significance, has now been proclaimed by one historian as perhaps the finest attainment of the Catholic Reformation.[3]

There was another dimension to the change in the structure of the seventeenth-century Church. This was the democratization of its personnel. More and more, the new secular institutes drew upon lower strata of society. For the first time, women "without veil or wimple"[4] – in other words, women unable to afford a dowry – were able to enter religious congregations. They became, from the very start of their involvement, the basic component in vast new structures of charity and education.

Quantitative change gives only the outline of inner psychological change. Throughout the seventeenth century, religious women influenced the tone of reformed Catholicism. A number of the most famous new devotions – to Saint Joseph, to the Holy Child, to the Sacred Heart – were promoted by nuns. Furthermore, to advance the active life to which they now laid claim, they endowed the Virgin with a new identity: she became a "vagabond," hurrying across the hills of Judah to serve her neighbour. "Virtue," in its old sense of courageous goodness, was no longer a male preserve. The literature is full of tributes by churchmen to the achievements of the new women. "They will be our judges," Vincent de Paul told his priests, "if we are not ready like them to risk our lives for God."[5]

How was the status of women within the Church affected by all this? According to one school of historians it remained uniformly dismal: the upper classes were kept confined within their cloisters, in frustration, dependence, and intellectual isolation, and the lower classes were assigned a position equivalent to that of a scullery maid in a rich and noble household. Another school argues that a promotion did, indeed, take place. If to all appearances the women's position remained humble and subordinate, in reality their prestige increased, and with it their influence. Jeanne-Françoise de Chantal, with her threadbare clothes and shabby shoes, and Marguerite du Saint-Sacrement, hidden in the cloister of her Carmel, were much more potent figures in their time than any medieval abbess with her vassals, her rights of justice and tithe, and her velour-covered throne.[6] As for the *filles séculières*, they were able, under the protection of their institutes, to develop what one historian calls "a professional life, consecrated to social action."[7]

I have argued for this second position. By modern standards the promotion left much to be desired, but we have only to return to the heated debates of the day to realize how serious a matter it was, and how much it was resented in more conservative circles. If in the final analysis the women did not get everything they hoped for, they got much more than some people thought they should have.

My second argument has concerned the process by which the promotion was effected. My contention has been that the principal agents of change were the women themselves. The great proliferation of schools and other charitable institutions which marked the times was made possible in the first place by the decisions of individual women to enter community life and undertake what they considered a meritorious and satisfying work. As community members, especially in the early days, they contributed to a common fund of ideas and practical methods which became the accepted wisdom, in many cases, for the rest of the Old Regime.

It should not be forgotten that they started from a position of disadvantage. Here and there, in the 1970s and 1980s, nuns have begun again to act as outsiders, challenging societies and governments and, sometimes, even the Church. But most Catholics throughout the last three hundred years would have considered such behaviour almost unthinkable. Before Vatican ii, as far back as memory could reach, nuns were the epitome of respectability within the community – pillars of the establishment. It would have been as difficult in 1950 as in 1850, or 1750, to recall that at one time nuns were outside the system, and that many of them, like the first Ursulines of Dijon, suffered for their nonconformity: "Whenever they passed in the streets, they were looked upon with scorn; the little children shouted after them and threw mud at them."[8]

Yet this, I must insist, was the starting point of their "promotion." Religious women entered new fields of activity in small stages, and with great difficulty. Their first efforts to "do all the good that is possible," and more especially, to catechize in the Catholic faith, were severely limited when they were ordered back into the cloister. However, they won the recognition that the instruction of girls was a worthy religious vocation; and this recognition was entrenched in their fourth vow. From within their monastery classrooms, double-locked so as not to violate clausura, they showed the clergy, and the public, that the instruction of girls was desirable.

As long as nuns remained in the cloister, a vast part of the population remained beyond their reach. Starting in the late 1630s, new approaches were explored, new ways in which women could work among the poor. These approaches were made under the rubric of charity, and they were made by women who were secular. Under this cover, which the authorities found less threatening, some women adopted elements of the religious life that they were denied; and among their charitable works they included teaching. Then, as the voluntary good works of the 1650s gave way to the institutions of the 1660s, charity schools for the poor were not only tolerated, but positively encouraged; and female teachers found themselves with a profession. Throughout the later years of the century, communities of teaching *filles séculières* appeared in growing numbers, and their teaching reached beyond the classrooms, to religious instruction *en mission*. Nun-educators became part of the Church's active personnel, pursuing an activity which the Crown, and society as a whole, now considered respectable.

It is misleading to say that the Church "called forth" these religious women. The Church of the Old Regime did not in general welcome change, and regarded this particular change with considerable suspicion. Where, then, did the impulse come from? From below? But the Catholic church was not then, any more than it is now, a democracy. No institutional channels existed by which the faithful could assist in its decision-making. Indeed, the structure of authority was never stronger than in the seventeenth century, when obedience was perceived as the supreme, the all-encompassing virtue.[9]

Yet women, who as a group were heirs to a subordinate status and a long tradition of obedience, nevertheless managed to break out of the state to which scripture and tradition had assigned them, and to establish a new identity for themselves. They had allies, and they had able leaders, many of whom were men. But the troops in this particular campaign were women. "They existed, they endured, and they made themselves known. They received their 'consecration' through the good that they did."[10] In the final analysis, it was by their numbers and their enthusiasm that the day was won.

Appendix: Entries and Professions in the Teaching Congregations (1611–1700)

Well-run monasteries kept records of their membership. Among these were two principal records: registers of clothings, and registers of professions. These were sometimes combined under a single cover, sometimes kept separate. Twelve of these records have been collected, for a total of 1141 subjects. Some of them list professions *and* clothings; some show only professions, others only clothings.

Clothing = entry: the aspirant, after a short period of testing, was given the religious habit and allowed to begin her noviciate. Clothing did not indicate permanent commitment. The novice was still free to leave, and the monastery was still free to send her away. A certain proportion of novices left before profession. This means that the register of clothings does not accurately represent the permanent membership of the community. What it does indicate, however, are the fluctuations in society's attraction to the monastery as an acceptable "retreat" for its daughters.

After approximately two years, the novice made her *profession*: in other words, she took her *solemn vows*. In the Old Regime, this act of profession signified a permanent change of "state." The professed nun expected to remain in her community for life, leaving only if she was required to assist in the foundation of another house. The book of professions is therefore an accurate indicator of a monastery's population.

METHOD

The years 1611–1700 have been divided into five-year periods: 1611–15, 1616–20, etc. Each period is indicated by its mid-point – e.q., 1611–15 = 1613, 1616–20 = 1618.

GRAPHS 2 AND 3

The registers of six monasteries were selected by reason of their almost complete record of professions. The professions have been charted through the seventeenth century. Each monastery shows a similar trend: a rush of entries in the years immediately after foundation, followed by a downward trend towards 1700. Individual monasteries are affected by local circumstances. Nancy, for example, was for a time in a war zone, and for this reason its professions show a marked decline. The general trend, however, shows a peak at mid-century and a decline thereafter.

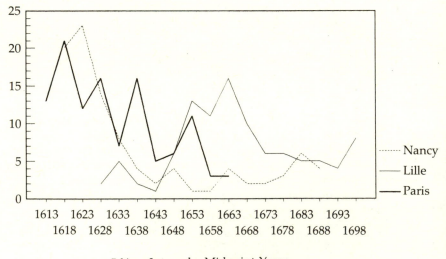

5-Year Intervals: Midpoint Years

Graph 2   Professions per year at Nancy, Lille, and Paris, 1611–1700.

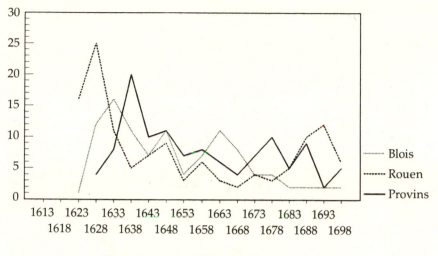

5-Year Intervals: Midpoint Years

Graph 3   Professions per year at Blois, Rouen, and Provins, 1611–1700.

GRAPHS 4, 5, AND 6

The various registers listed below contains 743 records of age at entry. Graph 4 shows the rising, then declining, curve of entries between 1611 and 1700. Graph 5 shows that as the social acceptability of the monasteries increased the average age of the entrants dropped. In the middle years of the century large numbers of young girls entered religious life – many of them, according to contemporaries, under pressure from their parents (see chapter 8, 186–7). As the monasteries became less fashionable, towards 1700, the number of young entrants can be seen to drop. Graph 6 indicates the percentage of young entrants – seventeen years and under, fifteen years and under – in the sample.

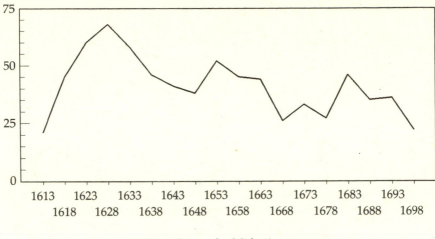

5-Year Intervals: Midpoint years

Graph 4   Entrants into teaching congregations, 1611–1700 (743 cases).

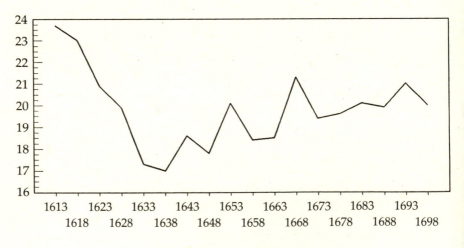

5-Year Intervals: Midpoint years

Graph 5   Average age at entry, 1611–1700 (743 cases).

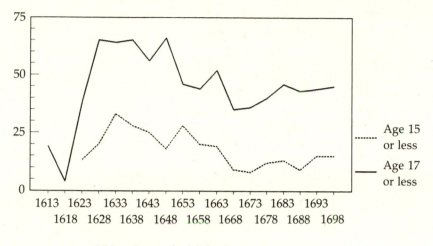

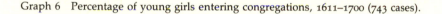

5-Year Intervals: Midpoint years

Graph 6   Percentage of young girls entering congregations, 1611–1700 (743 cases).

SOURCES

Ursulines, Paris (1612–61): 113 cases.
Source: Archives Ursulines de Québec: Registre des professions des Ursulines du Faubourg Saint-Jacques, ff.1–114, in Jégou, *Les Ursulines du Faubourg Saint-Jacques*, 168–74.
Congrégation de Notre-Dame, Nancy (1615–99): 99 cases.
Source: Liste des religieuses ayant fait leur profession de 1618 à 1789, in Aubry, "Le monastère nancéien de la Congrégation de Notre-Dame aux xviiᵉ et xviiiᵉ siècles," annexe 3, 156–62.
Ursulines, Rouen (1619–99): 139 cases.
Source: "Noms des Religieuses," in Reneault, *Les Ursulines de Rouen 1619–1906*, 294–311.
Filles de Notre-Dame, La Flèche (1623–1700): 99 cases.
Source: "Annales Manuscrites," cited in Calendini, *Le Couvent de Notre-Dame à La Flèche, passim.*
Ursulines, Blois (1625–99): 112 cases.
Source: Notter, "Les ordres religieux féminins blésois."
Ursulines, Carcassonne (1627–1700): 84 cases.
Source: AD Aude H 439: "Histoire de la fondation et annales du monastère, rédigés par les Soeurs Ursulines."
Congrégation de Notre-Dame, Provins (1629–99): 112 cases.
Source: BM Provins, MS 251: actes des professions.

Congrégation de Notre-Dame, Reims (1636–1700): 104 cases.

Source: Péchenard, *Congrégation de Notre-Dame de Reims* 2:372–9: noms des religieuses.

Ursulines, Lille (1633–1700): 102 cases.

Source: AD Nord H 149: Registre des professions.

Congrégation de Notre-Dame, Châteauroux (1641–1700): 83 cases.

Source: AD Indre H 904: Livre de la réception des religieuses.

Ursulines, Valenciennes (1654–1700): 50 cases.

Source: Loridan, *Les Ursulines de Valenciennes*, 300–1.

Ursulines, Saumur (1668–1700): 44 cases.

Source: AD Maine-et-Loire H 261 H 1: Registre des professions.

Glossary

Aa A religious sodality of laymen, under the direction of the Jesuits. These sodalities became a powerful social and political force during the Counter-Reformation.

Apostolate There are two forms of Christian activity: 1) the works of charity, and 2) the spreading of the faith, through teaching, preaching, and the conferring of the sacraments. The second form of activity is called "apostolic," and pertains principally to the priesthood. In the seventeenth century it was considered to pertain exclusively to the priesthood.

Bull (from the Latin word *bulla*, for seal) A written mandate of the pope, the seriousness of which is attested to by the papal seal.

Canons Secular clergy belonging to a cathedral or collegiate church.

Canons regular A body of canons living under a rule – usually the Rule of Saint Augustine. The nuns who adopted the Rule of Saint Augustine assumed the official title of canonesses.

Catechism A manual of religious knowledge, formulated to assist in the instruction of the faithful. First developed by the Protestant reformers, it was in use in Catholic circles by the mid-sixteenth century. The printed questions and answers were designed to be memorized, in preparation for catechism classes which were originally held by the clergy in the churches. Catechisms were designed for people of all ages, but it was in the instruction of children that they were most successful. Gradually they came to be used by catechists other than clergy, and in places other than the churches.

Civilité The group of conventions by which the relationship of the individual to society were regulated; thus, rules of polite conduct. An important subject in the schools of the seventeenth century.

Clausura 1) The living space reserved for religious, which they may not leave and others may not enter; commonly defined by walls and grilles which eliminate all access to and view of the outside.

2) The law which constrains religious to live in this space, and forbids others from entering it.

Cloister An enclosed space at the centre of the monastery; hence, figuratively, the enclosed religious life.

Clothing The formal ceremony in which a person aspiring to join a religious community received the dress, or habit, of that community. It usually took place several months after entrance into the community.

In Commendam The holding of the revenues of a benefice by a person not involved in the duties of that benefice.

Congréganiste This word had several meanings. In the first place, it was used to indicate a person or an institution belonging to a recognized congregation; e.g., the Jesuit colleges were known as *collèges congréganistes*.

It was also used to describe seculars who, like Marguerite Bourgeoys, worked under the supervision of a religious institution.

Later, the term was used to describe members of active religious congregations.

Congrégation 1) A community of persons living a consecrated life without taking solemn vows.

2) A group of monasteries following the same rule – e.g., the Ursuline congregation of Paris.

Congrégée A woman living in community without taking Solemn vows. This term was used in the early seventeenth century, but seems later to have disappeared.

Contemplative A monk or nun whose primary purpose is the worship of God.

Convent Originally (thirteenth century) a community, or gathering, of brothers. Later it came to designate a community of nuns. Also: the building in which the community lives.

Corporal Works of Mercy 1) feeding the hungry 2) giving drink to the thirsty 3) clothing the naked 4) harbouring the stranger 5) visiting the sick 6) ministering to prisoners 7) burying the dead. These obligations, which were laid upon all Christians, were taken from Christ's discourse on the Last Judgment (Matt. 25:35–7).

Divine Office (from the Latin *officium*: duty or responsibility) The official public prayer of the Church, complementing the Eucharist. By the late Middle Ages it was long and complicated, and was reserved to monasteries and cathedrals. Divine Office was divided into one night hour (Mattins) and seven day hours (Lauds, Prime, Terce, Sext, None, Vespers, Compline).

Easter Duties The obligation of all adult Catholics to receive the sacraments at least once a year, in the Easter season, in their own parish. The performance of Easter Duties was an indication of affiliation, and also of "state." Religious, who no longer had a civil identity, were exempted from the parish requirement.

Fille In seventeenth-century France, any unmarried woman or girl.

Fille de paroisse A devout woman, doing the good works of the parish, without claim to any special status.

First Communion A Catholic's first reception of the Eucharist. In the Counter-Reformation period the event was invested with new ceremony. It became a rite of passage, signalling entry into adulthood, and as such became a civil event of some significance.

Founder/foundress 1) The spiritual parent of a community, who set it up and gave it its original form.
2) The first temporal benefactor, who for his/her benevolence was given a permanent, and sometimes hereditary, status of privilege in the community.

Instruction Religious education.

Letters patent A sealed document, written on open sheets of parchment, authorizing the holding or enjoyment of some office; commonly less solemn than a charter, but more solemn than letters close.

Little Office of Our Lady An ancient office, often used in the Middle Ages in addition to Divine Office. After Trent, it was adopted in preference to the longer office by a number of women's congregations.

Mendicants Religious orders which live on alms: e.g., the Franciscans.

Monastery In English the word is usually reserved for male religious houses only; but it is used here, as it is used in French, to describe those female convents which were cloistered and subject to full monastic discipline. The communities of *filles séculières* would never be described as monasteries, although they might be called convents.

Novice A probationary member of a religious community.

Ordinary The bishop or his rightful replacement, who is responsible for teaching, governing, adjudication, and the administration of sacraments within the diocese.

Perfection A life totally conformed to the will of God. In the Middle Ages, this was understood as a life away from the world – "in contempt of the world" – i.e. a monastic life. The Reformation challenged this concept of "flight from the world," and in the seventeenth century Catholic theologians, too, began to argue that perfection could be achieved in the world. But the identification of perfection with the monastic life remained strong.

"Philothée" The person to whom François de Sales addressed his *Introduction à la vie dévote*. The name, which simply means "lover of God," was in fact a pseudonym for a real woman.

Profession The formal taking of religious vows, usually accompanied for nuns by the taking of the black veil. Before this ceremony, the novice was free to withdraw or to be sent away. After it, she was given altogether to the religious life.

Recusant A Catholic who refused to submit to the authority of the established Church of England, and was consequently subject to penalties.

Regular Clergy living under a religious rule and their own forms of government, as opposed to the secular clergy who were subject directly to their bishops.

Religion A recognized and approved association, whose members live under solemn vows of poverty, chastity, and obedience. This use of the word is seldom found in modern times, but was common in the seventeenth century. Thus "to enter religion" was to become a monk or a nun.

Religious A member, male or female, of the above.

Secular community According to a royal declaration of 1693, this was a community in which the members, though under the direction of a superior, still kept the legal right to own property.

Superior One who has authority over others by virtue of ecclesiastical rank. The head of a religious community.

Superior-General The central head of a religious order or congregation.

Tertiaries Secular members of religious orders, obliged by their act of profession to pursue perfection in the world. Directed by the religious order to which they belonged (usually one of the orders of friars), they wore a religious habit and passed through a period of noviciate.

Theologal The canon in charge of all preaching within the diocese.

Visitor An ecclesiastic designated to "visit" monasteries and to ascertain their regularity.

Vows Solemn and voluntary promises to perform something not otherwise required.

Vows of religion The vows of poverty, chastity, and obedience. Until the thirteenth century these were simple vows – i.e., they did not nullify actions taken in violation. After the thirteenth century they took on a solemn character. Once professed, a religious could not possess property, succeed to an inheritance, or marry.

Notes

INTRODUCTION

1 Ronzeaud, "La femme au pouvoir," 9.
2 This summarizes the argument made by Jean Delumeau, in his work *La peur en Occident*, chapter 10.
3 Philippe de Vitry, quoted in the introduction by Camillo Marazza to Ysambert de Saint-Léger, *Le miroir des dames* (Lecce: Milella n.d.), 10. Here and throughout the book, all translations from the French (unless otherwise specified) are mine.
4 Genesis 3:16 (Jerusalem Bible).
5 Delumeau, *La peur*, 408.
6 Brémond, *Histoire littéraire du sentiment religieux*, 10:178–9.
7 *Dictionnaire d'archéologie chrétienne et de liturgie*, article "nonne," 1559, 1563.
8 Letter 6, in C.K. Scott Moncrieff, *Letters of Abelard and Heloise* (New York: Cooper Square Publishers 1974), 110.
9 Parisse, *Les nonnes au Moyen Âge*, 84. The most notable exceptions were the Abbey of Fontevrault and its dependencies, which together formed a specifically female order; the Gilbertines in England, and later, the Brigittines, both of which orders were founded exclusively for women.
10 This reluctance was shared by the major orders, the Cistercians, the Carthusians, the Premonstratensians, and – later – the mendicant friars, the Dominicans and Franciscans. The majority of female religious houses in the Middle Ages were autonomous foundations, following the Benedictine Rule and supported by sympathetic individuals (often relatives). See Hourlier, *L'âge classique: les religieux*, 125–42; B. Bolton, "Mulieres Sanctae," in Stuard, ed., *Women in Medieval Society*, 141–58; and S. Thompson, "The Problem of the Cistercian

Nuns in the Twelfth and Early Thirteenth Centuries," in Baker, ed., *Medieval Women*, 227–52.

11 Vauchez, *La sainteté en occident*, 294–300, 316, 318. It should be remarked that after an initial hesitation, the Church took a positive approach to its "semi-religious" women – beguines and members of third orders.

12 Davis, "City Women and Religious Change in Sixteenth-Century France," in *Society and Culture*, 75.

13 Babeau, "L'Instruction dans les campagnes avant 1789," 2:44.

14 Delumeau, *La peur*, 422.

15 For example, Père Gontery, preaching to the Ursulines (1615), "exhorted the novices to practice a virtue which was not covered with hypocrisy but which was true and male, without a trace of the effeminate" (Jégou, *Les Ursulines du Faubourg Saint-Jacques*, 45).

16 Dagens, *Bérulle*, 105.

17 Brémond, *Histoire littéraire*, 2:36ff.

18 Chaunu, *L'église, culture et société*, 401.

19 Davis, "City Women," in *Society and Culture*, 85.

20 The word comes from Furet and Ozouf, *Lire et écrire*, 1:82.

21 The importance of this "intermediate state" to the modern Church is signalled in Lemoine, *Le droit des religieux*, and in its preface by Gabriel Le Bras.

22 Albistur and Armogathe, *Histoire du féminisme français*, 1:136.

23 Taveneaux, *Le catholicisme dans la France classique*, 1:82.

24 From 13,000 in 1808 to 130 000 in 1880 (Langlois, *Le catholicisme au féminin*, 307).

25 Perrel, "Sur l'enseignement féminin," 8.

26 Davis, "City Women," in *Society and Culture*, 93.

27 Langlois, *Le catholicisme au féminin*, 648.

CHAPTER ONE

1 Broutin, *La Réforme pastorale*, 1:14.

2 This climate of fear is most exhaustively described in Jean Delumeau's work, *La peur en Occident*. See, in particular, chapters 1–3.

3 Febvre, "Aspects méconnus," 645; Chaunu, *L'église, culture et société*, 457.

4 Dagens, *Bérulle*, 159.

5 Le Brun, in Rogier *et al.*, *Nouvelle histoire de l'Église* 3:246. Also see Delumeau, *La peur*, chapter 7: "Satan."

6 Chaunu, "Le xviie siècle religieux," 280–1. See also Delumeau, *Le catholicisme entre Luther et Voltaire*, 161; and Lebrun, *Histoire des catholiques en France*, 75–84.

7 Chaunu, "Le xviie siècle religieux," 286.

8 *Introduction à la vie dévote*, François de Sales, *Oeuvres*, 3:20–1.

9 Taveneaux, *Le catholicisme dans la France classique*, 2:404; Lebrun, *Histoire des catholiques*, 84.

10 Le Brun, in Rogier *et al.*, *Nouvelle histoire*, 244–5.

11 Ibid., 430–3.

12 Delumeau, *La peur en Occident*, 260.

13 Portemer, "Réflexion sur les pouvoirs de la femme," 191.

14 Leconte, *Le Docte Catéchisme*, quoted in Dhôtel, *Les origines du caté-chisme moderne*, 264.

15 Portemer, "Réflexion," 189–90.

16 Fagniez, *La femme et la société française*, 154.

17 Bossuet, *Politique tirée des propres paroles de l'Écriture Sainte*, ed. J. Le Brun (Genève: Droz 1967), 58.

18 Cordier, *La famille sainte*, 169.

19 Bossuet, *Politique*, 456.

20 Milton, *Paradise Lost*, book 4, lines 297ff.

21 Faguet, *Madame de Maintenon*, 160. Françoise d'Aubigné, Marquise de Maintenon (1635–1719), was the second wife of Louis xiv, and foun-dress of Saint-Cyr.

22 Segalen, *Mari et femme*, 181–3. Her study focuses on the nineteenth century, but she argues that peasant society was based upon systems of production, and therefore changed only when they did; therefore the patterns existing in the sixteenth century persisted, in many cases, until the twentieth.

23 Ibid., chapter 3.

24 Babeau, *Les artisans et les domestiques d'autrefois*, 166–7. Also see Davis, "City Women," in *Society and Culture*, 70–1.

25 Garapon, "Marie de l'Incarnation," in *Onze études*, 42.

26 Jadart, *Mémoires de Jean Maillefer*, 122–3.

27 Dulong, *La vie quotidienne*, 10–11.

28 Febvre, "Aspects méconnus," 643–4.

29 Fagniez, *La femme*, 57. As late as 1648, the young widow and heiress Marie Bonneau de Miramion, who was later to become one of the great *dévotes* of the century, was abducted by armed men on behalf of a suitor whom she did not know. Only her firm resolution prevented a forced marriage. See *Madame de Miramion*, by the comte de Bonneau-Avenant, 39–52.

30 Gaudemet, "Législation canonique," 15–30.

31 Mathieu Molé, *premier président au Parlement de Paris*, quoted in Sny-ders, *La pédagogie en France*, 232.

32 François de Sales, Advis pour les gens mariés, *Les femmes mariées*, (Paris: Ed. du Cerf 1967), 157. As always, the great saint's views were coloured by the aristocratic culture to which he belonged.

33 For a discussion of the qualities of a "good" marriage, see Arlette Farge's introduction to her collection of texts, *Le miroir des femmes*, 71.

34 Madame de Maintenon, "Du mariage," in Faguet, *Madame de Maintenon*, 111.

35 Fagniez, *La femme*, 203.

36 See Febvre, "Aspects méconnus"; also Roelker, "The Appeal of Calvinism to French Noblewomen," 391–413.

37 R.A. Knox, *Enthusiasm* (Oxford: Oxford University Press 1950), 20.

38 See Pietro Boglioni, "La perception de l'hérétique au moyen âge," in *L'altérité: vivre ensemble différents*, ed. M. Gourgues et G.-D. Mailhiot (Montreal: Ed. Bellarmin 1986), 337.

39 For feminine participation in Lollardy, see Claire Cross, "Great Reasoners in Scripture," in Baker, ed., *Medieval Women*, 359–71.

40 Febvre, "Aspects méconnus", 43.

41 Thomas, "Women and the Civil War Sects," 46–7.

42 Bossy, *The English Catholic Community*, 150–8.

43 A review of this argument may be found in Davis, "City Women," in *Society and Culture*. She concludes that the promotion was illusory, that "the Reformed model of the marriage relation subjected the wife as surely as did the Catholic one" (91).

44 Marguerite de Magnelay speaking to the Cardinal de Gondi. Quoted in Turin, "L'emprise de l'idéal monastique," 223.

45 Letter to Présidente Brulart, February 1609. François de Sales, *Oeuvres*, 14:134.

46 Fagniez, *La femme*, 310.

47 Barbe Avrillot (1566–1618), married to a prominent Parisian and former leaguer, Pierre Acarie. Brémond calls her the most influential person in Catholic France of the early seventeenth century (*Histoire littéraire*, 2:193).

48 Duval, quoted in ibid., 2:250.

49 Turin, "L'emprise," 366–7.

50 "Il faut doncques, en premier lieu / apprendre à bien parler de Dieu ... / Si faut-il faire la dévote, / porter le cordon Saint-François / Communion chaque mois ... / Aller aux vêpres a l'Oratoire, / Savoir où sont les Stations, / Ce qui est la méditation; / Visiter l'Ordre Sainte-Ursule, / Connaître le Père Bérulle, / Lui parler de dévotion ... / Avoir des tantes et des cousines / Dans le couvent des Carmélines" (J.Orcibal, *Jean Duvergier de Hauranne* [Paris 1947], 30, n.30.

51 Brémond, *Histoire littéraire*, 2:209.

52 Philippe d'Angoumois, quoted in Turin, "L'emprise," 372.

53 Cordier, *La famille sainte*, 169–70.

54 Père Jean Adam, quoted in Gueudré, "La femme et la vie spirituelle," 58.

55 Philippe d'Angoumois, quoted in Turin, "L'emprise," 379.

56 Quoted in Dechêne, "La veuve," in *Onze études*, 166.

57 Ibid., 165.

58 Nicolas Caussin, *La Cour sainte* (1655), quoted in Châtellier, *L'Europe des dévots*, 158.

59 Fénelon, "Entretien sur la vie religieuse," *Oeuvres complètes*, 5:691.

60 Claude Joly, *Avis chrétiens*, quoted in Dhôtel, *Les origines du catéchisme moderne*, 420.

61 *Le vrai dévot considéré à l'égard du mariage et des peines qui s'y rencontrent* (1679), quoted in Brémond, *Histoire littéraire*, 9:317.

62 Bardet, *Rouen aux XVIIe et XVIIIe siècles*, 1:90.

63 Ibid., 90.

64 Marion, *Dictionnaire des Institutions de la France*, art. clergé.

65 An anonymous chronicler of Châlons-sur-Marne, quoted in Babeau, *La ville sous l'Ancien Régime*, 462.

66 Boutiot, *Histoire de l'instruction publique et populaire à Troyes*, 71.

67 Notter, "Les ordres religieux féminins blésois," 147.

68 Poutet, *Origines lasalliennes*, 1:46.

69 At the end of the religious wars there were seven women's religious houses in the diocese of Paris, most with a population averaging between twelve and sixteen. See Ferté, *La vie religieuse*, 118–19.

70 This was the original idea of Alix Le Clerc of the Congrégation de Notre-Dame: "a new house of women, to do all the good that is possible." Quoted in Besancet, *Le bienheureux Pierre Fourier*, 44–5.

71 Chaunu, *Église, culture et société*, 401.

72 See appendix, graphs 4 and 5.

73 See glossary for a definition of this term.

74 See appendix, graph 4.

75 See appendix, graph 3.

76 By 1622 it had gone to forty editions. Pierre Chaunu considers this work the most important book of the Catholic Reformation. See *Église, culture et société*, 417.

77 Dagens, *Bérulle*, 172.

78 This lack of definition, combined with a sense of divine calling, is well described in the foreword to Gueudré, *Histoire des Ursulines*, 1:16.

CHAPTER TWO

1 Adrian VI's instruction to Chieregati, 1522, in John Olin, *The Catholic Reformation: Savanarola to Ignatius Loyola* (New York: Harper and Row 1969), 125.

2 Chambers, *Life of Mary Ward*, 1:378.

3 François de Sales, *Oeuvres*, 17:238, 250. These were Roman matrons who were praised by Saint Jerome for their devout lives.

4 The story of Mary Ward and her English Ladies has taken a long time to unfold. Contemporary sources are rich: Mary herself wrote an apologia, and a number of biographies were written by friends and acquaintances within a few years of her death. Her institute also figured frequently in the correspondence of the Jesuits. A series of paintings recording the principal events of her life is still in the possession of her institute. In modern times, a number of works have been written concerning her, the best of which is still the two-volume *Life of Mary Ward* by M.C.E. Chambers. However, the Holy See was slow to rehabilitate a person it had condemned. Books written in her defence in the eighteenth century were put on the Index. In 1745 an appeal by members of the institute for a re-examination of the case led to reiteration of the original judgment, in the bull *Quamvis justo*. Only in 1909 did Pope Pius x formally acknowledge her as a legitimate foundress. Shortly afterwards a Catholic historian, Peter Guilday, was able to examine the Vatican Archives, and to publish background information which helps to trace the ruin of the first institute. His book, *The English Catholic Refugees on the Continent*, completes what has been called "a sad page" in religious history.

5 Council of Trent, session 25:1, quoted in Schroeder, *Canons and Decrees of the Council of Trent*, 218.

6 Lemoine, *Le monde des religieux*, 3.

7 Ibid., 4–5.

8 Molette, *Guide des sources de l'histoire des congrégations féminines françaises*, 30.

9 Lemoine, *Le droit des religieux*, 40.

10 Taveneaux, *Le catholicisme dans la France classique*, 1:69.

11 For the increasing emphasis on chastity as the central feature of feminine monasticism, see J.T. Schulenburg, "Strict Active Enclosure and Its Effects on Female Monastic Experience (ca 500-1100)," in *Distant Echoes: Medieval Religious Women*, ed. J.A. Nichols and L.T. Shank (Kalamazoo 1984), 298–308. Also see Parisse, *Les nonnes au Moyen Âge*, 171ff; and Vauchez, *La sainteté en occident*, 405–10.

12 Council of Trent, session 25:5, in Schroeder, *Council of Trent*, 220–1.

13 *Dictionnaire de spiritualité*, 22, col. 994.

14 *Dictionnaire de droit canonique*, 3, cols. 895–6.

15 The council decreed that female monasteries, surrounded by their own walls, should be sheltered within cities (which of course had their own walls) so as to have double protection from outside interference. (Council of Trent, session 25:5, quoted in Schroeder, *Council of Trent*, 220–1).

16 Derréal, *Un missionaire de la Contre-Réforme*, 143.

17 Jean Hendrico, bourgeois of Saint-Omer, whose *Recueil Historique* is quoted in Chambers, *Mary Ward*, 1:272–3.

18 Memorial to Paul v, 1615, quoted in ibid., 1:375.

19 Mary Ward to Nuncio Albergati (c. 1621), quoted in ibid., 1:283.

20 Memorial presented to Paul v, 1616. For the complete text, see ibid., 1:375–84.

21 "The resemblance with the Company extended even to the words and the minutest details of the rule of Saint Ignatius" (J. Grisar, sj, "Der erste Verbot der Ordensgrndung Maria Wards," quoted in Lemoine, *Le monde des religieux*, 352, fn. 3). Because the Institute of Mary first took root in Germany, many of the works concerning it are in German.

22 Suarez's argument was as follows: "The Institute was expressly ordained and directed towards the salvation of souls; and it was a subject of serious consideration whether such a purpose could be approved of in the case of women; it seemed to be both against the Scripture and the Canon Law, and should by no means be consented to without consultation with the Holy See" (Salome, *Mary Ward*, xiii).

23 Father Lohner, *Gottsiliges Leben*, quoted in Chambers, *Mary Ward*, 2:185.

24 Bishop Richard Smith, quoted in ibid., 2:412. A complete discussion of the secular-Jesuit rivalry may be found in Bossy, *The English Catholic Community*, chapter 1.

25 Andrew White, sj, quoted in Salome, *Mary Ward*, 125. Andrew White later worked for many years in the colony of Maryland.

26 Letter of Richard Blount, English Provincial, written by order of Vitelleschi; quoted in Bernard Bassett, *The English Jesuits* (New York: Herder and Herder 1967), 171.

27 Memorial of the English Clergy, c. 1621, quoted in Chambers, *Mary Ward*, 1:183.

28 Bennett to Dr Bishop, quoted in ibid., 2:60.

29 Quoted in ibid., 1:132.

30 Ibid., 1:183ff.

31 Rant (agent of the English Clergy) to M.W., quoted in Salome, *Mary Ward*, 170.

32 Pillorget, "Mary Ward ou la Ténacité," 11.

33 Quoted in Salome, *Mary Ward*, 200. Among these enemies was Francesco Ingoli, secretary to the Congregation of Propaganda, who "was keenly opposed to the Jesuits" (Pastor, *History of the Popes* [London: Routledge and Kegan Paul 1938], 29:28).

34 Guilday, *English Catholic Refugees*, 190, 206.

35 *Analecta juris pontificii*, col. 2023. It should be remarked that the Holy See's bark was worse than its bite; Urban later privately assured Mary

that she was not a heretic, and gave her a pension. He also wrote secretly to the Elector Maximilian of Bavaria, authorizing him to keep the community in Munich open, as an asylum for the dispersed nuns. This explains the institute's continuing German connection.

36 *Analecta*, cols. 2022–3.

37 Ibid., col. 2023.

38 Fra Domenico de Gesù, quoted in Chambers, *Mary Ward*, 1:482.

39 Winifrid Wigmore, quoted in ibid., 2:297.

40 "Three Speeches of Our Reverend Mother Chief Superior," in ibid., 1:408ff.

41 Bossy, *The English Catholic Community*, 282.

42 Guilday, *English Catholic Refugees*, 193–203. Propaganda's blanket condemnation of "Jesuitesses" led to confusion and controversy. The archbishop of Cambrai argued at length in favour of his own teaching sisters, the *Filles de Sainte-Agnès*, that "they have never ... carried out any missions, which is what the aforesaid Congregation has chiefly forbidden women to do" (Lottin, "Reforme catholique," 26).

43 See chapter 3.

44 Lemoine, *Le monde des religieux*, 365, n. 28.

45 Religious women who took only simple vows were not recognized by the papacy as true religious until the end of the nineteenth century. Feminine religious congregations organized under a superior-general, after the model proposed by Mary Ward, were not recognized until the early 1900s (ibid., 358–9). Yet by this time, most religious women were in fact in congregations of this type (Langlois, *Le catholicisme au féminin*, 309).

46 Lemoine, *Le monde des religieux*, 306.

47 François de Sales (1567–1622); educated at Paris and Geneva; author of *Introduction à la vie dévote* and *Traité de l'amour de Dieu*; canonized by Alexander VII in 1665.

48 Jeanne-Françoise Fremyot de Chantal (1572–1641). Daughter of a *président à mortier* at Dijon, she became the foundress and first member of the congregation of the Visitation in 1610.

49 Brémond, *Histoire littéraire*, 2:565–6.

50 François de Sales to archbishop de Marquemont, June 1615, in *Oeuvres*, 17:17.

51 François de Sales to the baronne de Chantal, Dec. 1609. Ibid., 14:232.

52 François de Sales to the baronne de Chantal, s.d. Ibid., 14:110.

53 François de Sales to M. Philippe de Quoex, 20 December 1610. Ibid. 14:330.

54 Ibid., and his letter of 29 September 1608 to the baronne de Chantal, 14:69.

55 Lemoine, *Le monde des religieux*, 304.

56 François de Sales, *Oeuvres*, 25:291.

57 Ibid., 291–2. Here the bishop of Geneva was quoting from Saint-Basil.

58 Ibid., 311.

59 Ibid., 319–20.

60 Ibid., 322.

61 Ibid., 327.

62 Ibid., 328.

63 Ibid., 330.

64 Ibid., 323.

65 Ibid., 324.

66 Ibid., 17:139.

67 Ibid., 25:339.

68 Ibid., 332.

69 For a map of the Visitation's foundations, see Devos, *L'origine sociale des Visitandines*, opposite 89.

70 J.-P. Camus, *L'esprit du B. François de Sales* (Paris 1664), vi^e p., 5:196–7, quoted in Lemoine, *Le droit des religieux*, 185–6. This quotation from Camus was questioned by Brémond, who suspected him of exaggerating in order to support his own antimonastic bias. Brémond himself, who had the opposite bias, saw the translation of the Visitation into a contemplative order as the perfecting of the original design, in line with François de Sales's own wishes (*Histoire littéraire*, 2:19). However, there is other contemporary evidence to suggest that François de Sales was disappointed by the transformation. Vincent de Paul, who knew both the founders, more than once expressed the opinion that the cloistering of the Visitation was a distortion of its original purpose. Furthermore, François de Sales told Madame de Villeneuve, foundress of the Filles de la Croix, that the sisters of the Visitation had been cloistered "against his original design" (Molette, "Conclusion," *Les Religieuses enseignantes*, 155), and that he wished, if he lived long enough, to found another uncloistered congregation.

CHAPTER THREE

1 "To the councilmen of Germany" (1524), in Martin Luther, *Works*, ed. Walther I. Brandt (Philadelphia: Muhlenberg Press 1962), 45:368.

2 Convention signed between the Jesuits and the town of Aurillac, 12 February 1619, quoted in Compère, *Du collège au lycée*, 58.

3 Terms of foundation at Pau, cited in Bouzonnie, *Histoire de l'Ordre des Religieuses Filles de Notre-Dame* (1697), 1:233–5, quoted in Soury-Lavergne, *Chemin d'éducation*, 171.

4 Bouzonnie, *Histoire*, 1:53, quoted in Soury-Lavergne, *Chemin d'éducation*, 89.

5 Jeanne de Lestonnac (1556–1640), daughter of a *conseiller* to the Parlement of Bordeaux, niece of Michel de Montaigne. In 1563 she married Gaston de Montferrant, baron of Landiras (d. 1597).

6 Entraygues, *Une nièce de Montaigne*, 45.

7 François d'Escoubleau de Sourdis (1575–1628); appointed to the diocese of Bordeaux at the age of nineteen, while still in minor orders; received the cardinal's hat in 1599. He was a bishop in the best autocratic tradition. In his obituary the *Mercure de France* wrote that his was "a character that was intolerant of anything which prejudiced his jurisdiction." Quoted in *La Compagnie de Marie Notre-Dame*, 29.

8 *Constitutions*, quoted in ibid., 62.

9 Bull of Paul v, 7 April 1607, quoted in Molette, "Conclusion," *Les religieuses enseignantes*, 152.

10 Michel, "Une version modernisée," 59.

11 "Each religious or boarder shall have three dishes at each meal, morning and evening; to wit: a soup or an entree, a portion of meat and a dessert ... The customary portion of boiled meat for the Religious will be 4 ounces ... that of roast meat, 5 ounces" (quoted in ibid., 58–9).

12 Entraygues describes it as "tastefully made" (*Une nièce de Montaigne*, 85).

13 It was not uncommon for devout laymen to spend two or more hours a day in private prayer, as well attending mass and reciting the Little Office. See du Chesnay, "La spiritualité des laïcs," 31–3.

14 Constitutions of 1640, quoted in *La Compagnie de Marie Notre-Dame*, 67.

15 Constitutions of 1640, quoted in ibid., 69.

16 Documents d'Origine, 129, quoted in Soury-Lavergne, *Chemin d'éducation*, 84.

17 *Marie Notre-Dame*, 130.

18 See above, p. 27.

19 *Marie Notre-Dame*, 133–4.

20 Quoted in Calendini, *Le couvent des Filles de Notre-Dame de la Flèche*, 71.

21 Entraygues, *Une nièce de Montaigne*, 238.

22 *Marie Notre-Dame*, 136.

23 Numbering thirty houses in 1640, it increased to fifty-three by the end of the century. Thereafter it ceased to expand.

24 Gueudré, *Histoire des Ursulines*, 2:187. Compare this with the figures available for the major male congregations. In 1749 there were 3350 Jesuits; in 1720, 656 Oratorians; in 1725, 362 Fathers of Christian Doctrine; in 1700, 200 Sulpicians. See Viguerie, *Une oeuvre d'éducation*, 179.

25 Chalendard, *La promotion de la femme à l'apostolat*, 31.

26 Leymont, *Madame de Sainte-Beuve*, 127, and Lemoine, *Le monde des religieux*, 293. Note that under Borromeo the Ursulines began to concentrate on teaching as their principal apostolate.

27 M. Bourguignon, *La Vie du Père Romillon* (1649), quoted in Brémond, *Histoire littéraire*, 2:28.

28 Ibid., 29–30.

29 *Les chroniques de l'Ordre des Ursulines recueillies pour l'usage des Religieuses du Mesme Ordre par (M)ère (D)e (P)ommereu (U)rsuline* [hereafter *MDPU*] (Paris 1673), part 1:96.

30 Ibid., 72–9.

31 *Journal*, 2:53, quoted in Gueudré, *Histoire des Ursulines*, 1:158.

32 *MDPU*, part 1:85.

33 Quoted in Gueudré, *Histoire des Ursulines*, 1:156.

34 Ibid., 153.

35 Cardinal de Sourdis, pastoral letter (1609). Gueudré, *Histoire des Ursulines*, 1:330–42.

36 Beaurepaire, *Recherches*, 2:204.

37 Gueudré, *Histoire des Ursulines*, 1:153.

38 Lecler, *Chroniques ecclésiastiques du Limousin*, 2:20, quoted in Gueudré, *Histoire des Ursulines*, 1:42. For the reasons behind this opposition, see the petition of the four mendicant superiors of Lille (1639) against the establishment of an Ursuline house in that city, for fear of the damage they would do to the existing houses of "Religious and worthy *filles séculières*" (AD Nord 149 H 4).

39 *MDPU*, part 1:81.

40 Ibid., 84.

41 Père Marin, SJ, speaking to Madame de Sainte-Beuve, foundress of the Ursuline convent of Faubourg Saint-Jacques in Paris; quoted in *MDPU* Part 1:105.

42 Gueudré, *Histoire des Ursulines*, 1:131.

43 Quoted in Leymont, *Madame de Sainte-Beuve*, 246.

44 BM Chartres, 26-xv (Couvent des Ursulines), 189.

45 P. Le Merre, *Receuil des actes, titres, et memoires concernant les affaires du Clergé de France* (Paris 1716–50), 4, col. 1040; quoted in Gueudré, *Histoire des Ursulines*, 1:168.

46 *MDPU*, part 1:182.

47 Gueudré, *Histoire des Ursulines*, 1:50.

48 *MDPU*, part 1:142–3.

49 Ibid., 278–80.

50 Jégou, *Les Ursulines du Faubourg Saint-Jacques*, 54.

51 As in the case of a small local community in Gournay, which was constrained in 1625 to give way to an Ursuline house which enjoyed

the protection of the duchesse de Longueville (Beaurepaire, *Recherches*, 1:219).

52 In Blois, for instance, each of the four convents had its own network of supporting families. Between the different houses there could be considerable ill will. See Notter, "Les ordres religieux féminins blésois," 279, 124.

53 As in the case of Rennes, in October 1628. See Gueudré, *Histoire des Ursulines*, 1:90–1.

54 G. Augeri, *Vie de Catherine de Veteris du Revest* (Aix 1672), quoted in ibid., 177. Also see *MDPU*, part 3:416.

55 *MDPU*, part 3:84, 77, 5.

56 Vincent de Paul, *Correspondance*, 10:103.

57 François de Sales, *Oeuvres*, 25:323, n. 2.

58 Michel de Marillac (1563–1632), one of the leaders of the *dévot* party, and later keeper of the seals under Louis xiii. He was *chargé d'affaires* for the first Carmelite community, and temporal director of the Ursulines of Faubourg Saint-Jacques.

59 Jégou, *Les Ursulines du Faubourg Saint-Jacques*, 27–9.

60 Gueudré, *Histoire des Ursulines*, 1:318. The Ursulines of Dôle in Franche-Comté, under Anne de Xainctonge, continued to resist transformation; their success may be attributed to the fact that they were at the time in Spanish-controlled territory. They remained an uncloistered community.

61 Philippe d'Angoumois, quoted in Turin, "L'emprise," 233.

62 Quoted in Gueudré, *Histoire des Ursulines*, 1:274.

63 Mère de Pommereu of Paris, who was the order's first historian, counted nine congregations: Paris, Bordeaux, Lyon, Dijon, Arles, Tulle, Avignon, Toulouse, and Dôle. In fact, Madame Gueudré suggests that the number was more like thirty (*Histoire des Ursulines*, 1:5).

64 Lemoine, *Le monde des religieux*, 296.

65 Letter of 3 October 1645. Marie de l'Incarnation, *Correspondance*, 267. Marie de l'Incarnation (in secular life Marie Guyart) was an Ursuline of Tours who came to Quebec in 1639 to establish a religious teaching community.

66 Jégou, *Les Ursulines du Faubourg Saint-Jacques*, 66.

67 Papal bull to the Bordeaux house, 1610. See Gueudré, *Histoire des Ursulines*, 1:4.

68 Letter of 9 August 1659. Marie de l'Incarnation, *Correspondance*, 615.

69 *MDPU*, part 1:162–6.

70 See graph 1.

71 The sodalities were societies of laymen whom the Jesuits directed in devotion and charitable action. For a full account of their enormous effect upon Catholic urban society, see Châtellier, *L'Europe des dévots*.

72 J. Pitton, *Annales de l'église d'Aix* (Lyon 1668), quoted in Gueudré, *Histoire des Ursulines*, 1:3.

73 Fourier, *Correspondance*, 2:347.

74 This reputation was known even to Urban VIII. "He congratulated himself heartily ... that, by the grace of God, such a man had been given to the Church during his pontificate" (evidence from the *procès canonique, instruit à Toul, en 1682*, quoted in Derréal, *Un missionaire de la Contre-Réforme*, 378, n. 113).

75 J. Bedel, *La vie du Très R.P. Fourier, dit vulgairement le Père de Maitaincour* (Paris 1645), quoted in Bazelaire, *Le bienheureux Pierre Fourier*, 31–2.

76 Alix Le Clerc, *Relation à la gloire de Dieu et de sa sainte Mère, et au salut de mon âme* (Nancy 1666), quoted in Besancet, *Le bienheureux Pierre Fourier*, 44–5.

77 Derréal, *Un missionaire*, 149–53.

78 For the text of this document, see Fourier, *Correspondance*, 2:351–2.

79 Ibid., 350

80 *Vie de la Vénérable Alix Le Clerc* (Nancy 1666), 22.

81 Derréal, *Un missionaire*, 171.

82 An unnamed contemporary, quoted in Renard, *La Mère Alix Le Clerc*, 181.

83 Fourier to the sisters of Saint-Nicolas, 22 August 1605. *Correspondance* 1:9.

84 Decree of the Congregation of Bishops and Regulars, 22 January 1592.

85 *Supplique inédite au cardinal de Lorraine*, quoted in Derréal, *Un missionaire*, 62.

86 Ibid., 252.

87 Ibid., 265.

88 Fourier, *Correspondance*, 2:347.

89 *Evreux*, f.44, quoted in Derréal, *Un missionaire*, 252.

90 "Extrait de quelques articles du règlement provisionnel que gardaient les filles de la Congrégation de Notre-Dame avant qu'elles fussent religieuses" (1598). Fourier, *Correspondance*, 2:351–2.

91 Quoted in Derréal, *Un missionaire*, 215.

92 Ibid., 221–2.

93 Ibid., 284.

94 *Règles communes* MS B, 272, quoted in ibid., 276.

95 The suggestion for this seems to have come first from the nuns of Châlons-sur-Marne, and to have been taken up by Fourier. See Carrez, *Histoire du premier monastère de la Congrégation de Notre-Dame*, 118ff.

96 Derrèal, *Un missionaire*, 328–30.

97 Ibid., 336–7.

98 Fourier, *Correspondance*, 2:252.

99 Ibid., 302.

100 Ibid., 301.

101 Ibid., 452.

102 Ibid., 579.

103 Ibid., 612.

104 Bazelaire, *Le bienheureux Pierre Fourier*, 58–9.

105 AD Meurthe et Moselle, H 2571. Livre de l'Interrogatoire pour Examiner les Novices par un deputé du Seigneur Évêque selon l'Ordre du St-Concile pour la Profession.

106 Fourier, quoted in Péchenard, *Congrégation de Notre-Dame de Reims*, 1:35.

107 Gueudré, *Histoire des Ursulines*, 1:16.

108 "Mémoire concernant la Congrégation de la Visitation," in François de Sales, *Oeuvres*, 25:328.

109 This is a paraphrase of remarks made by Monsignor Ingoli, head of the *Propaganda fidei*, in 1629. See Guilday, *The English Catholic Refugees*, 199.

CHAPTER FOUR

1 Chaunu, "Le XVIIe siècle religieux", 291.

2 See Delumeau, *Le catholicisme entre Luther et Voltaire*, chapter 4, "Christianisation"; Taveneaux, *Le catholicisme dans la France classique*, 1:27.

3 See, for instance, Dhôtel, *Les origines du catéchisme moderne*, 13.

4 Broutin, *La Réforme pastorale*, 1:20.

5 Le Brun, in Rogier et al., *Nouvelle histoire de l'Église*, 3:10.

6 See Mandrou, *Introduction à la France moderne*, 273. "A good part of the movement of renewal during the years 1600–1640 was the work of the laity, and above all of devout women."

7 Quoted in Allier, *La "Cabale des Dévots,"* 260.

8 Adrien Bourdoise (d. 1655), founder of the seminary of Saint-Nicolas-du-Chardonnet. See below, chapter 5.

9 The Compagnie du Saint-Sacrement, founded by the duc de Ventadour in 1630, was a secret association of laymen and priests whose purpose was "to embrace with zeal every kind of good purpose, and to procure the glory of God by every kind of means." Its records show gypsy women locked away, a deist put into jail, a hermaphrodite banished from Paris, prostitutes prosecuted, butchers jailed for selling meat on Fridays – as well as continuing action against Protestants. On the other hand, it was active in a wide range of good works, including assistance to war-torn rural areas. See Argenson, *Compagnie du Saint-Sacrement, passim.*

10 For more on the political overtones of *Tartuffe*, see Châtellier, *L'Europe des dévots*, 176ff.

11 Dagens, *Bérulle*, 129–30.

12 Febvre, "Aspects méconnus," 641. See also du Chesnay, "La spiritualité des laïcs," 39.

13 François de Sales to Mme Présidente Brulart, 13 October 1604, in de Sales, *Oeuvres*, 12:347.

14 François de Sales, *Introduction*, part 3, chapter 15. This was clearly a counsel of perfection, seldom followed literally; but among those who did follow it were the first sisters of the Visitation, in the period before they were cloistered.

15 Du Chesnay, "La spiritualité des laïcs," 36–8; 43–5.

16 Gutton, *La société et les pauvres*, 93–4.

17 Deyon, "A propos du pauperisme," 151.

18 Gutton, *La société et les pauvres*, 111. For a discussion of contemporary English poor relief, see Valerie Pearl, "Puritans and Poor Relief: The London Workhouse, 1649–1660." in *Puritans and Revolutionaries: Essays in Seventeenth-Century History Presented to Christopher Hill* (Oxford: Clarendon Press 1978), 206–32.

19 François de Sales to Jean-François Ranzo, 6 May 1610. *Oeuvres*, 14:300.

20 Dulong, *La vie quotidienne des femmes*, 266.

21 Deyon, "A propos du pauperisme," 261.

22 Fléchier, "Oraison funèbre pour la duchesse d'Aiguillon," *Oeuvres complètes*, 10 vols. (Paris 1828), 1:59.

23 Jadart, *Mémoires de Jean Maillefer*, 120.

24 *Les justes complaints des Bourgeois de Paris addressées a Messieurs de Parlement* (Paris 1649), quoted in Jégou, *Les Ursulines du Faubourg Saint-Jacques*, 101.

25 Gutton, *La société et les pauvres*, 11–13.

26 *Ordre à tenir pour la visite des pauvres honteux*, following the *Reglements de la Charité de Saint-Germain de l'Auxerrois*, quoted in Allier, *La "Cabale des dévots,"* 95.

27 René Bourgeois, quoted in Desportes, *Histoire de Reims*, 200.

28 Allier, *"La Cabale des dévots,"* 99.

29 Vincent de Paul, *Correspondance*, 13:798.

30 Chalumeau, "L'assistance aux malades pauvres au xviie siècle," 76.

31 Vincent de Paul (1581–1660), born of peasant parents in a small village close to Dax, in Landes. Once a swineherd, he lived to become one of the most influential ecclesiastics of his time, when he was appointed to the king's *conseil de conscience*. He was the founder of the congregation of the Mission and of the Filles de la Charité, as well as the lay confraternities known as the parish *charités*.

32 Abelly, *Vie de S. Vincent de Paul*, 1:28.

33 Ibid., 55.

34 Coste, *Le grand saint du grand siècle*, 1:624–32.

35 Boudon, *La Science sacrée du catéchisme*, quoted in Germain, *Langages de la foi*, 86.

36 Abelly, *Vie de S. Vincent de Paul*, 1:237.

37 Vincent de Paul, *Correspondance*, 13:510.

38 Ibid., 14:125.

39 Ibid., 9:209.

40 Mademoiselle Le Gras, *Lettres de Louise de Marillac*, 12.

41 *Règlement de la Charité de Châtillon-les-Dombes* (1617), in Vincent de Paul, *Correspondance*, 13:423–38.

42 Père Desmoulins, Oratorian, quoted in ibid., 495.

43 Ibid., 496.

44 *Règlement de la charité mixte de Joigny*, in ibid., 447.

45 Ibid., 455.

46 Ibid., 4:11.

47 Coste, *Le grand saint*, 1:248.

48 Vincent de Paul, *Correspondance*, 9:209.

49 Ibid., 244.

50 Conference of December 1648, ibid., 445–56.

51 Louise de Marillac (1591–1660), niece of the chancellor and leader of the *dévot* party Michel de Marillac; married in 1613 to Antoine Le Gras, *secrétaire des commandements* to Queen Marie de Medicis. While her husband was occupied at court she adopted the lifestyle of a *dévote*, and in particular dedicated herself to visiting the sick. Her husband's death in 1625 left her free to pursue the life she had long desired.

52 Abelly, *Vie de S. Vincent de Paul*, 2:27.

53 Coste, *Saint Vincent de Paul et les dames de la Charité*, 162. Also see René Bady, "Vincent de Paul et les siens," in *Mélanges offerts à André Latreille*, 83–7.

54 Coste, *Le grand saint*, 1:443.

55 Abelly, *Vie de S. Vincent de Paul*, 2:38.

56 Vincent de Paul, *Correspondance*, 9:1–13.

57 Ibid., 221.

58 Mademoiselle Le Gras, *Lettres*, 899.

59 Conference of 7 December 1643. Vincent de Paul, *Correspondance*, 9:141.

60 Ibid., 9:658.

61 Ibid., 9:143.

62 Mademoiselle Le Gras to Abbé de Vaux, 29 June 56. Mademoiselle Le Gras, *Lettres*, 782.

63 Lemoine, *Le monde des religieux*, 309.

64 Conference to the sisters, 8 October 1655. Vincent de Paul, *Correspondance*, 9:102.

65 For a discussion of the case of the Visitation, see chapter 2.

66 Advice to the sisters leaving for Nantes, 22 October 1650. Vincent de Paul, *Correspondance*, 9:533–4.

67 Mademoiselle Le Gras, *Lettres*, 396.

68 Carrez, *Histoire du premier monastère de la Congrégation de Notre-Dame*, 255.

69 Vincent de Paul, *Correspondance*, 13:558.

70 Ibid., 13:567.

71 After Mademoiselle Le Gras's death, and just before his own, Monsieur Vincent was forced to make one final organizational decision. He chose for her replacement, not one of the Dames de la Charité, but a sister from inside the confraternity. For a canonist's perspective on the institution of this company, see Lemoine, *Le monde des religieux*, 309–13.

72 Abelly, *Vie de S. Vincent de Paul*, 2:38–9.

73 Vincent de Paul, *Correspondance*, 13:602.

74 Ibid., 10:662.

75 Ibid., 10:595.

76 Ibid., 13:555.

77 Mademoiselle Le Gras, *Lettres*, 589.

78 Conference of 16 March 1642. Vincent de Paul, *Correspondance*, 9:60–6.

79 Coste, *Le grand saint*, 1:464.

80 See, for instance, the *règlement* for the *charité* of Folleville, 1620. Vincent de Paul, *Correspondance*, 13:484.

81 Fosseyeux, *Les écoles de charité à Paris sous l'ancien régime*, 27.

82 Mademoiselle Le Gras, *Lettres*, 614.

83 Ibid., 853.

84 Any surplus cash was sent home to the mother house at the end of the year. Vincent de Paul, *Correspondance*, 9:51.

85 Mademoiselle Le Gras, *Lettres*, 854.

86 Coste, *Le grand saint*, 1:465–71.

87 It was still the practice to sentence criminals to forced service as oarsmen on the state's galleys. Before being shipped out to serve their sentence they might spend some time in prison. Vincent de Paul had always felt a personal concern for these galley-convicts, since he himself in his youth had been a slave of the Turks.

88 Abelly, *Vie de S. Vincent de Paul*, 2:36.

89 Mademoiselle Le Gras, *Lettres*, 808.

90 Vincent de Paul, *Correspondance*, 9:246.

91 Mademoiselle Le Gras, *Lettres*, 805.

92 Vincent de Paul, *Correspondance*, 9:118.
93 Coste, *Le grand saint*, 1: chapter 19, 461–528 *passim*.
94 Conference of March 1647. Vincent de Paul, *Correspondance*, 9:306–7.
95 Chill, "Religion and Mendicity in Seventeenth-Century France," 403.
96 Allier, *La "Cabale des dévots,"* 63.
97 Chill, "Religion and Mendicity," 413.
98 Ibid., 415.
99 A. Arnauld to P. de Cort, 6 April 1657, quoted in Taveneaux, *Le catholicisme dans la France classique*, 1:220.
100 Quoted in Gutton, *La société et les pauvres*, 134.
101 Coste, *Le grand saint*, 2:495.
102 Abelly, *Vie de S. Vincent de Paul*, 1:194.
103 Quoted in ibid., 144.
104 Coste, *Le grand saint*, 2:506.
105 Chill, "Religion and Mendicity," 424.
106 Vincent de Paul, *Correspondance*, 13:430.
107 Pensées de Louise de Marillac, quoted in Coste, *Le grand saint*, 2:497.
108 Fagniez, *La femme et la société française*, 362.
109 Gutton, *La société et les pauvres*, 149.
110 Deyon, "À propos du paupérisme," 152.
111 "Sentiment de M. Loisel Docteur de la Maison et Société de Sorbonne, Chancelier de l'Eglise et Universite de Paris, Curé de St-Jean," in the preface to the *Reglement et pratique chrestiens, en forme de constitutions des Filles et vefves Seculières, du Seminaire nommé de l'Union Chrestienne, establies dans plusieurs Dioceses* (1673).

CHAPTER FIVE

1 Abelly, *Vie de S. Vincent de Paul*, 2:38.
2 Lottin, "Réforme catholique et instruction des pauvres," 22.
3 Vincent de Paul, *Correspondance*, 10:549–50.
4 See, for instance, AN, S 7046–7 for the model contract contained in the 1657 *Règlement* of the Filles de l'Instruction chrétienne, a small teaching community in Paris.
5 To give one example among many: a tiny community of women was set up in Reims to provide job training for poor girls. A rule was drawn up for them, and they remained active, though secular, until the Revolution. See BM Reims, E 2, t 2: Articles pour servir de regle et conduite dresses par les soins de Mme de Magneux (1636), and Gosset, *Les Magneuses*, 11.
6 See below, chapter 7.
7 One story is enough to illustrate his approach. Somewhere outside Paris he met a wealthy and pious woman, whose practice it was to attend mass in a private chapel. He took her to her parish church,

showed her its decay and dereliction, and so overwhelmed her with remorse that she swept and cleaned it with her own hands, and saw to its maintenance thereafter (Darche, *Le saint abbé Bourdoise* 1:78–9).

8 Ibid., 1:465.

9 Ibid., 1:466.

10 Coste, *Saint Vincent de Paul et les dames de la Charité*, 88–9.

11 These are the *Vie de Madame de Miramion* by the abbé de Choisy (1707), which is reprinted in G.J.A.J. Jauffret, *Des services que les femmes peuvent rendre à la religion* (Paris 1801); and *Madame de Miramion* by the comte de Bonneau-Avenant. The constitutions, which have survived, along with a pamphlet entitled "De l'esprit de la Communauté des filles de Sainte-Geneviefve," provide the rest of my information on the community.

12 Bonneau-Avenant, *Madame de Miramion*, 200.

13 Ibid., 199–200. As will be seen below, Marguerite Bourgeoys came from Montreal to seek her advice on the foundation of the congregation.

14 Ibid., 172; Coste, *Le grand saint*, 364.

15 "De l'Esprit de la Communauté des filles de Sainte-Geneviefve," chapter 3.

16 AN, série LL 1679, 1681. Filles de Sainte-Geneviève, Constitutions, introduction.

17 "De l'Esprit," fol. 6.

18 Bonneau-Avenant, *Madame de Miramion*, 240–1.

19 Constitutions (1679), 36.

20 Vincent de Paul, *Correspondance*, 13:758.

21 Mademoiselle Le Gras, *Lettres*, 396. See above, p. 86.

22 See, for instance, the handwritten rule for the community of Filles de Saint-Joseph et de Sainte-Geneviève à Senlis – one of the houses that Madame de Miramion reformed (Bibliothèque Ste-Geneviève, MS 1718).

23 "Esprit," fol. 3.

24 "Règles et statuts des filles de Saint-Joseph et de Sainte-Geneviève à Senlis," fol.4.

25 "Esprit," fol. 2.

26 Constitutions (1680), 89.

27 "Esprit," fol. 2.

28 Constitutions (1680), 33.

29 Constitutions (1679) 1:9.

30 Bonneau-Avenant, *Madame de Miramion*, 196.

31 Ibid., 415–17.

32 Letter of 29 March 1696, quoted in ibid., 353.

33 The word is Pierre Deyon's. See his article "A propos du paupérisme," 137.

34 Vincent de Paul, *Correspondance*, 10:664.

35 For a full study of her spiritual background, see Plante, *Marguerite Bourgeoys, fille de France*, and Caza, *La vie voyagère*.

36 The description comes from her friend, Marie Morin, a *hospitalière* in Montreal from 1662 to her death in 1730. See her *Histoire simple et véritable*, 75.

37 *Le Vray Esprit de l'Institut des Soeurs Séculières de la Congrégation de Notre Dame*, 18–19.

38 *Conduite de la Providence dans l'établissement de la Congrégation de Notre-Dame, qui a pour son instituteur Pierre Fourier, dit vulgairement de Mattaincourt, supérieur général et réformateur des chanoines réguliers de la Congrégation de Notre Sauveur*, quoted in Jamet, *Marguerite Bourgeoys*, 1:33.

39 Marguerite used the term "vie voyagère," to express the idea that the Blessed Virgin was dedicated to the service of others, even to the point of leaving her home and going out into "the world." The same principle was found in the devotion to the Visitation, which was promoted for the first time during the seventeenth century. See below, chapter 8.

40 Marguerite Bourgeoys to Louis Tronson, September 1695. *Écrits de Mère Bourgeoys*, 204.

41 Jamet, *Marguerite Bourgeoys*, 1:40.

42 "Sainte Mère de Dieu, pure Vierge au coeur royale, gardez-nous une place en votre Montreal" (*Écrits*, 38).

43 "As there were many sick she nursed them all with a care that defies description, not only on board ship but even after they had reached Quebec." Dollier de Casson, "Histoire de Montréal," 101. The author was superior of the seminary of Montreal, and knew Marguerite personally.

44 *Ecrits*, 42.

45 Ibid., 38.

46 Ibid., 56. Marguerite secured labour for the chapel by barter – doing sewing in return for building.

47 Morin, *Histoire simple et véritable*, 73.

48 Faillon, *Vie de la Soeur Bourgeoys*, 1:219.

49 Soeur Saint-Damase-de-Rome, *L'intendante de Notre-Dame*, 37–8.

50 Jamet, *Marguerite Bourgeoys*, 2:432.

51 Audet, "L'éducation au temps de Mgr de Laval," 65. It appears that a temporary concession was made for the colony.

52 Jamet, *Marguerite Bourgeoys*, 1:335.

53 Lahaise, *Les édifices conventuels du vieux Montréal*, 110–11.

54 For the text of the letters patent see Soeur Sainte-Henriette, *Histoire de la Congrégation de Notre-Dame de Montréal*, 1:113–15.

55 Ibid., 1:135–6.

56 Quoted in ibid., 1:270. The francization of the Indians was one of the few colonial educational endeavours which the government was prepared to subsidize. The Montagne mission received four thousand livres from Paris for this purpose. See Soeur Saint-Damase-de-Rome, *L'intendante de Notre-Dame*, 52.

57 Soeur Sainte-Henriette, *Histoire de la Congrégation*, 1:109.

58 *Ecrits*, 257.

59 Soeur Sainte-Henriette, *Histoire de la Congrégation*, 1:213, 257.

60 Ibid., 329–30.

61 Ibid., 333.

62 Jamet, *Marguerite Bourgeoys*, 2:744.

63 *Ecrits*, 278.

64 Dollier de Casson, "Histoire de Montréal," 136–7.

65 *Ecrits*, 61.

66 See, for instance, the 1673 contract between Zacharie Dupuy and his wife and the sisters, by which the former donated all their property to the latter, in return for a commitment to "Nourir et Entretenir Lesdits donateurs Sains et Malades, pendant leur Vie" (quoted in Chicoine, *La métairie de Marguerite Bourgeoys*, 112).

67 Morin, *Histoire simple et véritable*, 75.

68 Soeur Saint-Damase-de-Rome, *L'intendante de Notre-Dame*, 69–70.

69 Quoted in Faillon, *Vie de Soeur Bourgeoys*, 1:202.

70 *Ecrits*, 248.

71 Ibid., 256.

72 Ibid., 248.

73 Soeur Saint-Damase-de-Rome, *L'intendante de Notre-Dame*, 34.

74 Morin, *Histoire simple et véritable*, 75.

75 Fifty-four at the time of the foundress's death. Glandelet to Monsieur Henri Boudon, archdeacon of Evreux, 5 October 1700, quoted in Jamet, *Marguerite Bourgeoys*, 2:788.

76 Ibid., 713.

77 The particular circumstances surrounding the foundation of the Congrégation had made Marguerite, from the very beginning, much older than most of her companions. This contrast in age was increased when the fire of 1683 killed the two French sisters (both recruits of 1658) who had been considered most likely to succeed her. When the first election was finally held, in 1693, the four women elected to office were all Canadians, between the ages of twenty-seven and thirty-three. See Caza, *La vie voyagère*, 44.

78 See the petition of the *habitants* of Lachine (1680), quoted in Soeur Sainte-Henriette, *Histoire de la Congrégation*, 2:279.

79 De Meulles to Seignelay, 4 November 1683. Quoted in Jamet, *Marguerite Bourgeoys*, 2:552.

80 Ibid., 721.

81 See n. 28.

82 Notre-Dame de Bon Secours.

83 *Relation* de 1667, quoted in Jamet, *Marguerite Bourgeoys*, 323. Mère Morin was speaking for her own community of *hospitalières*, who took solemn vows only in 1671.

84 Marks of social respect included the privilege of receiving the *pain bénit* at mass. Soeur Bourgeois disapproved of such honours: "Since we are only poor women, we ought not to receive public honours in church" (*Ecrits*, 272).

85 60 per cent of the sisters recruited under the French regime originated among the people, as against 41 per cent of the Ursulines (Hurtubise, "Origine sociale des vocations canadiennes," 47).

86 Colbert to Talon, 11 February 1671. Talon, "Correspondance échangée entre le Cour de France et l'Intendant Talon," 147.

87 Quoted in Soeur Sainte-Henriette, *Histoire de la Congrégation*, 1:114.

88 According to Olivier Maurault, p.s.s., Saint-Sulpice, from the time it was "granted" the Seigneury, sent only individuals of private means to Montreal, with the understanding that they would spend their own funds in its service. By 1763, the company had spent over seven million livres on the colony. See his article, "Nos Messieurs," quoted in Soeur Saint-Damase-de-Rome, *L'intendante de Notre-Dame*, 56, and another article quoted in ibid., 87, n. 116.

89 Lanctot, *Montréal sous Maisonneuve*, 229.

90 See Talon, "Mémoire de Talon sur le Canada," 127.

91 Letter to the Ursulines of Tours, September-November 1671, Marie de l'Incarnation, *Correspondance*, 936.

92 Soeur Sainte-Henriette, *Histoire de la Congrégation*, 2:186–7.

93 Ibid., 1:288.

94 See above, p. 103.

95 Letter to the archbishop of Tours, 25 September 1670, in Marie de l'Incarnation, *Correspondance*, 894. Though the Ursulines argued that their presence would not affect the work of the Congrégation, everyone else agreed that there would be room for only one female teaching community in Montreal.

96 See above, p. 104.

97 *Ecrits*, 69.

98 Ibid., 70–2.

99 For a full account of this confrontation between the bishop and the sisters, see Soeur Sainte-Henriette, *Histoire de la Congrégation*, 2:46–8.

100 See the sisters' own account of the crisis, in their memoir to Tronson, paraphrased in ibid., 2:57–69. "Monseigneur wishes to give us rules and constitutions which will tend, for the most part, to make us into religious."

101 The same memoir as above, quoted in Jamet, *Marguerite Bourgeoys*, 2:746.
102 Tronson to Leschassier, 6 March 1695, quoted in ibid., 748.
103 *Ecrits*, 203–8; 221–3.
104 *Correspondance de Louis Tronson*, 2:351.
105 Ibid., 360.
106 *Ecrits*, 286.
107 Caza, *La vie voyagère*, 46.
108 The minister to the bishop of Quebec, 16 May 1710, quoted in Jean, *Évolution des communautés religieuses*, 34.
109 Jamet, *Marguerite Bourgeoys*, 2:790.
110 Lemoine, *Le monde des religieux*, 2.

CHAPTER SIX

1 Viguerie, *L'institution des enfants*, 62–3.
2 See above, chapter 3.
3 See chapter 3.
4 Madame Gueudré suggests that intellectual stimulation was "written out" in the Ursulines' bulls, while traditional jobs, such as sewing, were specified (*Histoire des Ursulines*, 1:108). Certainly the early practice of teaching Latin to the novices was soon discontinued (ibid., 2:235).
5 *Règlements* of the Ursulines of Saint-Brieuc, quoted in ibid., 2:166.
6 Mère de Pommereu, in her dedicatory letter at the beginning of her *Annales*, quoted in Jégou, *Les Ursulines du Faubourg Saint-Jacques*, 138.
7 Quoted in Babeau, *La ville sous l'Ancien Régime*, 465.
8 One of the nuns later commented: "we couldn't help smiling, since we could not understand how anyone would think that six women could do damage to a great city like Troyes." *La vie à Troyes sous Louis XIII* (Troyes: Centre de Recherche et d'Etudes Pierre et Nicolas Pithou 1984), 224–5.
9 Quoted in Derréal, *Un missionaire de la Contre-Réforme*, 191. See above, chapter 3.
10 Derréal, *Un missionaire*, 327, 325.
11 See above, chapter 3.
12 Jeanne Françoise de Chantal to Noël Brulart de Sillery, quoted in Devos, *L'origine Sociale des Visitandines*, 121.
13 Ibid., 259. It is interesting to note that according to Pillorget, in his work *La tige et le rameau: Familles anglaises et françaises 16–18 siècle* (Paris: Calmann-Levy 1979), 149–50, the number of spinsters in eighteenth-century France was considerably lower than that in England (15 per cent against 26 per cent). This must have been the case

partly because of the existence of an alternative to marriage in the religious communities.

14 1 Corinthians 14:34 (Jerusalem Bible).

15 1 Timothy 2:11–14 (Jerusalem Bible).

16 Didascalia Apostolorum, chapter 15.

17 S. Hosias, *De expresso dei verbo* (1561), quoted in Thomas, "Women and the Civil War Sects," 60, n.70. English Protestant writers seized gleefully upon this text, as proof of the way in which "the Jesuits" barred women "from all conference touching the word of God."

18 Dhôtel, *Les origines du catéchisme moderne*, 123.

19 According to the book of instructions put out in 1657 by the priests of Saint Nicolas-du-Chardonnet, "the catechist should at least be a lector" (ibid., 162).

20 Regarding the instruction of the poor by the charitable confraternities, Vincent de Paul ruled that "the brothers should not teach in the church" (quoted in Germain, *Langages de la foi*, 74).

21 Chambers, *Mary Ward*, 2:64.

22 Quoted in Darche, *Le saint abbé Bourdoise*, 2:115. For Père Anselme, catechizing was in the same category as preaching and offering the sacrifice of the mass.

23 *MDPU*, part 1:81.

24 Rule for the *regentes* of Alet, founded by Nicolas Pavillon (Taveneaux, *La vie quotidienne des jansenistes*, 78). Vincent de Paul gave a similar instruction to the dames de la Charité who worked among the sick of the Hôtel-Dieu of Paris (Coste, *Saint Vincent de Paul et les dames de la Charité*, 9–10).

25 Renard, *La Mère Alix Le Clerc*, 182.

26 Leymont, *Madame de Sainte-Beuve*, 267.

27 In François de Sales, *Oeuvres*, 25:330.

28 Furet and Ozouf, *Lire et ecrire*, 1:72.

29 François de Rochefoucauld, bishop of Senlis, "Avertissements aux curés" (ca.1614), quoted in Broutin, *La Réforme pastorale*, 1:49.

30 Dhôtel, *Les origines du catéchisme moderne*, 266.

31 Roger Duchêne attests to this outpouring in his commentary on the talk by Chedozeau, "Les petites écoles de Pierre Nicole," 19. "I have not found many testaments which do not mention … a financial bequest for the schools."

32 Poutet, "L'enseignement des pauvres," 88.

33 Fénelon, *Education des filles*, 8. 1

34 Fourier, *Primitif et légitime esprit*, 8–10.

35 Chartier, Compère, and Julia, *L'éducation en France*, 244. However, it has been noted, both by them and by others, that this rule was honoured in the breach as well as in the observance, since royal and

episcopal denunciations of the practice of coeducation continued in many schools throughout the Old Regime.

36 Ibid., 237.
37 Poutet, *Origines*, 1:494.
38 Ibid., 530.
39 Beaurepaire, *Recherches*, 1:303.
40 Ibid., 314.
41 Ibid., 283.
42 AD Seine maritime, G 1177. Visite paroissiale de Joseph de Serau-court, 1698, quoted in Bardet, *Rouen*, 1:248.
43 Poutet, *Origines*, 1:533.
44 Barré, "Memoire instructif," *Statuts et reglemens des escoles chrestiennes et charitables.*
45 Poutet, *Origines*, 1:497.
46 Aroz, *Nicolas Roland*, 72, n. 1.
47 Poutet, "L'influence du Pere Barré dans la fondation des Soeurs du Saint-Enfant-Jésus de Reims," 23.
48 Marguerite Lestocq, "Mémoire," quoted in Grèzes, *Vie du R.P. Barré*, 157–8.
49 Barré, *Lettres spirituelles*, 345.
50 Ibid., 319.
51 Barré, *Statuts et reglemens*, 1–2.
52 Ibid., 1–2.
53 Vincent de Paul, *Correspondance*, 10:567.
54 See below, p. 133.
55 "Mémoire," in Grèzes, *Barré*, 159.
56 Ibid., 158.
57 Ibid., 160.
58 Ibid., 159.
59 Ibid., 230.
60 See below, p. 137.
61 Barré, "Mémoire instructif," 3.
62 Servien de Montigny, *secrétaire des commandements* to the late queen mother, before he resigned to become a priest; the sieur de Grain-ville, councillor in the Parlement of Rouen, whose mother lent space in her house for the first charity classes held in the city; Pierre Fau-vel, seigneur de Touvens; the abbé de l'Epinay. These men took over full supervision of the Rouen house after Barré's death.
63 Memoir of the administrators of Ernemont to the archbishop, 1727, quoted in Beaurepaire, *Recherches*, 1:253.
64 Farcy, *Providence de Rouen*, 82.
65 Quoted in ibid., 66.
66 MS of 1696, Bayeux, printed in ibid., 65.

67 Request by the administrators of the Providence for letters patent, 26 February 1679, quoted in ibid., 67–8.
68 Bardet, *Rouen*, 2, table 103.
69 Grèzes, *Barré*, 180.
70 Ibid., 188.
71 *Abrégé de l'histoire*, by Servier de Montigny, in Barré, *Lettres spirituelles*, 372.
72 Chateauneuf to Montigny, 30 April 1686, quoted in Grèzes, *Barré*, 220.
73 Arch. de Saint-Maur, printed in Grèzes, *Barré*, 215.
74 M. Langlois, *Correspondance de Madame de Maintenon*, 3:121, quoted in Lemoine, *Le monde des religieux*, 339.
75 Grèzes, *Barré*, 338–9.
76 Hermant, *Histoire des ordres religieux et des congrégations régulières et séculières de l'Eglise*, 454.
77 Lemoine, *Le monde des religieux*, 326.
78 Barré, "Mémoire instructif," 2.
79 Barré, *Statuts et reglemens*, chapter 1, art. 5.
80 *Abrégé*, in Barré, *Lettres spirituelles*, 374–5.
81 "Maximes de conduite chrétienne," in Barré, *Lettres spirituelles*, 356.
82 Quoted in Farcy, *Providence de Rouen*, 77.
83 Barré, *Statuts et reglemens*, chapter 9, art. 9.
84 Quoted in Farcy, *Providence de Rouen*, 57.
85 Poutet, "L'influence du Père Barré," 34–47.
86 Barré, *Maximes particulières pour les Ecoles charitables*, ix and x, in *Lettres spirituelles*, 344–5.
87 Barré, *Statuts et reglemens*, chapter 8, art. 11.
88 Quoted in Farcy, *Providence de Rouen*, 56.
89 Grèzes, *Barré*, 383–4.
90 *Abrégé*, in Barré, *Lettres spirituelles*, 372.
91 Poutet, *Origines*, 1:520–5; Grèzes, *Barré*, 194–5.
92 P. Raffron, *Vie du R. P. Francois Giry* (Paris 1691), quoted in Grèzes, *Barré*, 343.
93 Desportes, *Histoire de Reims*, 182–3.
94 Loriquet, *Mémoires d'Oudard Coquault*, 1:475.
95 Ibid., 1:375.
96 G. Laurent, *Reims et la région rémoise à la veille de la Révolution* (Reims: Imprimerie Matot-Briane 1930), xx.
97 Poutet, *Origines*, 1:123.
98 Péchenard, *Congrégation de Notre-Dame à Reims*, 1:86.
99 Ibid., 2:374.
100 Poutet, *Origines*, 1:393.
101 Most of the information on Roland's life comes from a collection of

posthumous tributes, made in the year 1693 by the Soeurs du Saint-Enfant-Jésus of Reims. A number of these personal recollections were collected into a single manuscript, entitled "Mémoires sur la Vie de Monsieur Nicolas Roland, Prêtre, Chanoine Théologal de l'Eglise de Reims, et Fondateur de la Communauté du Saint Enfant Jésus, Décedé le 27 avril 1678, age de 35 ans et 5 mois." The author is unknown, though there is some reason for believing that he was Jean-Baptiste de La Salle, who was Roland's executor. This document, and the various letters from which it draws, are reproduced in *Un précurseur méconnu*, a collection of documents published in Reims in 1963, as part of the process towards Roland's canonization. The "Mémoires" are the first biography of Roland.

102 See Poutet, *Origines*, 2, for an appreciation of the influence which this community had on Roland and, through him, on his friend Jean-Baptiste de La Salle.

103 "Mémoires," *Un précurseur méconnu*, 157.

104 Faillon, *Vie de M. Démia* (Lyon 1829), quoted in Aroz, *Nicolas Roland*, 63.

105 "Mémoires," *Un précurseur méconnu*, 163.

106 Ibid., 165.

107 BM Reims, MS. 1704, 97: "Mémoires de René Bourgeois," quoted in Aroz, *Nicolas Roland*, 38. These memoirs are invaluable, since they present the council's point of view in its battle of wills with Roland.

108 Ibid, quoted in ibid., 74.

109 "Mémoires," *Un précurseur méconnu*, 166.

110 René Bourgeois, Mémoires, 782, quoted in Hannesse, *Vie de Nicolas Roland*, 188–9.

111 "Mémoires," *Un précurseur méconnu*, 176.

112 Ibid., 170.

113 Aroz, *Nicolas Roland*, 107–12.

114 "Mémoires," *Un précurseur méconnu*, 171.

115 Ibid., 177.

116 Ibid., 207.

117 Hannesse, *Nicolas Roland*, 191.

118 "Mémoires," *Un précurseur méconnu*, 199.

119 Letter from P. Valentin, Minime, in ibid., 136.

120 Henri Brémond, "La vie religieuse d'un bourgeois de Reims au XVIIe siecle," *Etudes* 89 (1901):622–38.

121 See above, chapter 3.

122 Arch. Soeurs de l'Enfant-Jesus de Reims: Proces verbal des premiers Voeux, 8 février 1684.

123 When he received a note criticizing this usage, he immediately recognized his fault: "he said that they were right, and that the sisters

should be quickly told that henceforth they should only be addressed by the title of 'ma Soeur'" ("Mémoires," *Un précurseur méconnu*, 208).

124 Ibid., 207.

125 René Bourgeois, Mémoires, 3, 697, quoted in Hannesse, *Nicolas Roland*, 184.

126 Bourgeois, Mémoires, 3, 1078. In fact, the sisters did not confine themselves to the limitations set by the city. From the very beginning, their schools accepted girls of all ages ("Memoires," *Un précurseur méconnu*, 166). By the 1680s, when their school rules were written down, they were teaching writing to advanced students.

127 See above, p. 125.

128 Arch. Ville de Reims, carton 691, liasse 14, no. 5, printed in Aroz, *Nicolas Roland*, 94.

129 "Mémoires," *Un précurseur méconnu*, 167.

130 Nicolas Roland to Jean Roland, 1678, printed in ibid., 7.

131 BN MSS. 20712, Lettres et mémoires, 1704–6, fol. 159, cited in Aroz, *Nicolas Roland*, 14.

132 BM Reims, MS. 1851, "Constitutions Pour la Com^te des filles du St Enfant Jésus Etablie à Reims" given by Charles-Maurice Le Tellier, 12 November 1683, chapter 7, no. 2.

133 Aroz, *Nicolas Roland*, 123.

134 Archives Soeurs de l'Enfant-Jésus, MS. 17, f. 19.

135 Poutet, *Origines*, 1:575.

136 Nicolas Roland to Jean Roland, 1678. *Un précurseur méconnu*, 7.

137 Arch. Soeurs de l'Enfant-Jesus, Reims, MS. 17, f. 158.

138 Aroz has recorded this list of professions of the fathers of students at a school run by the Christian Brothers, "which imitated that of the sisters," in the Saint-Rémi quarter; he suggests that it resembles the clientèle of the sisters' schools (Aroz, *Nicolas Roland*, 156).

139 See Desportes, *Reims*, 209 for map.

140 BM Reims, MS. 1851, 3–4.

141 Jean-Baptiste de La Salle drew heavily upon the experience of the sisters, as well as other communities, in the creation of his Christian Brothers. Two historians of the Christian Brothers acknowledge his debt to the sisters. See Aroz, *Nicolas Roland*, n.137, and Poutet, *Origines*, 1: "Pauvre avec les pauvres de Reims."

142 Albistur and Armogathe, *Histoire du féminisme français*, 1:136.

143 Brémond, *Histoire littéraire*, 2:37.

144 Chaunu, *L'église, culture et société*, 401.

145 Poutet, "Nicolas Barré, Nicolas Roland, Charles Démia et leurs 'filles séculières,'" 42.

146 *Ecrits*, 114–15.

CHAPTER SEVEN

1 Avant-propos, *Les religieuses enseignantes*, 7.
2 Langlois, *Le catholicisme au féminin*, 625.
3 Anne de Xainctonge, quoted in Morey, *La vénérable Anne de Xainctonge*, 2:33.
4 *Les vrayes constitutions des religieuses de la Congregation de Nostre Dame* (1646), preface.
5 Morey, *Anne de Xainctonge*, 2:33.
6 Fourier, *Vrayes constitutions*, quoted in Maggiolo, "L'oeuvre pédagogique de Pierre Fourier," 212.
7 *MDPU*, part 1:8–9, quoted in Jégou, *Les Ursulines du Faubourg Saint-Jacques*, 138.
8 Morey, *Anne de Xainctonge*, 1:250–1.
9 Quoted in Viguerie, *L'institution des enfants*, 64.
10 Bull of erection for the Bordeaux monastery of the Filles de Notre-Dame, 7 April 1607, quoted in Molette, "Conclusions," *Les religieuses enseignantes*, 152.
11 Derréal, *Un missionaire*, 374, n. 75.
12 Ibid., 139–40.
13 *MDPU*, quoted in Jégou, *Les Ursulines du Faubourg Saint-Jacques*, 44.
14 Michel, "Une version modernisée," 56.
15 Père Orset, quoted in Morey, *Anne de Xainctonge*, 2:384.
16 Ursulines, *Constitutions* (1640), part 1:21–2, quoted in Jégou, *Les Ursulines du Faubourg Saint-Jacques*, 139.
17 *MDPU*, part 1:14.
18 Fourier, *Vrayes constitutions*, 6.
19 See above, chapter 6.
20 Barré, *Lettres spirituelles*, maxime 10, 344–5.
21 Ménard, *Une histoire des mentalités religieuses*, 375ff.
22 Fénelon, *Education des filles*, 5.
23 See, for instance, the various articles of Jean Perrel, especially "Sur l'enseignement féminin avant la Révolution," in *Penelope* 2 (1980): 9–10.
24 Chedozeau, "Les petites écoles de Pierre Nicole," 15.
25 "Relation à la gloire de Dieu" by Alix Le Clerc, quoted in Bazelaire, *Le bienheureux Pierre Fourier*, 1; *MDPU*, part 1:161. Stories of this sort abound in the various annals, and they are probably true: after all, the schools were free.
26 Leymont, *Madame de Sainte-Beuve*, 154–5; Morey, *Anne de Xainctonge*, 1:378.
27 Pingaud, *Saint Pierre Fourier*, 60.
28 Salome, *Mary Ward*, 77.

29 Père Orset, quoted in Morey, *Anne de Xainctonge*, 2:63.
30 Michel, "Une version modernisée," 59–60.
31 Ibid., 72.
32 Fourier, *Vrayes constitutions*, art. 14, 15.
33 Morey, *Anne de Xainctonge*, 2:71.
34 For the Jesuit model, see Dainville, *La naissance de l'humanisme moderne*, 1:144. For their debt to older Calvinist practice, see Soury-Lavergne, *Chemin d'éducation*, 74.
35 *Reglemens des Ursulines* (Paris 1705), part 1:144.
36 *Bref Discours* (1608), quoted in Dainville, *La naissance de l'humanisme moderne*, 151–2.
37 Pierre Fourier (1645), quoted in Maggiolo, "L'oeuvre pédagogique," 219. Also see the school rule of the Filles de Notre-Dame, quoted in *La Compagnie de Marie Notre-Dame*, 77: "The student will be made to stand up to recite the lesson which she is supposed to know by heart, and the counterpart or adversary of the girl who is reciting will stand up on the other side, opposite her, teaching her or correcting her if there is need."
38 Maggiolo, "L'oeuvre pédagogique," 229.
39 Quoted in Rohan-Chabot, "Les écoles de campagne," 170.
40 Montaigne, *Essais*, 1:26: De l'Institution des Enfants.
41 Maggiolo, "L'oeuvre pédagogique," 228.
42 Quoted in Gueudré, *Histoire des Ursulines*, 2:244.
43 Quoted in Grosperrin, *Les petites écoles*, 110.
44 Quoted in Gueudre, *Histoire des Ursulines*, 2:245.
45 Fénelon, *Education des filles*, 31.
46 *Règlement et methode pour les écoles* (Paris 1709), quoted in Fosseyeux, *Les écoles de charité*, 70.
47 Thuillier, *Diarium patrum*, 64.
48 Dainville, *La naissance de l'humanisme moderne*, 117.
49 Perrel, "Les filles à l'école avant la Révolution," 314.
50 Many monasteries considered the training of secular teachers as part of their apostolate. Marguerite Bourgeoys learned her trade in the monastery of Troyes; the pedagogy which she brought to Montreal was that of Pierre Fourier. See Soeur Sainte-Gertrude, "L'oeuvre pédagogique de Marguerite Bourgeoys," 58ff. Sometimes whole new communities would undergo training at neighbouring monasteries. This was the case with the Soeurs du Saint-Enfant-Jésus of Reims, who were trained by the cloistered Congrégation. Their methods, in turn, influenced those of the Christian Brothers.
51 Poutet, *Origines*, 1.
52 Letter to the nuns of Bar-le-Duc, 30 October 1621. Fourier, *Correspondance*, 1:297.

53 Coste, *Le grand saint*, 1:457.

54 See above, chapter 6.

55 Poutet, "Nicolas Barré, Nicolas Roland, Charles Démia et leurs 'filles séculières,'" 40.

56 *Ecrits de Mère Bourgeoys*, 70.

57 *Reglemens des Ursulines* (1705), 3:33. In this case, the practice under discussion was the folding of the boarders' linen.

58 Ibid., 2:75.

59 Calendini, *Le couvent des Filles de Notre-Dame*, 179.

60 For instance, a catechism by Marguerite Filloleau, in use among the Filles de Notre-Dame (ibid., 220), and a memoir on the method of preparing children for first communion, drawn up by Elisabeth Desnots, Ursuline of Faubourg Saint-Jacques, which was included in the *règlements* of 1640 (Jégou, *Les Ursulines du Faubourg Saint-Jacques*, 120).

61 Quoted in Gueudré, *Histoire des Ursulines*, 2:260.

62 Jégou, *Les Ursulines du Faubourg Saint-Jacques*, 125; Gueudré, *Histoire des Ursulines*, 2:220

63 Ibid, 2:248.

64 "Avis de M. de Fénelon à une dame de qualité sur l'éducation de mademoiselle sa fille," *Education des filles*, 121–2.

65 Argenson, *Annales de la Compagnie du Saint-Sacrement*, 69.

66 Paul Beurrier, *Oeuvres*.

67 *Instructions et reglemens pour celles qui désirent servir Dieu en la Communauté des pauures filles dites de Saincte Marthe*, 1651.

68 Reglement pour les petites Ecoles Chretiennes.

69 Barré, Mémoires et instructions pour la sanctification des Soeurs, in *Lettres spirituelles*, 356.

70 Barré, *Statuts et reglemens*, chapter 3, art. 15.

71 Ibid., chapter 2, art. 20.

72 Grèzes, *Barré*, 216. According to Barré's rule, this was too many: "each mistress will ordinarily be charged with no more than seventy or eighty children" (*Statuts et reglemens*, chapter 8, art. 8).

73 Ibid., chapter 9, art. 8.

74 As, for instance, in the years after the Revocation of the Edict of Nantes, when they acted as re-educators of new Catholics in the cities of southern France. See Chartier, Compère and Julia, *L'Education en France*, 242.

75 Arch. Soeurs du Saint-Enfant-Jesus de Reims, MS. 17, f. 20.

76 Soeur Sainte-Gertrude, "L'Oeuvre pédagogique," 63.

77 Furet and Ozouf, *Lire et écrire*, 1:73. Also see Poutet, "L'enseignement des pauvres," 90.

78 Chartier, Compère, and Julia, *L'éducation en France*, 294.

79 Grosperrin, *Les petites écoles*, 142.

80 Quoted in Poutet, "Spiritualité des enseignants," 323.

81 *MDPU*, part 1:12.

82 Mademoiselle Le Gras, *Lettres*, 357.

83 *Statuts et reglemens*, chapter 8, art. 13; chapter 3, art. 15.

84 Gueudré, *Histoire des Ursulines*, 2:231.

85 Dhôtel, *Les origines du catéchisme moderne*, 272–4.

86 *Vrayes constitutions*, art. 23.

87 Archbishop de Grammont of Besançon, 1688, quoted in Grosperrin, *Les petites écoles*, 103.

88 Grosperrin, *Les petites écoles*, 104.

89 Reglement pour les petites Ecoles Chretiennes, f. 139.

90 Dhôtel, *Les origines du catéchisme moderne*, 425.

91 Fourier, *Vrayes Constitutions*, part 3, art. 13.

92 Quoted in Jégou, *Les Ursulines du Faubourg Saint-Jacques*, 56. This is not to say, however, that boarders were discouraged from entering religion. Of the fifty-eight nuns living in the monastery of Faubourg Saint-Jacques in 1662, thirty-nine were ex-boarders (ibid., 107).

93 A saying attributed to the Ursulines, cited in A. Loth, *La charité catholique en France avant la Révolution* (Tours 1896), 378.

94 *Reglemens des Ursulines*, 4:62.

95 Barré, Reglemens manuscrits, 2.

96 Fourier, quoted in Maggiolo, "L'oeuvre pédagogique", 222–3.

97 Furet and Ozouf, *Lire et écrire*, 86.

98 For this false delicacy the nuns of Saint-Cyr were roundly scolded by Madame de Maintenon (Faguet, *Madame de Maintenon*, 153–4).

99 Soeurs du Saint-Enfant Jésus, Reims, Extraits du livre des usages, f.4.

100 Barré, Reglements manuscrits, 18.

101 Soeurs du Saint-Enfant Jésus, Usages, f.9.

102 See, for instance, Marguerite Lestocq's "Mémoire," quoted in Grèzes, *Barré*, 158.

103 *Education des filles*, 62.

104 Quoted in Faguet, *Madame de Maintenon*, 99.

105 Furet and Ozouf, *Lire et écrire*, 1:90.

106 *Vrayes Constitutions*, part 3, art. 14, 3.

107 Barré, Reglemens manuscrits, 3.

108 *Reglemens des Ursulines de Paris*, part 1:30–1.

109 Morey, *Anne de Xainctonge*, 79. The practice of bringing such documents into school continued in Franche-Comté, according to Morey, until after the Revolution.

110 Fénelon, *Education des filles*, 11.

111 Meyer, "Essai sur l'instruction populaire," 343.

112 Ibid., 333.

113 Barré, Reglements manuscrits, 27.

114 Meyer, "Essai sur l'instruction populaire," 339. It should be noted that metal pen nibs were already in use in the *petites écoles* of Port-Royal (Delforge, *Les petites écoles de Port-Royal*). Their use did not become general until much later.

115 *Reglemens des Ursulines*, chapter 8, 144.

116 Ibid., chapter 6, 75ff.

117 *Vrayes Constitutions*, part 3, art. 40.

118 Barré, Reglements manuscrits, 4.

119 Reglement pour les petites Ecoles Chretiennes, 108.

120 Fourier, quoted in Maggiolo, *L'oeuvre pédagogique*, 225–6.

121 Quoted in Dulong, *La vie quotidienne*, 12.

122 Beaurepaire, *Recherches*, 2:276.

123 *Mémoire* of 1667, quoted in Dainville, *La naissance de l'humanisme moderne*, 134.

124 Quoted in Furet and Ozouf, *Lire et écrire*, 1:356.

125 Ibid., 1:356–7, and 85.

126 See above, chapter 6.

127 L. Franquet, *Voyages et mémoires sur le Canada* (Montreal: Ed. Elysée 1974), 31–2.

128 *Reglemens des Ursulines*, chapter 8, art. 84, 85.

129 Jadart, *Mémoires de Jean Maillefer*, 122–3. Also see above, p. 13.

130 "De l'esprit de la communauté des Filles de Sainte-Genevièfve," chapter 2, art. 1.

131 *Education des filles*, 125.

132 *Reglemens des Ursulines*, chapter 7, 82–3.

133 Ibid., chapter 3, 34–5.

134 Morey, *Anne de Xainctonge*, 2:82.

135 Fourier, *Vrayes Constitutions*, part 3, art. 46.

136 Morey, *Anne de Xainctonge*, 2:74.

137 Fourier, *Vrayes Constitutions*, part 3, art. 48.

138 Quoted in Morey, *Anne de Xainctonge*, 2:378.

139 Barré, Reglements manuscrits, 7.

140 "Reglemens à faire dans les Ecoles Chrétiennes du travail manuel ... dressez et écrits de la main du R. Père Barré," in Barré, *Lettres spirituelles*, 359–66.

141 Fénelon, *Education des filles*, 94.

142 Gueudré, *Histoire des Ursulines*, 2:187.

CHAPTER EIGHT

1 "Reglement Provisionnel" (1598), in Fourier, *Correspondance*, 2:351.

2 Ibid., 352.

3 Viguerie, *Une oeuvre d'éducation*, 25.

4 Langlois, *Le catholicisme au féminin*, 308.

5 Ibid., 78. It should be emphasized that many cloistered nuns were engaged in active service, as teachers or as nurses. They should really be classed as "active contemplatives."

6 Council of Trent, session 25:5. See above, chapter 2, n. 12.

7 This paraphrase of Ingoli's remarks is found in Guilday, *The English Catholic Refugees*, 199.

8 Fourier, *Correspondance*, 2:347. See chapter 3, n. 73.

9 Cardinal Bellarmine to François de Sales, 29 December 1616, François de Sales, *Oeuvres*, 17:416.

10 Quoted in Poutet, "Spiritualités d'enseignants," 51.

11 Prospectus of the Filles de la Croix, quoted in Poutet, *Origines*, 1:574.

12 Flachaire, *La dévotion à la Vierge, passim*, but especially 168ff.

13 Bérulle, quoted in Caza, *La vie voyagère*, 101.

14 Including the primitive Visitation of Annecy, whom François de Sales first called "soeurs de Sainte-Marthe," to indicate their duty to the poor (Lemoine, *Le monde des religieux*, 302).

15 Morey, *Anne de Xainctonge*, 2:33. Barré, also, invoked the patronage of the guardian angels for his schoolmistresses. See his Reglements manuscrits, 24.

16 Caza, *La vie voyagère*, 63.

17 Flachaire, *La dévotion à la Vierge, passim*, but especially 34ff. and 121.

18 Ibid., 140, 104, 160.

19 See above, chapter 7, n. 21.

20 *La vie du chrestien ou le catechisme de la mission* of Jean Eudes (1668), quoted in Ménard, *Une histoire de mentalités religeuses*, 371.

21 *Vie de la vénérable Alix Leclerc (1773)*, 269.

22 *Ecrits*, 91.

23 François de Sales, *Oeuvres*, 25:214.

24 Denis de Marquemont, Mémoire, in ibid., 25:328.

25 Vincent de Paul, *Correspondance*, 13:419.

26 Olier, *Vie intérieure de la Très Sainte Vierge*, quoted in Caza, *La vie voyagère*, 86. Jean-Jacques Olier (1618–59), cousin of Pierre Seguier, keeper of the seals, was a member of the Compagnie du Saint-Sacrement and founder of Saint- Sulpice. In 1640 he became the co-founder, with Jerome Royer de la Dauversière, of the Société de Notre-Dame pour la conversion des Sauvages de la Nouvelle-France. He ardently supported the work of the teaching *filles séculières* in France.

27 *Ecrits*, 204.

28 Acts of the Apostles 1:14 (Jerusalem Bible).

29 Quoted in Caza, *La vie voyagère*, 90.

30 Fourier, *Le primitif et legitime esprit* (1650).

31 *Ecrits*, 78.

32 Ibid., 81. Her answer was simple: "The Blessed Virgin was never cloistered" (ibid., 82).

33 Quoted in Lemoine, *Le droit des religieux*, 202.

34 Conference of 2 February 1653, in Vincent de Paul, *Correspondance*, 9:584.

35 "Maximes pour les Ecoles charitables," in Barré, *Lettres spirituelles*, 341–2.

36 Quoted in Bonneau-Avenant, *Madame de Miramion*, 243.

37 Taveneaux, *Le catholicisme*, 1:158.

38 Robert Bellarmine to François de Sales, 29 December 1616. François de Sales, *Oeuvres* 17:416.

39 Constitutions of the Visitation: Formula for profession. Francois de Sales, *Oeuvres* 25:186, 193.

40 Mademoiselle Le Gras, *Lettres*, 473.

41 Vincent de Paul, *Correspondance*, 9:661–2.

42 Lemoine, *Le monde des religieux*, 309.

43 E.g., the Soeurs du Saint-Enfant-Jésus of Reims, Constitutions, chapter 1, art. 8.

44 E.g., Constitution of the Filles de l'Instruction Chrestienne (1657), f. 11, formula for the contract signed upon admission: "The aforesaid sister will remain for the rest of her days in the aforesaid house ... Equally, the aforesaid ladies and Senior Sister have promised to feed and board her, in sickness and in health as long as she remains in the service of the said house" (AN s 7046–7). This was the type of agreement that the schoolmistresses who came to Montreal in 1658 made with Soeur Bourgeoys (*Ecrits*, 60–2).

45 Barré, *Statuts et reglemens*, chapter 1, art. 5.

46 Ibid., chapter 6, art. 4.

47 Soeur Sainte-Henriette, *Histoire de la Congrégation*, 2:73. It should be remarked that even in the seventeenth century, monasteries were expected to provide a prison cell for recalcitrants.

48 Morey, *Anne de Xainctonge*, 1:248.

49 *MDPU*, part 1:50.

50 Olier, *Lettres*, 2:453, quoted in Faillon, *Vie de M. Olier*, 1:632.

51 Barré, *Lettres spirituelles*, 353.

52 Vincent de Paul, *Correspondance*, 9:683–4.

53 Pocquet du Haut-Jussé, *La vie temporelle des communautés de femmes à Rennes*, 66.

54 Aubry, "Le monastère nancéien," 112. This became a matter of serious importance during the Jansenist controversy, when many feminine communities showed Jansenist leanings.

55 Jégou, *Les Ursulines du Faubourg Saint-Jacques*, 118.

56 Mère Juchereau, *Les annales de l'Hôtel-Dieu de Québec*, introduction, xxiv.

57 For an account of the process of drawing up the final rule, see Jégou, *Les Ursulines du Faubourg Saint-Jacques*, 118–22.

58 Gueudré, *Histoire des Ursulines*, 2:208. They won their argument.

59 Devos, *Les Visitandines d'Annecy*, 55.

60 Jégou, *Les Ursulines du Faubourg Saint-Jacques*, 119.

61 *Constitutions de Nancy* (1647), quoted in Aubry, "Le monastère nancéien," 103.

62 Ursulines of Rouen, Declaration de lestat du temporel. AD Seine Maritime, D 404.

63 AD Pas-de-Calais, H 402.

64 AD Seine Maritime, D 394. Marguerite went on to become superior of the house. Also see Pocquet du Haut-Jussé, *La vie temporelle*, 25ff, 87, for further examples of founders' privileges.

65 Fourier, *Correspondance*, 1:238.

66 Registre des Actes du chapitre, 1641, quoted in Jégou, *Les Ursulines du Faubourg Saint-Jacques*, 98.

67 AD Haute-Loire, série L, quoted in Gaussin and Vallet, "L'instruction secondaire des filles," 461.

68 Gueudré, *Histoire des Ursulines*, 2:51–2; Morey, *Anne de Xainctonge*, 2:373–4. In Bordeaux, the Filles de Notre-Dame were advised by the bishop "to spin wool, and make lace and trimmings that can be sold so as to comfort them in their poverty" (Entraygues, *Une nièce de Montaigne*, 251).

69 AD Pas-de-Calais, H 402.

70 Perrel, "Les filles à l'école," 300; Jégou, *Les Ursulines du Faubourg Saint-Jacques*, 102. During the same period the Visitation of Riom was charging a *pension* of 360 livres (Perrel).

71 Jégou, *Les Ursulines du Faubourg Saint-Jacques*, 103.

72 Devos, *Visitandines*, 170.

73 Fagniez, *La femme*, 32.

74 A good discussion of *constitutions de rente*, and their importance in the monastic economy, may be found in Pocquet du Haut-Jussé, *Vie temporelle*, 101ff.

75 Conclusion des Assemblees du Conseil, 8 April 1661, quoted in Jégou, *Les Ursulines du Faubourg Saint-Jacques*, 99.

76 Gueudré, *Histoire des Ursulines*, 2:141.

77 Ibid., 2:132.

78 E.g., Montluçon, 23,000 livres; Montbrison, 12,000 livres; Rennes, 10,666 livres (ibid., 2:138; Pocquet du Haut-Jussé, *La vie temporelle*, 127).

79 Lemoine, *Le monde des religieux*, 369.

80 Viguerie, "La vocation religieuse et sacerdotale," 34. Jean-Claude Dubé has pointed out an added disadvantage suffered by women's monasteries: as a rule, their share of charitable donations was smaller than that of their male counterparts.

81 Le Brun, in Rogier *et al.*, *Nouvelle histoire de l'Eglise*, 3:424.

82 *Un précurseur méconnu*, 7.

83 Vincent de Paul, conference of 29 September 1655, in *Correspondance*, 10:114.

84 See above, chapter 6.

85 Union Chrestienne, *Constitutions* (1673), 20.

86 Vincent de Paul, conference of 30 April 1643, in *Correspondance*, 9:122–3.

87 *Ecrits*, 221–2.

88 Barré, *Statuts et reglemens*, chapter 9, art. 2. Also see Mademoiselle Le Gras, *Lettres*, 657.

89 Farcy, *Providence*, 111.

90 Barré, *Statuts et reglemens*, chapter 10, arts. 18, 19.

91 Beaurepaire, *Recherches*, 2:234–40.

92 Aroz, *Nicolas Roland*, 38, and above, chapter 5, n. 68.

93 AD Seine-Maritime, D 436.

94 Ordinance of 22 February 1689, quoted in Lembrez, "Institut du Saint-Enfant-Jésus," 162.

95 ANS 7051: Etat de la maison de Bonnetable, quoted in Grèzes, *Barré*, 364.

96 See the testament of the duchesse de Guise, 1686: "I order that all the schoolmasters and mistresses who are employed by me on my domains, and who are there on the day of my death, shall be maintained there in perpetuity at a salary of two hundred livres for each schoolmaster, and fifty écus for each schoolmistress" (quoted in ibid., 609).

97 Vincent de Paul, *Correspondance*, 9:51–2. This was also the practice among the sisters of Montreal.

98 Quoted in Gueudré, *Histoire des Ursulines*, 2:217.

99 François de Sales, *Oeuvres*, 25:61.

100 Quoted in Calendini, *Couvent des Filles de Notre-Dame*, 94.

101 Devos, *Visitandines*, 250.

102 Jégou, *Les Ursulines du Faubourg Saint-Jacques*, 89–90.

103 Pocquet du Haut-Jussé, *La vie temporelle*, 85–6.

104 Notter, "Les ordres religieux féminins blésois," 189.

105 Pocquet du Haut-Jussé, *La vie temporelle*, 70.

106 Ibid., 72.

107 Loriquet, *Mémoires d'Oudart Coquault*, 1:379–80.

108 Cordier, *La famille sainte*, 395–6, quoted in Châtellier, *L'Europe des dévots*, 158–9.

109 Vincent de Paul, *Correspondance*, 5:563–4.

110 See appendix, graphs 3, 4, 5.

111 Viguerie, "La vocation religieuse," 34.

112 See appendix, graph 4.

113 Conference of 9 June 1658. Vincent de Paul, *Correspondance*, 10:509.

114 *Ecrits*, 286. Neither Bishop Saint-Vallier nor Tronson was impressed by this argument. The rule drawn up in 1697 for the congregation stipulated dowries.

115 Letter to Guillaume Deluile, Arras, 18 February 1657, Vincent de Paul, *Correspondance*, 6:189.

116 Mademoiselle Le Gras, *Lettres*, 537.

117 Ibid., 615.

118 *Ecrits*, 81.

119 Rule of the *confrérie* of the Filles de la Charité. Vincent de Paul, *Correspondance*, 13:555.

120 Ibid., 10:661.

121 "Mémoire instructif," 2.

122 Ursulines of Quebec, archives: Annales manuscrites du premier couvent de Paris pendant les 50 premières années de son existence, 1612–1662, fol. 92.

123 "Mémoire instructif," 3.

124 See above, chapter 7, n. 6.

125 Conference of June 1642. Vincent de Paul, *Correspondance*, 10:81–2.

126 Ibid., 10:103. For correspondence on the question of headgear, see ibid., 14:index, under *coiffure*.

127 A document drawn up in 1666 and bearing the signatures of the community includes names of some of the best families of Rouen, such as Corneille, Tiberge, l'Espinay, de la Pommeraye, le Bras de Fer. For the complete list, see Farcy, *Providence*, 39–40.

128 Which usually remained uncut. There were some exceptions to this rule, e.g., the Soeurs du Saint-Enfant-Jésus of Reims, whose hair was cut at time of profession. This community, since it took simple vows, was more "religious" than many others.

129 Montigny-Servien, "sur la simplicite des habits," in Grèzes, *Barré*, 394.

130 "Maximes particulieres pour les Ecoles charitables," in Barré, *Lettres spirituelles*, 353.

131 Mère Juchereau, *Annales*, 229.

132 *Ecrits*, 72.

133 Vincent de Paul, *Correspondance*, 9:312–13.
134 Conference of December 1648. Ibid. 9:455–6.

CONCLUSION

1 *Analecta juris pontificii* (1885), col. 2022–3. See chapter 2.
2 Lemoine, *Le monde des religieux*, 9.
3 Chaunu, *L'église, culture et société*, 401.
4 *Ecrits de Mère Bourgeoys*, 204.
5 Abelly, *Vie de Saint-Vincent de Paul*, 2:36.
6 These rights belonged to the abbess of Remiremont in Lorraine, who was also, by virtue of her position, a princess of the Holy Roman Empire (Renard, *La Mère Alix Le Clerc*, 4).
7 Poutet, "Nicolas Barré, Nicolas Roland, Charles Démia et leurs 'filles séculières,'" 42.
8 *MDPU*, part 3:5.
9 See chapter 1, n. 13.
10 Lemoine, *Le monde des religieux*, 2.

Note on the
Use of Sources

"The name of a religious ought to be as unknown and solitary as her person; she should rather work to inscribe her name in the Book of Life than on a thesis of theology." (The Marquise de Saint-Martin, Ursuline prioress of Metz; quoted in Gueudré, "La femme et la vie spirituelle," 47–8.

The feminine congregations of early modern France were almost buried from modern view, under the disruption of the Revolution, which put an end to many of them, the contempt of nineteenth-century republican historians (fuelled in no small part by the continuing hold which the congregations exercised on female education), the condescension of major male religious historians who, at least until recently, respected nuns more for their virtue than for their social value, and outright dismissal by the modern historians who have tended all too easily to accept at face value the women's own lowly and humble self-image. Only lately have historians begun to investigate the possibility that these thousands of women may have had a real effect both upon their times and upon their own condition.

The changing attitude was signalled by a book published in 1974: Charles Molette's *Guide des sources de l'histoire des congrégations féminines françaises de vie active*. Molette's work had been inspired by a different concern. The shrinking numbers of many communities had raised the possibility that whole congregations might disappear, and that their records might be irretrievably lost. Therefore a campaign was mounted to persuade them to set up archives. The campaign has had a dual benefit: nuns have learned how to be archivists, and interest in this sub-branch of women's history has grown, encouraged by the co-operation which many religious congregations now offer to researchers.

I ORIGINAL SOURCES

Nuns as a group are better documented than most seventeenth-century women. In the first place, many of them were covered by official records.

Every cloistered nun made a solemn profession of vows, which was entered in a register. In most cases, her age, place of origin, and parents' names were entered. Less frequently, her death was also recorded, sometimes with a brief eulogy which allows some insight into her character, or at least what her sisters thought was most important about her. Furthermore, since entry into a cloistered monastery entailed the payment of a dowry, agreements were drawn up, notarized, and preserved. Many of these records may still be found. In recent years, historians have begun to use them to analyse the population of congregations, both male and female. The study by Roger Devos, *L'origine sociale des Visitandines d'Annecy* (1973), was an early model for such works. Unfortunately, the *filles séculières*, nuns who did not take solemn vows, and therefore were not covered by legal records, have left no such consistent trace of themselves; their numbers and social composition may only be deduced from random contemporary references.

Every religious community, monastic or secular, had its code of behaviour. Monastic communities began with one of the four recognized rules. But it was only a beginning; around the rule there developed a host of *règlements* and *coûtumes* which translated its general prescriptions into everyday practices. The institutes of *filles séculières* did not follow monastic rules, but they developed their own *règlements*, dealing mainly with the work, discipline, and prayer life of the community. Many of these documents, printed or handwritten, still exist, to provide insight into the schedules and demands of daily life.

Of course, rules are only rules; there is no way of knowing how closely they were followed. It was recognized at the time that some communities were less "regular" than others. However, what the succession of rules, taken together, shows is the way that religious idealism evolved over time. Each community expressed its own particular bias, or *esprit*, through its rules. As one community after another was created, new ideas and values were gradually introduced into the tradition of religious communities. The rules show that the *filles séculières* of 1700 saw life very differently from the cloistered nuns of 1630.

Another contemporary source of information about the congregations was a sort of prospectus which described a community, its particular characteristics and purpose. It was usually entitled "L'Esprit de ...", and was written by a churchman acquainted with the community. It may be assumed that these documents were circulated for purposes of recruitment. Needless to say, they are public-relations documents and therefore have nothing bad to say about their subjects. But, again, they show the way that ideals and objectives altered over time.

In recent years, the history of the *mentalité*, or mind-set, of ordinary people of the past has been probed through the study of their proverbs, stories, songs, and superstitions. In the same way, much can be learned about the mind-set of religious communities from their prayers, or "devotions." Counter-Reformation spirituality put new demands upon pious Catholics. The saints, and particularly the Blessed Virgin, were no longer perceived simply as protectors of the faithful; they were now their role models, exhorting them to imitation. However, devotion, like art, was really an improvement on life. The character with which religious men and women invested their patron saints was their own ideal character – contemplative or active, ascetic or charitable, remote from the world or deeply involved in it. Devotions created in the seventeenth century – many of which are still observed in the congregations today – serve as a valuable insight into the mind of their times.

To the evidence of their rules, their prayers, and their books of professions may be added the records which communities kept with the conscious purpose of perpetuating their tradition. Almost every major religious community observed a deep respect for its founder/foundress. Sermons, spiritual conferences, maxims, and correspondence were preserved, firstly out of pure filial piety, secondly with an eye towards possible canonization proceedings. The principal religious personalities of the day are as well documented as any political "great." For the purpose of social commentary, the value of the literature varies. Sermons were a genre designed to inspire listeners, not to inform historians; their oratorical exaggerations were not meant to be taken literally. Spiritual conferences and maxims, also, were more a comment on the ideal than the real. Most of our insight into the practical experiences of the founders and their associates comes from their correspondence. In one case – that of Vincent de Paul – conferences with the sisters, which included question-and-answer sessions, were recorded *viva voce*, and offer a fascinating insight into the way the community functioned. Similarly, extensive minutes were taken of the meetings of the council of the Filles de la Charité. Behind the discussions and disagreements of Monsieur Vincent and Mademoiselle Le Gras and the sister-councillors, we can see the whole company at work, in its tentative and controversial beginnings. Records like this provide the truest insight into the foundation period. Unfortunately, they are few and far between.

Finally, references to religious houses often appear in every level of official record, both ecclesiastical and secular. The communities were subject to inspection by the bishops, to scrutiny by the parlements, the *intendants*, the municipalities; they were involved in lawsuits and in every sort of notarized transaction. The value of this evidence is that it presents other points of view, less biased in their favour. It also provides material history which is otherwise lacking: details of their holdings, their investments, their interaction with their neighbours.

Communities often developed their own histories. In many cases, annals were kept. One distinguished *annaliste*, Mère de Pommereu of the Ursuline house of Faubourg Saint-Jacques, asked for information from other Ursuline monasteries before drawing up her chronicles. Works such as these mixed two styles. In dealing with present events they were practical and, it may be believed, reliable. But when they turned to the past they became frankly hagiographical. Their purpose was not to record historical fact, but to provide examples of sanctity and heroism for the community to follow. The founding generation was furnished with haloes, and an air of serenity which did not accord well with the anxieties and uncertainties that their actual correspondence reveals. What the annals did contribute, however, was a broader view of community life: all sorts of sisters, whose virtues or experiences were considered worth sharing with their successors, appear in their pages.

II SECONDARY WORKS: CONGREGATIONS

Histories of congregations continued to be written in succeeding centuries, and the hagiographical motive continued to underlie these histories. Late in the nineteenth century, it became, if anything, more pronounced. The anticlericalism which had been unleashed by the French Revolution a century before now reached its climax, as also did the opposing force which for lack of a better name we may call proclericalism. During the fierce Church-State confrontations of the Third Republic, from about 1880 onwards, a number of books appeared, dedicated to specific communities, and highly defensive in tone. At that time the teaching congregations were under political attack, and in serious danger of being suppressed. Then came the Law of Separation of 1905, after which most religious congregations were exiled and their houses closed, and suddenly, the tone changed: the literature became a eulogy, full of regret for the good old days. Even after the crisis was over, histories of congregations continued to be written, mostly characterized by strong partisanship and a loyalty that tolerated no imputation of fault or weakness.

This hagiographical tradition is obviously a highly impure source for historical research. Yet it is indispensable. The authors, usually good friends of the communities which they eulogized, had access to information which does not appear elsewhere – which, indeed, may since have been lost. What the modern reader must do is ignore the polemics and concentrate on the "passive testimony" – the commonplace and virtually incidental observations which lie about unnoticed. In a style which seems peculiar to the nineteenth century, whole documents, as well as all sorts of pieces of unrelated information, may be found incorporated in the texts. These can be picked up and used for purposes that were never intended. What we must regret, and continue to search for, is evidence that was suppressed because it seemed, at the time, uncomfortable or irrelevant. This evidence often relates to the difficulties which the communities experienced within the Church.

Two principles were always observed in older Catholic historiography. First: everything turned out in the end as Providence intended. This philosophy can be found, for instance, in every work which dealt with the imposition of clausura upon the female congregations. Church historians, especially those writing for the benefit of the many cloistered nuns of the nineteenth and twentieth centuries, were not prepared to question the "two stakes put in cross in form of enclosure" which Mary Ward had so firmly rejected. None of them would consider the possibility that the Ursulines, among others, lost in effectiveness when they were enclosed. Rather, these authors insisted on treating clausura as a providential perfection of the feminine apostolate. A corollary to this optimistic view of history was that the official Church could never be wrong, or at fault. Thus – to take one example – the nineteenth-century clerical author who wrote for the cloistered Congrégation in Reims was able to praise the wisdom of Pierre Fourier in continuing the practice of clausura, and the wisdom of the papal court in its handling of the nuns' petitions, even though this meant not giving them what they asked for.

These attitudes of unswerving loyalty were later called into question by two religious historians, members of the two congregations involved. Marie de Chantal Gueudré, in her *Histoire de l'Ordre des Ursulines*, published in 1957, took previous historians to task for neglecting the history of the Ursulines in the days before clausura was imposed, and for remaining silent on the subject of their suffering. While she admired the tradition of spirituality which the nuns developed, and their pedagogical achievements, she saw in their isolation and dependence a potential for weakness and stagnation. Later, in 1965, Hélène Derréal, in her biography of Pierre Fourier, *Un missionaire de la Contre-Réforme*, depicted the papal court, and Pope Urban himself, in all their limitations, and described Fourier's distress at the decisions which led to the Congrégation's loss of its original spirit. Both religious invited a new, more critical, look at the history of their congregations.

Pope John XXIII's symbolic opening of a window, to allow air into the Church, also opened an age of unprecedented self-examination in the religious orders. One of the benefits of this has been the appearance of a number of scholarly studies of congregations, male and female, usually conducted by members of the same congregation. Outstanding examples of this new historiography are the work by Marie-Andrée Jégou, *Les Ursulines du Faubourg Saint-Jacques à Paris, 1607–1662* (1981), and that by Françoise Soury-Lavergne, *Chemin d'éducation: sur les traces de Jeanne de Lestonnac* (1984). On the whole, however, such historians do not move far outside the limits of their own congregations. The result has been that islands of erudition have been created in a sea which still remains dark. No serious synthesis has yet been attempted of the multiple religious-educational endeavours of seventeenth-century France. The experiences of the different congregations remain discrete and unrelated to each other and to the general situation. Furthermore, our historiography has concentrated almost exclusively upon the congregations that still exist. Nobody has yet attempted a head-count of the little communities of women, created by the dozen during the Catholic Reformation, which served their neighbourhoods for years before dying a natural death or being obliterated by the Revolution. And yet nobody can really take the measure of female education in seventeenth-century France until this is done.

III SECONDARY WORKS: EDUCATION

No study of feminine education in seventeenth-century France would be complete without reference to the famous work of Fénelon, *Education des filles*, first published in 1687, and the letters of Madame de Maintenon. In these works, conventional female education, which was convent education, received a bad press. Until recently, the criticisms of these two educators formed the bulk of all that was known about girls' schools in the seventeenth century. However, it must be pointed out that both Fénelon and Madame de Maintenon were concerned with the education of upper-class girls. Thus while their ideas were interesting, and sometimes ground-breaking, they concerned only a small elite group. The same is true of the pedagogy of *petites écoles* of Port-Royal, which have received considerable attention. They no more represented the mass of French schools than the Utopian communities of the nineteenth century represented employer-worker relationships as a whole. A general investigation of schools and schoolteachers must quickly move beyond them.

There has always been a certain interest in the history of public education. Large numbers of works on the subject appeared in the later days of the nineteenth century, motivated, no doubt, by the same concerns that have been mentioned above. One of these is particularly worthy of mention: the article on Fourier by Maggiolo, which rediscovered the great educationist of the seventeenth century. In recent times, especially in the 1970s, interest in the history of public education has grown, and new studies have appeared. In 1970 and in 1971, two conferences, at Reims and at Marseille, devoted their attention to seventeenth-century education in France. In 1976, the most comprehensive book yet written on the subject, *L'éducation en France du XVIe au XVIIIe siècle* by Chartier, Compère, and Julia, was published. In the following year, an equally important work appeared: *Lire et écrire*, a study of literacy in France, by Furet and Ozouf. In 1978, Jean de Viguerie brought out yet another work, *L'institution des enfants*. Throughout these years, numerous articles on old-regime schooling appeared in the journals.

Here and there, in all these works, mention is made of feminine education, but it is of secondary importance, reflecting, no doubt, the true position of this education in the Old Regime. In the work mentioned above, by Chartier, Compère, and Julia, out of three hundred pages only fifteen deal directly with girls' education. However, the brevity of the chapter results more from paucity of source material than from lack of will; the authors regret the lack of studies from which to compose their synthesis. This lack is gradually being made good: a number of monographs have appeared on feminine education, often distinguished by region. Then, in 1981, the Presses de l'Université d'Angers published the acts of the fourth meeting of religious historians at Fontevraud, dedicated (as its title suggests) entirely to *Les religieuses enseignantes*. The teaching sisters have been recognized, and doubtless many more works about them will appear.

For the purposes of this study, many of the works listed – whether on the congregations or on education as a whole – have three serious drawbacks: 1) They concentrate on the *pensionnats* of the rich. These institutions, which in obedience to the laws on clausura held their pupils almost incommunicado throughout their adolescence, have been seen by every educationist since Fénelon as semi-prisons, and hothouses of religiosity. But the vast majority of schoolgirls of the Old Regime, as Madame Aubry has pointed out in her study of the *grand couvent* of Nancy, were day students who went home after school, and therefore probably mixed a little water with their wine. The preoccupation with the rich has resulted in a distortion.

2) Most historians treat the Old Regime as a whole. They classify a period of almost two hundred years as a single unit, and thus, by their methodology, create a supposition of immobility without even having to argue for it. Then, drawn by an understandable attraction to the part of that period which is richest in data, they come to rest in the eighteenth century. But the eighteenth century's ideals were very different from the seventeenth century's, and any extrapolation will be likely to have misleading results.

This work argues not for immobility but for movement. Leaving the eighteenth century aside, with its cooling religious fervour and its "great glaciation of social mobility," we can discern even within the seventeenth century great changes of spirit, great movements of ideas. The foundation period of the first religious congregations – sometimes so brief that it almost escapes attention – was characterized by an intense idealism in society at large. The idealism could not perpetuate itself, and mysticism subsided into moralism. The second wave of foundations answered to a new-found concern for charitable action, and allowed religious women to explore new avenues of social service. The third wave of foundations gave official recognition to these women, and made them an integral part of the system – but often at the cost of a certain containment of early aspirations. The congregations as they survived bore, and in many cases still bear, within themselves markings specific to the date and circumstances of their foundation.

3) The literature, especially the older histories of the congregations, is institutional in character. Each work endows its own congregation, from the beginning, with a special character and purpose. Its "apartness" – an important component of its identity, according to Claude Langlois – is emphasized. The Mystical Body is pictured as a collection of corpuscles, each functioning very nicely on its own. Modern historians have accepted this approach, and have gone on to calculate feminine achievement in the seventeenth century simply by adding up the number of congregations known to have existed. But in fact, the *congréganistes* were born in the secular world, out of the intense involvement of women of all kinds with the new reformed Catholicism. They worked alongside a great crowd of *dames, tantes, veuves,* and *filles âgées,* in parish *charités,* schools, and hospitals. Only later did they accept, and enhance, their own distinctiveness. To project back to the beginnings the institutional character of later years is to make a true appreciation of seventeenth-century feminine activism impossible.

And without a true appreciation of feminine activism, there can be no true appreciation of the charitable and educational activity of the Catholic church of the *grand siècle.*

Bibliography

MANUSCRIPT SOURCES

Archives Nationales
LL 1679, 1681. Filles de Sainte-Geneviève, Constitutions.
LL 1713. Constitutions des Ursulines de Paris, dressés par P. Charles de la Tour, SJ.
L 425 (45) Statuts des congregées parisiennes, dressés par leurs supérieurs ecclésiastiques, 1610.
L 1962. Filles de Sainte-Geneviève (Miramionnes) 1669–1732.
S 7046–7. Filles de l'Instruction chrétienne. Reglement du 22 août 1657.
S 7048. Filles de Sainte Geneviève. Ecoles de Saint Etienne du Mont.
Public Archives of Canada
MG 17, A 7.1. Bibliothèque du Séminaire du Saint-Sulpice (Paris): Correspondance de M. Tronson, 1675–99.
MG 17, A 7.2. Séminaire du Saint-Sulpice, Montréal.
AD Indre
Série H 904. Livre de la reception des Religieuses du Monastere de la Congregation Notre Dame soubz la Reigle de St Augustin Erigé en cette Ville de Chateauroux.
AD Maine-et-Loire
Série H 261 H 1. Ursulines de Saumur, Registre des Professions 1668–1789.
AD Meurthe et Moselle
Série H 2571. Livre de l'interrogatoire pour examiner les novices par un député du Seigneur Evêque selon les ordres du Saint Concile pour la Profession.
AD Nord
Série H 149. Ursulines de Lille.
AD Pas-de-Calais
Annexe de Boulogne H 402. Ursulines de Boulogne.

AD Seine Maritime

Série D 408. Ursulines 1624–1768.

Série D 418. Ursulines 1622–1780.

Série D 427. Regles et statuts des Dames Filles de Notre-Dame Ordre de Saint-Augustin. 1617.

D 428. Congrégation de Notre-Dame. Titres de fondation et de dotation.

D 436. Soeurs du Saint Enfant-Jésus: débuts.

BM Provins

MS 99 t. IV: 1050. Etablissement des filles Devotes de l'Ecolle de Jesus a Provins transferé a Bray sur Seine.

MS. 251. Recueil de tous les actes et des professions de toutes les religieuses qui ont esté recues dans ce Mon^r depuis de son commancement qui fut l'an MVICXXIV le troisiesme jour de May. MVICXLII.

BM Reims

MSS. 1702–5. Memoires de René Bourgeois, avocat au Parlement et échevin de la ville de Reims, sur tout ce qui s'est passé en la dite ville et au Conseil d'icelle (1640–1679).

MS. 1891. Constitutions pour La Com^té des filles du St Enfant Jesus Etablie a Reims, 1683.

E 2, t 2. Articles pour servir de règle et conduite dressés par les soins de Mme de Magneux, 1636.

Bibliothèque Ste-Geneviève, Paris

MS. 703. fol. 36. Etablissement d'Ecoles des filles.

MS. 1686. Constitutions des Religieuses de la Congrégation de Notre-Dame, 1673.

MS. 1718. Regles et statuts des filles de Saint-Joseph et de Sainte-Geneviève à Senlis.

MS. 1885–8. Autobiographie et oeuvres du P. Paul Beurrier (1608–96).

Arch. Soeurs de la Providence de Rouen

Statuts, MS. de 1677.

"De l'Esprit de la Communauté des Filles de Sainte-Genevièfve," s.d.

Arch. Soeurs de l'Enfant-Jésus de Reims

Carton 12. Livre des mortuaires.

15–4. Procez verbal de la reception des premières Filles, 8 novembre 1684.

16–3.Constitutions.

17. Reglement pour les petites Ecoles Chretiennes.

25–9. Recueil de pièces diverses.

42. Prières en usage.

Arch. Soeurs de l'Enfant Jésus, Paris

Reglements manuscrits pour les Ecoles Charitables.

Arch. Soeurs Ursulines de Québec

Annales manuscrites du premier couvent de Paris pendant les 50 premières années de son existence, 1612–1662.

PRINTED SOURCES

Abelly, Louis. *Vie de S. Vincent de Paul*. 2 vols. Paris: Debécourt, Librairie-Editeur 1843. (First edition published in 1666, under the title *La Vie du Venérable Serviteur de Dieu Vincent de Paul*.)

Alphabet, ou Instruction chrétienne à l'usage des Ecolières de la Congrégation de Notre Dame à Troyes, 1708.

Argenson, Comte René de Voyer d', *Annales de la Compagnie du Saint-Sacrement*, publiées et annotées par le R.P. Dom H. Beauchet-Fillieau. Marseilles 1900.

Barré, Nicolas. *Statuts et reglemens des escoles chrestiennes et charitables du Saint-Enfant Jésus*. Paris: Le Cointe 1685.

– *Lettres spirituelles*. Toulouse: Douladoure 1876.

Belmont, François Vachon de. "Eloges de quelques personnes mortes en odeur de sainteté a Montreal, en Canada. Marguerite Bourgeoys." *RAPQ* 10 (1929–30):167–89.

– "Histoire du Canada (1720)." *Collection de Mémoires et de relations sur l'histoire ancienne du Canada*. Quebec 1840.

Béthencourt, Jacques de. *Instruction méthodique pour l'Escole paroissiale, dressée en faveur des petites écoles*, par M.I.D.B., prêtre. Paris 1669. Edition postérieure de *L'Escole paroissiale ou la manière de bien instruire les enfants dans les petites écoles*, par un prêtre d'une paroisse de Paris. Paris 1654.

Beurrier, Paul. *Reglemens de l'école charitable entretenue pour l'instruction des pauvres filles de la paroisse St. Estienne du Mont par la compagnie des dames, instituée pour le soulagement des pauvres familles honteuses ... Arrestez par M. le Curé Paul Beurrier le 7 sept. 1675*. Paris 1675.

Blain, J. *La vie de M. Jean-Baptiste de la Salle*. Cahiers lasalliens 7,8. Rome: Maison St Jean-Baptiste de la Salle 1961.

Bourgeoys, Marguerite. *See Les Ecrits*.

Chantal, Jeanne-Françoise Fremyot de. *Correspondance 1605–25*. 2 vols. Paris: Editions du Cerf 1986.

Choisy, Abbé T. de. *Vie de Madame de Miramion*, in Jauffret, Gaspard-Jean-André-Joseph. *Des services que les femmes peuvent rendre à la religion*. Paris 1801.

Les Chroniques de l'Ordre des Ursulines recueillies pour l'usage des Religieuses du mesme Ordre, par M(ère) D(e) P(ommereu) U(rsuline). Paris 1673.

Condren, Charles de. *Lettres (1588–1641)*. Publiées par Paul Auvray et André Jouffrey. Paris: Editions du Cerf 1943.

Cordier, Jean, sj. *La famille sainte, où il est traité de toutes les personnes qui composent une famille*. Paris 1885.

Démia, Charles. *Remonstrances à Messieurs les Marchands, Echevins et principaux habitants de la Ville de Lyon touchant la nécessité des écoles pour instruire des enfans pauvres*. Lyon 1666.

– *Reglemens pour les Ecoles de la Ville et Diocèse de Lyon.* Lyon 1688.

Descourveaux, Philibert. *La Vie de Monsieur Bourdoise, premier prestre de la communauté de Saint-Nicolas-du-Chardonnet. Sentences chrétiennes et ecclesiastiques de Messire Adrien Bourdoise.* Paris 1714.

Dollier de Casson, François. "Histoire de Montréal, 1640–1672." *Mémoires de la société historique de Montréal* (quatrième livraison). Montreal 1868.

Les Ecrits de Mère Bourgeoys. Montreal: CND 1964.

Fénelon, François de Salignac de la Mothe. *Education des Filles.* Paris: Flammarion 1937.

Fourier, Pierre. *Sa Correspondance 1598–1640,* ed. Hélène Derréal and Madeleine Cord'homme. 2 vols. (1598–1628). Nancy: Presses Universitaires de Nancy 1986, 1987.

– *Le primitif et légitime esprit de l'institut des filles de la Congrégation de Nostre Dame.* Pont-à-Mousson 1650.

– *Les vrayes constitutions des religieuses de la Congregation de Nostre Dame.* NP 1646.

François de Sales. *Introduction à la vie dévote.* Paris: Nelson 1947.

– *Oeuvres complètes.* 25 vols. Annecy 1892–1908, 12–21, 25.

Giry, François. *Méditations pour les Soeurs maîtresses des écoles charitables du Saint-Enfant Jésus.* Paris 1810.

Glandelet, Charles de. *Le Vray Esprit de l'institut des Soeurs séculières de la Congrégation de Notre-Dame établi à Ville-Marie en l'Isle de Montréal en Canada.* Montreal: CND 1976.

Hermant, J. *Histoire des ordres religieux et des congrégations régulières et séculières de l'Eglise.* Rouen 1710.

Instructions et reglemens pour celles qui désirent servir Dieu en la Comunauté des pauvres filles dites de Saincte Marthe, fondée a Reims par Demoiselle Barbe Martin vefve de feu sieur de Magneaux. Reims 1651.

Jadart, Henri. *Mémoires de Jean Maillefer continués par son fils jusqu'en 1716.* Paris-Reims 1890.

Juchereau, Mère Jeanne-Françoise de Saint-Ignace. *Les annales de l'Hôtel-Dieu de Québec 1636–1716.* Québec: Hôtel-Dieu 1939.

La Salle, Jean-Baptiste. *Conduite des Ecoles chretiennes.* Edition comparée du manuscrit dit de 1706 et du texte imprimé de 1720. Rome: Maison Saint Jean-Baptiste de la Salle 1965.

– *Les regles de la bienséance et de la civilité chrestiennes.* Metz 1754.

Le Gras, Mademoiselle. *Lettres de Louise de Marillac.* 2 vols. Privately published 1890.

Loriquet, Charles. *Mémoires d'Oudart Coquault bourgeois de Reims (1649–1668).* 2 vols. Reims 1875.

Marie de l'Incarnation. *Correspondance.* New edition by Dom Guy Oury. Solesmes 1971.

MDPU. See *Les Chroniques de l'Ordre des Ursulines ...*

Morin, Marie. *Histoire simple et véritable: Les annales de l'hôtel-dieu de Montreal, 1658–1725*. Edition critique par Ghislaine Legendre. Montreal: Presses Universitaires de l'Université de Montréal 1979.

Un précurseur méconnu, Monsieur le Chanoine Roland, Fondateur de la Congrégation des Soeurs du Saint-Enfant-Jésus de Reims. Reims: Imprimerie du Nord-Est 1963.

Règle de Sainct Augustin à l'usage des religieuses de la Congrégation de Notre-Dame, approuvée par Mgr. l'Illustrime et Reverendissime Charles-Maurice Le Tellier, Archevêque de Reims. Reims 1673.

Regle de Sainct Augustin pour ses Religieuses. Tours 1635.

Reglemens des religeuses ursulines de la Congregation de Paris, divisez en trois livres. Paris 1705.

Règlemens faits par Monseigneur l'Illustrime et Revérendissime Evesque et comte de Chaalons, Pair de France, pour la direction spirituelle et temporelle pour la communauté des Regentes etablie par luy dans la ville de Chaalons et dans les autres villes de son Diocèse. Châlons-sur-Marne 1677.

Reglement et pratique chrestiennes, en forme de constitutions des Filles et Vefves Seculières, du Seminaire nommé de l'Union Chrestienne, establies dans plusieurs Dioceses. Paris 1673.

Règlement pour la communauté des Filles établis pour l'instruction des pauvres filles de la paroisse St-Roch. Paris 1687.

Saint-Vallier, Monseigneur de. *Etat présent de l'Eglise et de la colonie française dans la Nouvelle-France*, ed. Robert Pepin. 1688.

Statuts des Religieuses Ursulines de la Ville et Diocese de Tours. Paris 1661.

Talon, Jean. "Correspondance échangée entre la Cour de France et l'Intendant Talon pendant ses deux administrations de la Nouvelle-France." *RAPQ* 11 (1930–1):1–182.

Tronson, Louis. *Correspondance de Louis Tronson, troisième supérieur de la Compagnie de Saint-Sulpice; lettres choisies, annotées et publiées par L. Bertrand*. Paris: V. Lecoffre 1904.

Thuillier, René. *Diarium patrum*. 1686.

Vachon de Belmont, M. "Eloges de quelques personnes mortes en odeur de sainteté à Montréal, en Canada" *RAPQ* 10 (1929–30):167–89.

Vie de la vénérable Alix Leclerc co-institutrice de l'ordre de la Congrégation de Notre-Dame. Par un Carme Déchaussé de la Province de Lorraine. Liège 1773.

Vie de la vénérable Alix Le Clerc, fondatrice, première Mere et religieuse de l'Ordre de la Congrégation de Notre-Dame. Contenant la relation d'icelle ecrite signée de la Mesme Mere. Nancy 1666.

Vincent de Paul. *Correspondance, Entretiens, Documents*. Edition publiée et annotée par Pierre Coste. 14 vols. Paris: Librairie Lecoffre 1923.

SECONDARY WORKS

Albistur, Maite, and Armogathe, Daniel. *Histoire du féminisme français du moyen-âge à nos jours.* 2 vols. Paris: Editions des femmes 1978.

Allaire, Micheline d'. *L'Hôpital-Général de Québec, 1692–1764.* Montreal: Fides 1971.

Allier, Raoul. *La Compagnie du Très Saint-Sacrement de l'Autel: La "Cabale des dévots" 1627–1666.* Paris: Librairie Armand Colin 1902.

Ariès, Philippe. *Centuries of Childhood: A Social History of Family Life.* Translated from the French by Robert Baldick. New York: Random House 1962.

Armengaud, A. *La famille et l'enfant en France et en Angleterre du XVIIᵉ et XVIIIᵉ siècle.* Paris: SEDES 1975.

Aroz, Léon de Marie. *Nicolas Roland, Jean-Baptiste de La Salle et les Soeurs de l'Enfant-Jésus de Reims.* Cahiers lasalliennes, fasc. 38. Rome: Maison St-Jean-Baptiste de La Salle 1972.

Aubry, M.E. "La Congrégation de Notre-Dame à Nancy et l'éducation des filles aux XVIIᵉ et XVIIIᵉ siècles." *Annales de l'Est* 26 (1974):76–96.

– "Le monastère nancéien de la Congrégation de Notre-Dame aux XVIIᵉ et XVIIIᵉ siècles." Mémoire de maîtrise presenté à la Faculté des Lettres et des Sciences Humaines de Nancy, 1970.

Audet, Louis-Philippe. "L'instruction des dix mille colons, nos ancêtres." *Cahiers des Dix* 37 (1972):9–43.

– "L'éducation au temps de Mgr de Laval." *SCHEC* 25 (1957–58): 59–78.

Babeau, Albert. *La ville sous l'Ancien Régime.* Paris 1880.

– *Les artisans et les domestiques d'autrefois.* Paris 1886.

– "L'Instruction primaire dans les campagnes avant 1789." *Annuaire de l'Aube* 2 (1876):3–84.

Baker, Derek, ed. *Medieval Women.* Oxford: Blackwell 1978.

Bardet, Jean-Pierre. *Rouen aux XVIIᵉ et XVIIIᵉ siècles.* 2 vols. Paris: SEDES 1983.

Bazelaire, Edouard de. *Le bienheureux Pierre Fourier.* Clermont-Ferrand 1853.

Beaurepaire, Charles Robillard de. *Recherches sur l'instruction publique dans le diocèse de Rouen avant 1789.* 2 vols. Evreux 1872.

Bernonville, Gaetan. *Un précurseur de Saint Jean-Baptiste de La Salle: Nicolas Roland, fondateur de la Congrégation du Saint-Enfant Jésus de Reims.* Paris: Ed. Alsatia 1950.

Bertout, Anne. "Les Ursulines de Paris sous l'ancien régime." Thèse pour le Doctorat d'Université 1935.

Besancet A. de. *Le bienheureux Pierre Fourier et la Lorraine.* Paris 1864.

Bonneau-Avenant, Le Comte de. *Madame de Miramion et ses oeuvres charitables.* Paris: Didier et Cie 1875.

Bossy, John. *The English Catholic Community.* London: Darton, Longman and Todd 1975.

Bourgeon, Jean-Louis. *Les Colbert avant Colbert, destin d'une famille marchand.* Paris: PUF 1973.

Boutiot, T. *Histoire de l'instruction publique et populaire à Troyes.* Troyes 1865.

Braudel, Fernand, Ernest Labrousse, et al. *Histoire économique et sociale de la France.* Vol. 2: Des derniers temps de l'âge seigneuriale aux préludes de l'âge industriel (1660–1789). Paris: PUF 1970.

Brémond, Henri. Vols. 2 and 9 of *Histoire littéraire du sentiment religieux en France, depuis la fin des guerres de religion jusqu'à nos jours.* 12 vols. Paris: Bloud et Gay 1916–33.

Broutin, Paul, SJ. *La réforme pastorale en France au XVIIe siècle.* 2 vols. Paris: Desclée et Cie, Editeurs 1956.

Cabourdin, Guy, and Georges Viard. *Lexique historique de la France d'ancien régime.* Paris: Armand Colin 1981.

Cadet, Félix. *L'Education à Port-Royal.* Paris 1887.

Calendini, Paul. *Le couvent des Filles de Notre-Dame de la Flèche.* La Flèche: Imprimerie Eugène Besnier 1905.

Calvet, J. *Saint Vincent de Paul.* Paris: Editions Albert 1948.

Carrez, L. *Histoire du premier monastère de la Congrégation de Notre-Dame établi à Châlons-sur-Marne.* Châlons-sur-Marne 1906.

Catta, E. *La Visitation Sainte-Marie de Nantes (1630–1792).* Paris: Vrin 1954.

Caza, Lorraine, CND. *La vie voyagère, conversante avec le prochain, Marguerite Bourgeoys.* Montreal: Cerf 1982.

Chalendard, Marie. *La promotion de la femme à l'apostolat 1540–1650.* Paris: Editions Alsatia 1950.

Chaline, Nadine-Josette. *Le diocèse de Rouen-Le Havre.* Paris: Editions Beauchesne 1976.

Chalumeau, R.P. "L'assistance aux malades pauvres au XVIIe siècle." *XVIIe Siècle* 90–1 (1971):75–86.

Chambers, M.C.E. *The Life of Mary Ward.* 2 vols. London 1882.

Chartier, Roger, Marie-Madeleine Compère, Dominique Julia. *L'éducation en France du XVIe au XVIIIe siècle.* Paris: SEDES 1976.

Châtellier, Louis. *L'Europe des dévots.* Paris: Flammarion 1987.

Chaunu, Pierre. *L'église, culture et société: Essais sur réforme et contre-réforme.* Paris: SEDES 1984.

– "Le XVIIe siècle religieux. Réflexions préalables." *AESC* March-April 1967:279–302.

Chedozeau, Bernard. "Les petites écoles de Pierre Nicole." *Marseille* 88 (1972):15–19.

Chesnay, Charles B. du. "La spiritualité des laïcs." *XVIIe Siècle* 62–3 (1964):30–46.

– "Ecriture sainte et vie spirituelle au XVIIe siècle." *Dictionnaire de spiritualité* 4, col.226.

Chicoine, Emilia, CND. *La métairie de Marguerite Bourgeoys à la Pointe Saint-Charles*. Montreal: Fides 1986.

Chill, E. "Religion and Mendicity in Seventeenth-Century France." *International Review of Social History* 7, no. 3 (1962):400–25.

La Compagnie de Marie Notre-Dame. Vol. 8 in *Les ordres religieux*. Paris: Letouzey et Ané 1926.

Compayré, Gabriel. "Charles Démia et l'origine de l'enseignement primaire à Lyon." *Revue d'Histoire de Lyon* 4 (1905).

– *Charles Démia et les origines de l'enseignement primaire*. Paris 1905.

Compère, Marie-Madeleine. *Du collège au lycée (1500–1850)*. Paris: Editions Gallimard/Julliard 1985.

Coste, Pierre. *Le grand saint du grand siècle: Monsieur Vincent*. 2 vols. Paris: Desclée de Brouwer et Cie 1931.

– *Saint Vincent de Paul et les dames de la Charité*. Paris: Bloud et Gay 1918.

Cressy, David. *Literacy and the Social Order: Reading and Writing in Tudor and Stuart England*. Cambridge: Cambridge University Press 1980.

Dagens, Jean. *Bérulle et les origines de la Restauration catholique (1575–1611)*. Paris: Desclée de Brouwer 1952.

Dainville, François de, SJ. *La naissance de l'humanisme moderne*. Paris: Beauchesne 1940.

– *L'éducation des Jésuites XVIIe – XVIIIe siècles*. Textes réunis et présentés par Marie-Madeleine Compère. Paris: Editions de Minuit 1978.

Danielou, Madeleine. "Fénelon éducateur." *XVIIe siècle* 12,13, 14 (1951, 1952).

– *Madame de Maintenon éducatrice*. Paris: Bloud et Gay 1946.

Darche, Jean. *Le saint abbé Bourdoise*. 2 vols. Paris 1884.

Darmon, Pierre. *Mythologie de la femme dans l'Ancienne France*. Paris: Seuil 1983.

Daveluy, Marie-Claire. *La Société de Notre-Dame de Montréal*. Montreal: Fides 1965.

Davis, Natalie Z. *Society and Culture in Early Modern France*. Stanford: Stanford University Press 1975.

Delforge, Frederic. *Les petites écoles de Port-Royal, 1637–1660*. Paris: Editions du Cerf 1985.

Delumeau, Jean. *La peur en Occident*. Paris: Fayard 1978.

– *Le catholicisme entre Luther et Voltaire*. Paris: PUF 1971.

– "Les chrétiens au temps de la Réforme." *Histoire sociale – Social History* 10 (Nov. 1977):235–48.

– *Naissance et affirmation de la Réforme*. Paris: PUF 1968.

Derréal, Hélène. *Un missionaire de la Contre-Réforme*. Paris: Librairie Plon 1965.

Desportes, Pierre. *Histoire de Reims*. Toulouse: Privat 1983.

Devos, Roger. *L'origine sociale des Visitandines d'Annecy aux XVIIe et XVIIIe siècles*. Annecy: Academie Salésienne 1973.

Deyon, Pierre. "A propos du pauperisme au milieu du xvıı^e siècle: peinture et charité chrétienne." *AESC* 22 (Jan.–June, 1967):137–53.

Dhôtel, J.-C. *Les origines du catéchisme moderne, d'après les premiers manuels imprimés en France.* Paris: Aubier 1967.

Dompnier, B. "Un aspect de la dévotion eucharistique dans la France du xvıı^e siècle: Les Prières des Quarante Heures." *RHEF* 67(1981):5–31.

Douville, R. "L'instruction primaire dans la région tri-fluvienne au début de la colonie." *Cahiers des Dix* 34(1969):39–60.

Dubois, Elfrieda. "The Education of Women in Seventeenth-Century France." *French Studies* 32, no. 1 (1978):1–19.

Duby, J., and A. Wallon. *Histoire de la France rurale.* Paris: Seuil 1975.

Dulong, Claude. *La vie quotidienne des femmes au grand siècle.* Paris: Hachette 1984.

"Education des filles, enseignement des femmes." *Penelope* 2 (1980):1–116.

Entraygues, Chanoine L. *Une nièce de Montaigne: la bienheureuse Jeanne de Lestonnac.* Perigueux, chez l'auteur 1938.

Fagniez, Gustave. *La femme et la société française dans la première moitié du XVIIe siècle.* Paris: J. Gambler 1929.

Faguet, M. Emile. *Madame de Maintenon Institutrice: Extraits de ses lettres, avis, entretiens, conversations et proverbes sur l'éducation.* Paris 1887.

Faillon, M. *Vie de la Soeur Bourgeoys.* 2 vols. Tours 1853.

– *Vie de M. Olier.* 2 vols. Paris 1841.

Farcy, Chanoine. *L'institut des soeurs du Saint Enfant Jésus dites de la Providence de Rouen.* Rouen: Imprimerie commerciale du Journal de Rouen 1938.

Farge, Arlette. *Le miroir des femmes.* Textes presentés par Arlette Farge (Bibliothèque bleue collection dirigée par Daniel Roche). Paris: Montalba 1982.

Febvre, L. "Aspects méconnus d'un renouveau religieux en France entre 1590 et 1620." *AESC* 13 (Oct.–Dec.1958):639–50.

Ferrier, F. "La Compagnie du Saint-Sacrement en Limousin." *Les Provinciaux sous Louis XIV*, 5e Colloque de Marseille, Revue Marseille no. 10 1/2 trim. 1975.

Ferté, Jeanne. *La vie religieuse dans les campagnes parisiennes (1622–1695).* Paris: Vrin 1962.

Flachaire, Charles. *La dévotion à la Vierge dans la littérature catholique au commencement du XVIIe siècle.* Paris: Apostolat de la Presse 1957.

Fosseyeux, Marcel. *Les écoles de charité à Paris sous l'ancien régime et dans la première partie du XIXe siècle.* Paris 1912.

Froeschlé-Chopard, M.H. "Univers sacré et iconographie au xvııı^e siècle: églises et chapelles des diocèses de Vence et de Grasse." *AESC* 31 (1976):489–511.

Furet, F., and J. Ozouf. *Lire et écrire: l'alphabétisation des français de Calvin à Jules Ferry.* 2 vols. Paris: Editions de minuit 1977.

Gaudemet, J. "Legislation canonique et attitudes séculières à l'égard du lien matrimoniale au xviiᵉ siècle." *XVIIᵉ Siècle* 102–3 (1974):15–30.

Gaussin, Pierre-Roger, and Madeleine Vallet. "L'instruction secondaire des filles en Forez aux xviiᵉ et xviiiᵉ siècles." *Religion et politique: Melanges offerts à André Latreille*. Lyon: Audin 1972.

Germain, Elisabeth. *Langages de la foi à travers l'histoire: mentalités et catéchèse*. Paris: ISPC 1972.

Gosset, Pol. *Les Magneuses: Fondation de Mme Colbert de Magneux (1635–1799)*. Reims: Mance et Cie 1924.

Goubert, Pierre. *La vie quotidienne des paysans français au XVIIᵉ siècle*. Paris: Hachette 1982.

Grèzes, Henri de, OFM. *Vie du R.P. Barré, religieux minime, fondateur de l'Institut des Ecoles charitables du Saint-Enfant-Jésus de Saint-Maur*. Bar-le-Duc 1892.

Grosperrin, Bernard. *Les petites écoles sous l'Ancien Régime*. Rennes: Oeust France 1984.

Gueudré, Marie de Chantal. *Histoire de l'Ordre des Ursulines en France*. 3 vols. Paris: Editions St-Paul 1957.

– "La femme et la vie spirituelle." *XVIIᵉ Siècle* 62–3 (1964):47–77.

Guigue, G. *Les papiers des dévots de Lyon*. Lyon 1922.

Guilday, Peter. *The English Catholic Refugees on the Continent, 1558–1795*. London and New York: Longmans, Green and Co. 1914.

Gutton, Jean-Pierre. "Dévots et petites écoles: l'exemple du Lyonnais." *Marseille* 88: 9–14.

– *Domestiques et serviteurs dans la France de l'Ancien Régime*. Paris: Aubier Montaigne 1981.

– *La société et les pauvres. L'exemple de la généralité de Lyon, 1534–1789*. Paris: PUF 1974.

– "Les compagnies paroissiales de charité à Lyon au xviiᵉ siècle." *Religion et politique: Melanges offerts à André Latreille*. Lyon: Audin 1972.

Hannesse, Albert. *Vie de Nicolas Roland*. Reims, 1888.

Hoffer, P. *La dévotion à Marie au déclin du XVIIᵉ siècle*. Paris: Editions du Cerf 1938.

Hourlier, Jacques. *L'âge classique (1140–1378): les religieux*. Vol. 10 in *Histoire du Droit et des Institutions de l'Eglise en Occident*, published under the direction of Gabriel Le Bras. Paris: Editions Cujas 1974.

Hudon, Leo. "Monseigneur de Laval et les communautés de femmes." *SCHEC* 25 (1957–8): 35–57.

Hurtubise, Pierre. "Origine sociale des vocations canadiennes de Nouvelle-France." *SCHEC* 45 (1978) 41–56.

Hunt, David. *Parents and Children in History: The Psychology of Family Life in Early Modern France*. New York: Basic Books 1970

Jaenen, Cornelius. *The Role of the Church in New France*. Montreal: McGraw-Hill Ryerson 1976.

Jamet, Dom Albert. *Marguerite Bourgeoys, 1620–1700.* 2 vols. Montreal: La Presse Catholique Panaméricaine 1942.

Jean, Marguerite. *Evolution des communautés religieuses de femmes au Canada de 1639 à nos jours.* Montréal: Fides 1977.

Jeanblanc, Henri. "Charles Demia et l'enseignement primaire à Lyon au xviie siècle." *Religion et politique: Mélanges offerts à André Latreille.* Lyon: Audin 1972.

Jégou, Marie-Andrée. *Les Ursulines du Faubourg Saint-Jacques à Paris 1607–1662.* Paris: PUF 1981.

Join-Lambert, M. "La pratique religieuse dans le diocèse de Rouen sous Louis XIV." *Annales de Normandie* 3 (1953):247–74.

Lahaise, Robert. *Les édifices conventuels du vieux Montréal.* Quebec: Editions Hurtubise, HMH 1980.

Lanctot, Gustave. *Montréal sous Maisonneuve, 1642–1665.* Montreal: Beauchemin 1966.

Langlois, Claude. *Le catholicisme au féminin: les congrégations françaises à supérieure générale au XIXe siècle.* Paris: Editions du Cerf 1984.

Latreille, André, E. Delaruelle, and J.R. Palanque. *Histoire du Catholicisme en France.* 3 vols. Paris: Ed. Spes 1957–62.

Le Bras, Gabriel (under the direction of). *Les ordres religieux.* 2 vols. Paris: Flammarion 1980.

Lebrun, François (under the direction of). *Histoire des catholiques en France du XVe siècle à nos jours.* Toulouse: Edouard Privat 1980.

– *La vie conjugale sous l'Ancien Régime.* Paris: Armand Colin 1978.

Legois, Jeanne-Marie. "Etude du vocabulaire de l'enseignement dans les statuts et règlements des écoles chrétiennes et charitables fondées par Nicolas Barré et Jean-Baptiste de La Salle." Mémoire de Maîtrise de Lettres Modernes, Lille, faculté de lettres 1980.

Legué, Gabriel, and Gilles La Tourette. *Soeur Jeanne des Anges.* Paris 1886.

Lembrez, Anne-Marie. "Institut du Saint-Enfant-Jésus (Saint Maur) à Toulouse, 1688–1959." Mémoire de Maîtrise redigé sous la direction de M. Louis Trénard 1985.

Lemoine, Robert (Dom, OSB) *Le droit des religieux du concile de Trente aux instituts particuliers.* Paris: Desclée de Brouwer 1956.

– *Le monde des religieux: l'époque moderne 1563–1789.* Vol. 15 (part 2) of *Histoire du Droit et des Institutions de l'Eglise en Occident,* ed. Gabriel Le Bras and Jean Gaudemet. Paris: Editions Cujas 1976.

Lestocquoy, Jean. *La vie religieuse en France du VIIe au XXe siècle.* Paris: Albin Michel 1964.

Leymont, Hélène de. *Madame de Sainte-Beuve et les Ursulines de Paris, 1562–1630.* Lyon 1890.

Loridan, J. *Les Ursulines de Valenciennes: avant et pendant la Terreur.* Paris: Desclée de Brouwer 1901.

Lottin, Alain. "Réforme catholique et instruction des pauvres dans les pays-bas meridionaux." *Les religieuses enseignantes*, Actes de la quatrième rencontre d'Histoire religieuse de Fontevraud. Angers, Presses de l'Université d'Angers 1981.

Maggiolo, M. "L'oeuvre pédagogique de Pierre Fourier." *Mémoires de l'Academie de Stanislas 1892*. 5th series, vol. 10.

Magnan, Charles-Joseph. "Les idées pédagogiques de Marguerite Bourgeoys." *Enseignement primaire* (June 1924):665–9.

Mandrou, Robert. *De la culture populaire aux XVIIᵉ et XVIIIᵉ siècles: La Bibliothèque bleue de Troyes*. Paris: Stock 1964.

– *Introduction à la France moderne 1500–1640*. Paris: Ed. Albin Michel 1974.

Mélanges offerts à André Latreille. Lyon: Audin 1972.

Ménard, Michèle. *Une histoire des mentalités religieuses aux XVIIᵉ et XVIIIᵉ siècles: Mille rétables de l'ancien diocèse du Mans*. Paris: Editions Beauchesne 1980.

Mesnard, P. "La pédagogie des jésuites." *Les grands pédagogues*, under the direction of J. Cateau. Paris: PUF 1972.

Meyer, Jean. "Essai sur l'instruction populaire en Bretagne du XVIᵉ au XIXᵉ siècle." *Actes du Congrès national des societés savantes* 1 (Reims 1970):333–53.

Michel, Pierre. "Une version modernisée des règles et constitutions des Filles de Notre-Dame." *B. Soc. Amis de Montaigne* ser. 5, 16 (1975):47–62.

Molette, Charles. *Guide des sources de l'histoire des congrégations féminines françaises de vie active*. Paris: Editions de Paris 1974.

Morey, Jean. *La vénérable Anne de Xainctonge, fondatrice de la congrégation de Sainte-Ursule au Comté de Bourgogne*. 2 vols. Besancon: Jacquin 1901.

Mousnier, Roland. *Les institutions de la France sous la monarchie absolue, 1598–1789*. 2 vols. Paris: PUF 1974.

Notter, Marie-Thérèse. "Les ordres religieux féminins blésois: leurs rapports avec la société, 1580–1670." Doctorat de troisième cycle, Université de Tours 1982.

Onze études sur l'image de la femme dans la littérature française du XVIIᵉ siècle. Under the direction of Wolfgang Luner. Tubingen: Verlag Gunter Narr; Paris: Ed. J-M. Place 1978.

Parenty, Abbé. *Histoire de Sainte Angèle Fondatrice de l'Ordre de Sainte-Ursule*. Arras 1842.

Parias, Louis-Henri, ed. *Histoire générale de l'enseignement et de l'éducation en France*. Paris: Editions Labat 1981.

Parisse, Michel. *Les nonnes au Moyen Age*. Le Puy: Christine Bonneton 1983.

Péchenard, P.L. *La Congrégation de Notre-Dame de Reims*. 2 vols. Reims 1886.

Perrel, Jean. "Les écoles de filles dans la France d'ancien régime." In *The Making of Frenchmen 1679–1979*, ed. Donald Baker and Patrick Harrington. Waterloo: Historical Reflections Press 1980.

– "Les filles à l'école avant la Révolution." *Revue d'Auvergne* 94 (1980): 291–316.

– "Sur l'enseignement féminin avant la Révolution." *Penelope* 2 (1980): 9–10.

Perrel, M. "L'enseignement féminin sous l'Ancien Régime: les écoles populaires en Auvergne, Bourbonnais et Velay." *Cahiers Historiques* 23, no. 2 (1978):193–210.

Pillorget, René. "Mary Ward ou la Ténacité (1585–1645)." *Les religieuses enseignantes.* Actes de la quatrième rencontre d'Histoire Religieuse de Fontevraud. Angers: Presses de l'Université d'Angers 1981.

– "Vocation religieuse et Etat en France aux xvie et xviie siècles." *La vocation religieuse et sacerdotale en France, XVIe – XIXe siècles.* Fontevraud 1978, 1979:9–18.

Pinard, P. "Méthodes pédagogiques." *Information historique* 2 (1981).

Pingaud, Léonce. *Saint Pierre Fourier.* Paris: Librairie Victor Lecoffre 1902.

Pirard, E. "Le vocabulaire en rapport avec l'enseignement dans l'oeuvre de Saint Pierre Fourier." Mémoire presenté pour l'obtention du grade de licencié en Philologie romain. Louvain 1968.

Plante, Lucienne, CND. *Marguerite Bourgeoys, fille de France: 1620–1653.* Montreal: CND 1978.

Pocquet du Haut-Jussé, Bernard. *La vie temporelle des communautés de femmes à Rennes au XVIIe et au XVIIIe siècles.* Paris: Librairie Ancienne Honoré Champion 1916.

Portemer, Jean. "Réflexion sur les pouvoirs de la femme selon le droit français au xviie siècle." *XVIIe Siècle* 144 (July–Sept. 1984):189–99.

Positio sur la cause de béatification du serviteur de Dieu P.Nicolas Barré. Rome: Typis polyglottis vaticanis 1970.

Poutet, Yves. "La compagnie du Saint-Sacrement et les écoles populaires de Marseille." *Provence historique* (December 1963):341–95.

– *Le XVIIe siècle et les origines lasalliennes; recherches sur la génèse de l'oeuvre scolaire et religieuse de Jean-Baptiste de La Salle.* 2 vols. Rennes: Imprimeurs réunis 1970.

– "L'enseignement des pauvres dans la France du xviie siècle." *XVIIe siècle* 90–1 (1971):87–110.

– "L'influence du Père Barré dans la fondation des Soeurs du Saint-Enfant-Jésus de Reims." *RHEF* 46 (1960):18–53.

– "Nicolas Barré, Nicolas Roland, Charles Démia et leurs 'filles seculières.'" *Les religieuses enseignantes* 1981.

– "Spiritualités d'enseignants: Anne de Xainctonge et Jean-Baptiste de la Salle." *Revue d'ascétique et de mystique* 139 (1959):304–28; 140 (1959):409–26; 141 (1960).

Prévost, A. *Saint Vincent de Paul et ses institutions en Champagne méridionale.* Bar-sur-Seine: L. Goussard 1928.

Prévot, Jacques. *La première institutrice de France, Madame de Maintenon.* Paris: Editions Belin 1981.

Quéniart, Jean. "Deux exemples d'alphabétisation: Rouen et Rennes à la fin du xviiᵉ siècle." *Actes du congrès national des sociétés savantes* 1 (Reims 1970):355–66.

Les religieuses enseignantes. Actes de la quatrième rencontre d'Histoire Religieuse de Fontevraud. Angers, Presses de l'Université d'Angers 1981.

Reneault, Abbé. *Les Ursulines de Rouen (1619–1906).* Fécamp: Imprimeries réunies L. Durand et fils 1919.

Renard, Edmond. *La Mère Alix Le Clerc.* Paris: J. de Gigord 1935.

Reynes, Geneviève. *Couvents de femmes.* Paris: Fayard 1987.

Rogier, L.J., R. Aubert, and M.D. Knowles. *Nouvelle histoire de l'Eglise.* Paris: Seuil 1963. Vol. 3: *Réforme et Contre-Réforme,* by Hermann Tuchle, C.A. Bouman, and Jacques Le Brun.

Roelker, Nancy L. "The Appeal of Calvinism to French Noblewomen of the Sixteenth Century." *Journal of Interdisciplinary History* 4 (Spring 1972): 391–418.

Rohan-Chabot, Alix de. "Les écoles de campagne en Lorraine au xviiiᵉ siècle." Unpublished thesis 1969.

Ronzeaud, Pierre. "La femme au pouvoir ou le monde à l'envers." *XVIIᵉ siècle* 108 (1975):9–33.

Saint-Damase-de-Rome, Soeur, CND. *L'intendante de Notre-Dame: la bienheureuse Marguerite Bourgeoys et son administration temporelle.* Montreal: CND 1958.

Sainte-Gertrude-de-la-Croix, Soeur, CND. "L'oeuvre pédagogique de Marguerite Bourgeoys." Université Laval 1951, unpublished thesis.

Sainte-Henriette, Soeur, CND. *Histoire de la Congrégation de Notre-Dame de Montréal.* Vols 1 and 2. Montreal: CND 1910.

Salome, Mother M. *Mary Ward: A Foundress of the 17th Century.* London: Burns and Oates 1901.

Sauvage, Michel. *Tricentenaire de Nicolas Roland 1678–1978.* Privately published 1978.

Schoenher, P. *Histoire du Seminaire de Saint-Nicolas du Chardonnet, 1612–1908.* 2 vols. Paris: Desclée De Brouwer 1909–11.

Schroeder, H.J. *Canons and Decrees of the Council of Trent.* St Louis 1941.

Segalen, Martine. *Mari et femme dans la société paysanne.* Paris: Flammarion 1980.

Simard, Jean. *Une Iconographie du clergé au XVIIᵉ siècle.* Québec: Presses de l'Université de Laval 1976.

Snyders, Georges. *La pédagogie en France aux XVIIᵉ et XVIIIᵉ siècles.* Paris: PUF 1965.

Soury-Lavergne, Françoise. *Chemin d'éducation sur les traces de Jeanne de Lestonnac, 1556–1640.* Chambray-les-Tours: CLD 1984.

Stone, Lawrence, ed. *Schooling and Society: Studies in the History of Education.* Baltimore and London: Johns Hopkins University Press 1976.

– *The Family, Sex and Marriage in England 1500–1800.* London: Weidenfeld and Nicolson 1977.

Stuard, Susan Mosher, ed. *Women in Medieval Society*. University of Pennsylvania Press 1976.

Taveneaux, René. *La vie quotidienne des jansenistes aux XVIIᵉ et XVIIIᵉ siècles*. Paris: Hachette 1973.

– *Le catholicisme dans la France classique*. 2 vols. Paris: SEDES 1980.

Thomas, K.V. "Women and the Civil War Sects." *Past and Present* 13 (1958): 42–62.

Trudel, Marcel. *Montréal: la formation d'une societé*. Montreal: Fides 1976.

Turin, Second de. "L'emprise de l'idéal monastique sur la spiritualité des laïcs au xviiᵉ siècle." *Revue des sciences religieuses* 40 (1966): 209–38; 353–83.

Vauchez, André. *La sainteté en occident aux derniers siècles du Moyen Age*. Rome: Ecole française de Rome 1981.

Veissière, M. "L'enseignement à Provins aux xviiᵉ et xviiiᵉ siècles." *Actes du Congrès national des sociétés savantes* (Reims 1970):565–87.

Viguerie, Jean de. "La vocation religieuse et sacerdotale en France aux xviiᵉ et xviiiᵉ siècles. La théorie et la réalité." *La Vocation religieuse et sacerdotale en France, XVIIᵉ–XVIIIᵉ siècles*, 2ᵉ Rencontre Hist. rel., Fontevraud 1978, 1979:27–39.

– *L'institution des enfants: l'éducation en France, 16ᵉ–18ᵉ siècle*. Paris: Calmann-Levy 1978.

– *Une oeuvre d'éducation sous l'Ancien Régime*. Paris: Publications de la Sorbonne, Editions de la nouvelle Aurore 1976.

La vocation religieuse et sacerdotale en France. XVIIᵉ–XIXᵉ siècles. Actes de la deuxième rencontre d'histoire religieuse de Fontevraud. Angers: Presses de l'Université d'Angers 1979.

Index